SHACKLETON'S
HEROES

SHACKLETON'S
HEROES

THE EPIC STORY OF THE MEN WHO KEPT
THE *ENDURANCE* EXPEDITION ALIVE

WILSON McORIST

FOREWORD BY
SIR RANULPH FIENNES

The Robson Press

First published in Great Britain in 2015 by
The Robson Press (an imprint of Biteback Publishing Ltd)
Westminster Tower
3 Albert Embankment
London SE1 7SP

ISBN 978-1-84954-815-1

10 9 8 7 6 5 4 3 2 1

A CIP catalogue record for this book is available from the British Library.

Set in Bulmer

Printed and bound in Great Britain by
CPI Group (UK) Ltd, Croydon CR0 4YY

CONTENTS

AUTHOR'S PREFACE

THERE IS NOTHING quite like sitting at a table in the deathly silent Archives Room of the Scott Polar Research Institute Library in Cambridge, wearing white gloves, with a grimy, seal-blubber-oil-splattered diary, reading words that were written by one of your own heroes; words that were written in Antarctica in 1915–16.

My 'heroes' are six men who were in a support party placing food depots for Shackleton's planned crossing of Antarctica in 1915. I call these six men the 'Mount Hope Party' because their most southerly depot was placed at Mount Hope, 360 miles onto the continent from their base at McMurdo Sound.

The rough, handwritten scrawl of their diaries often required a number of readings to ensure the words written were interpreted correctly. Did he write 'heavy' or was the word 'leaving'? Did he simply describe yet another day of hauling a sledge through waist-deep snow as 'worse than awful'? Did he really write that they ate half a biscuit and drank one cup of weak warm tea, for the entire day? He mentions his toes – does he not realise his toes are frostbitten, and they may need to be amputated? Does he have any idea that the blizzard will continue for another five days? Or that his colleague will die in two days? Such was my life, on and off, for six years as I researched the diaries of the men of the Mount Hope Party for this book.

Over this time I badgered the staff at various institutions for any diary, document, letter or journal related to the Mount Hope Party: the Scott Polar Research Institute in Cambridge, the Canterbury Museum in Christchurch, the James Caird Library at the National Maritime Museum in London, the Royal Geographical Society in London, the Alexander Turnbull Library in Wellington and the Federation University in Victoria (formerly University of Ballarat).

I searched for more details of the six men: Mackintosh, Joyce, Wild, Spencer-Smith, Hayward and Richards. I spent time with Anne Philips, granddaughter of the leader of the party, Aeneas Mackintosh, and she gave me even more background information on him. I tracked down Ernest Joyce's original diary (in private hands in the USA) and the owner, Betsy Krementz, obligingly sent me a complete copy of it for my work. I visited obscure places like the tiny village of Eversholt, the home of Ernest Wild. I met the late Michael Weaver, archivist at Woodbridge School in Suffolk, who was also entranced with the exploits of a past pupil, A. P. Spencer-Smith. I wrote to hundreds of people named 'P. Hayward' before finding Peter Hayward, the grand-nephew of Victor Hayward, who shared with me the history of his family. I had tea and biscuits in Adelaide with Dick Richards's daughter, the most charming nonagenarian, Patricia Lathlean.

We can hardly imagine what life was really like in Antarctica in the early 1900s, so I travelled there on the Heritage Expeditions ship *Spirit of Enderby* to try and gain a better understanding of the Antarctic environment, and the conditions under which the men lived. Invercargill in New Zealand was our starting point at latitude 46° S and our destination was McMurdo Sound in Antarctica, latitude 77.5° S. Day after day the ship rolled its way across the Southern Ocean, covering no more than a few degrees of latitude each day. We encountered wild weather and rough seas. We saw our first icebergs drifting up from the south. Like past explorers we were stopped by pack ice. After ten days at sea we could see Antarctica, highlighted by the ice cliffs of the Great Ice Barrier. In the distance we could see the Trans-Antarctic Mountains, a range of mountains that went southward into Antarctica. We were in the hallowed ground of Scott and Shackleton. We had reached McMurdo Sound.

We stood silently by bunks at the Cape Evans hut (abandoned by Captain

R. F. Scott's expedition of 1910–13) that the men of the Mount Hope Party had slept on. We read a scribbled inscription on the wall by Dick Richards and, in the dim light, wondered who wore the blubber-stained improvised canvas trousers. We saw unopened tins of McDoddies dried vegetables on the shelves. We saw a game of 'Bobs' that the men entertained themselves with over the winter months. We stared unbelievingly at a pile of seal blubber, stacked by the men of the Mount Hope Party in 1916, frozen and untouched since that time. Outside the hut we were transfixed by the anchor and broken cables from the ship *Aurora*, embedded in the gravel beach since May 1915. At *Discovery* hut we walked around the one blubber stove, with a frying pan still on the plate, complete with seal chunks, also frozen and untouched for almost 100 years. We saw the few wooden planks raised up from the floor which men slept on during winter. We walked up the hill nearby where, in 1916, three men of the Mount Hope Party watched two of their comrades attempt to walk to Cape Evans, only 13 miles away.

We attempted a trek up Observation Hill, a prominent landmark at the foot of McMurdo Sound, but a sudden blizzard came on when only half the ship's party had reached the summit so we were forced to return to the ship. It was probably nothing more than a strong wind with snow drift, but we experienced a little of what the men of the early 1900s may have experienced; we in our fleecy underwear and duck-down windcheaters, they with frostbitten fingers and toes, wearing worn and threadbare clothing.

But even with a trip to Antarctica, and armed with a mass of information from diaries, books, letters and journals, I found it impossible to accurately convey how and why these men of the early 1900s acted the way they did. One could make assumptions, surmise and guess, but what was the true story of the Mount Hope Party? Then I realised that the story could be told; by the men themselves. We have their diaries, almost all of them. And on most days we have a number of diary entries by more than one man to describe what happened. There are even explanations as to why they took a certain step, or what they thought of another man's action or what was on their own mind. Their private thoughts are in the diaries. There is no better way to learn about the heroics of the six men of the Mount Hope Party than for these men to tell the story, in their own words – and that is through their diaries.

A number of relatives of the Mount Hope Party, and others who own copyright, have kindly given me permission to publish diary extracts. These include:

Anne Phillips, the granddaughter of Aeneas Mackintosh.

Betsy Krementz, the owner of Ernest Joyce's original diary.

Julie George (Francis) and Judy Murray, relatives of Ernest Wild.

Debby Horsman and Clifford Smith, relatives of Arnold Patrick Spencer-Smith.

Peter Hayward, grand-nephew of Victor Hayward.

Canterbury Museum in Christchurch, New Zealand, who have copyright of Richard Walter Richards's diary.

My talented brother Ian McOrist has added to the diary words with maps and my equally talented sister Jessie-Jean Walker has painted the portraits of the six men of the Mount Hope Party. Dr David Harrowfield, the Antarctic historian and geographer, offered to read my manuscript and made a number of excellent suggestions which I have incorporated. He has written a Postscript for which I am most grateful. I am indebted to Sir Ranulph Fiennes for his Foreword.

To Sheila Drummond and Anna Carmichael I am especially grateful, who, as literary agents, saw some value in my work, as did Heather Lane at SPRI. I have a special thank you for Victoria Godden, the Editorial Assistant at Biteback Publishing. Her attention to detail in the final editing and correcting of my manuscript was absolutely brilliant.

And last to thank is the lady who for years has put up with me idolising men from 100 years ago. Enough is enough, Suzanne said, so she decided to help, and more than help, she edited my book from page one to the end.

FOREWORD BY
SIR RANULPH FIENNES

I WAS INTRODUCED TO Wilson McOrist, the author of *Shackleton's Heroes*, by Dr David Harrowfield. David is a close colleague and a highly respected author, geographer and researcher of Antarctica. He had reviewed a draft manuscript of Wilson's book and not only did he find it a most enjoyable read, but he was enthused by Wilson's use of original diaries; diaries written in 1915–16.

Shackleton's Heroes is told through the diaries of six men. The narrative adds a new and highly significant chapter to the early 1900s British Heroic Age of Antarctic Exploration. The six men were the Mount Hope Party, a small team who placed food depots out to Mount Hope on the Great Ice Barrier in 1915 and 1916. Shackleton intended to use the depots on the last 360 miles of his planned crossing of Antarctica; from Mount Hope near the foot of the Beardmore Glacier to *Discovery* hut in McMurdo Sound. I personally can appreciate Shackleton's logic in needing such food depots. In 1993 Mike Stroud and I had walked across the Antarctic continent unsupported and had reached the start of the Great Ice Barrier, next to Mount Hope. We too were 360 miles from our support base at McMurdo Sound and we had only eight days of food left. For us to march that final 360 miles we would have needed food depots to have been laid for us.

The story of the Mount Hope Party is almost unknown because it has been dwarfed by Shackleton's epic escape from the ice after his ship *Endurance* was crushed, the landing of his men on Elephant Island, his boat journey to South Georgia, his trek across that island and the rescue of all his men.

The release of the diaries to the public view exposes the intimate details of the Mount Hope Party story. We experience Antarctic life of 1915–16 with the words of the men who were there. It is a gripping tale with the most tragic of endings. An integral part of the story is the six months from October 1915 to March 1916 when the men were out on the Great Ice Barrier, man-hauling sledges, battling freezing conditions, severe blizzards, crevasses, sastrugi, waist-deep snow, and succumbing to frostbite, snow-blindness and scurvy. The six men of the Mount Hope Party were halted by a prolonged blizzard, only 10 miles from a food depot and within 80 miles of their hut. In their diaries they write of Scott because they knew they were in a similar predicament, and in close proximity to where he died just four years before. Many of these struggles I can relate to, having endured similar conditions during the ninety-three days of my crossing of Antarctica in 1992–3.

What also makes the diary release significant is that we have six diaries, one from each of the six men of the Mount Hope Party. We see events told from different perspectives. We read different points of view. And, beyond the immediacy of their writing, what makes the story even more interesting is the cast of characters. Six men of varied backgrounds, education, experience and personalities performed unbelievably heroic work, under harrowing and difficult conditions. For 100 years these diaries have remained hidden, except for the release of selected quotes in a small number of books.

I believe the diaries of the Mount Hope Party are an Antarctic literary treasure. I congratulate Wilson McOrist for not only bringing them out of obscurity but for weaving them together so they tell the fascinating, but true and definitive story of the Mount Hope Party: *Shackleton's Heroes*.

Ranulph Fiennes

INTRODUCTION

IN THE BOOK *South*, the story of his attempt to cross Antarctica in 1914–17, Shackleton wrote: 'I think that no more remarkable story of human endeavour has been revealed than the tale of that long march.' [1]

He was not referring to his retreat from Antarctica when, from January 1915 until April 1916, with his ship the *Endurance* trapped in the ice in the Weddell Sea and then crushed, he led his men, finally escaping in three lifeboats to Elephant Island.

His comment was unrelated to his famous 800-mile boat journey across the Southern Ocean.

And he was not alluding to his own efforts to trek across South Georgia to reach a whaling station so he could rescue his men stranded on Elephant Island.

Shackleton was referring to a march on the Great Ice Barrier of Antarctica by the 'Mount Hope Party'. This party of six men were members of his support team based on the opposite side of the continent to the Weddell Sea. The Mount Hope Party consisted of five Englishmen: the leader, Captain Aeneas Lionel Acton Mackintosh, ex-Petty Officer Ernest Edward Mills Joyce, Petty Officer Harry Ernest Wild, the Reverend Arnold Patrick Spencer-Smith, and Victor George Hayward; and an Australian, Richard 'Dick' Walter Richards.

The 'march' Shackleton referred to was a 360-mile return journey made by these men from Mount Hope at the foot of the Beardmore Glacier in the Trans-Antarctic Mountains to the safety of Hut Point at McMurdo Sound in the Ross Sea. This is what Shackleton was describing as a remarkable story of human endeavour.

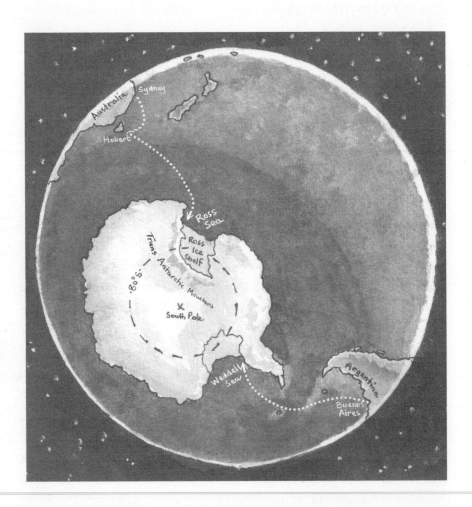

Background

After the conquest of the South Pole by Amundsen in December 1911, Shackleton had written: '…there remained but one great main object of Antarctic journeyings – the crossing of the South Polar continent from sea to sea.'[2]

In an attempt to cross Antarctica, Shackleton planned the 1914–17 Imperial Trans-Antarctic Expedition, which involved the use of two ships, the
Endurance and the *Aurora*. The *Endurance* would take Shackleton's party
to the Weddell Sea and Shackleton would set off across the continent. His
aim was to reach the South Pole and then continue on to McMurdo Sound,
on the opposite side of Antarctica, coming down the Beardmore Glacier.

He would have a supporting party in the second ship, the *Aurora*. This
party would sail from Australia to McMurdo Sound in the Ross Sea, establish camp there and lay a series of vital supply depots out across the Great
Ice Barrier to Mount Hope at the foot of the Beardmore Glacier. These
depots would support Shackleton's final step, his last 360 miles crossing
the continent.

Shackleton's own story is well known. In early 1915 his ship the *Endurance* became caught in the pack ice in the Weddell Sea and, with the men,
camped on the ice; the ship was squeezed, then smashed and broken
up before it disappeared below the ice. The pack ice drifted slowly north
before Shackleton and his men escaped in their three lifeboats, landing
on Elephant Island, a mountainous, ice-covered and barren island off the
coast of Antarctica. From there, in April 1916, Shackleton and five of his
men set sail for help in one of the lifeboats, across 800 miles of the Southern Ocean to the island of South Georgia. After being forced to land on
the opposite side of the island to a whaling port located there, Shackleton,
with two of his men, crossed the mountains and glaciers on the island to
reach the port, and assistance, so he could arrange for his men at Elephant
Island, and two still on South Georgia, to be picked up.

Not knowing of Shackleton's aborted attempt to land on the opposite
side of the continent, his supporting party established base at a hut in
McMurdo Sound in the Ross Sea and made preparations for their sledging
journey. They planned to lay two depots in the late summer of 1915 (January to March), one at 70 miles south of their base, at latitude 79°S, and the
other 70 miles further south, near latitude 80°S. Then, after the winter of
1915, their plan was to lay more depots, at 81°S, 82°S, 83°S, then a final
depot for Shackleton at 83° 30´S, next to Mount Hope by the Beardmore
Glacier. This depot would be 360 miles from Hut Point.

Shackleton's Heroes

There have only been a limited number of books written on the experiences of the Mount Hope Party, possibly because the story was dwarfed by Shackleton's tale, which even today remains the classic story of adventure. Moreover, the Mount Hope tale can first appear to be little more than a story of wasted efforts to lay food depots that were not needed.

Two members of the Mount Hope Party did write books of their exploits. In 1929 Ernest Joyce's book, *The South Polar Trail: The Log of the Imperial Trans-Antarctic Expedition*, was published. It is a loose transcript of his field diary. Many years later, in 1962, Dick Richards wrote a slim volume titled *The Ross Sea Shore Party*. In forty pages he covers his appointment by Mackintosh to join the expedition through to meeting with Shackleton when finally rescued. Like Joyce's book, it is one man's opinion and take on events. It was 2001 before the journalist Lennard Bickel wrote *Shackleton's Forgotten Men* (originally titled *Shackleton's Argonauts*), a novel about the Mount Hope Party. However, at his time of writing only a few primary source documents were available. In 2004, Richard McElrea and Dr David Harrowfield wrote a complete and accurate account of the entire Ross Sea Party story, titled *Polar Castaways*. Their book covers the period from 1914 to 1917 so there is limited space available to describe in full the critical three months, January–March 1916, when the six men returned from Mount Hope. In 2006 Kelly Tyler-Lewis also wrote of the Ross Sea Party in her book *The Lost Men* but only a small number of pages covered the months of January–March 1916. In Shackleton's book on the Imperial Trans-Antarctic Expedition, *South*, he devoted a significant proportion (almost a third of his book) to the exploits of the men of his Ross Sea support party. He used selected diary extracts from only two of the men, Mackintosh and Joyce, to describe events, rather than his own words.

We see that the epic struggle of the six men to return from Mount Hope has been barely documented… In addition, as well as the books of Joyce and Richards, we have a number of interviews with Richards later in his life (with Bickel, his son-in-law Peter Lathlean, Phillip Law, the first Director of Australia's Antarctic Division, and ABC radio), and letters he wrote to various Antarctic historians.

Having access to every diary from the one expedition in the Scott–Shackleton exploration era is exceptional and it allows us to glimpse a truer picture of life than would be obtained from the diary of one man, or when only one person's recollection of events is given. In bringing many of these diaries from obscure library storage to published volume we also honour the courage and spirit of these lesser-known, but equally brave and heroic, Antarctic explorers.

Apart from Mackintosh, who as the leader had an obligation to write up a daily record of events, the other men had no duty to catalogue their achievements, but fortunately they did write, when times were good and bad. When they were sledging they wrote their notes at lunch stops, when they had finished for the day or while waiting out a blizzard. On most occasions they wrote while inside their tent and lying inside their sleeping bags. Through the diaries we read a remarkable story of six men and their dogs in a battle with nature in a bitter and hostile environment with many illuminating human touches. The diaries not only bring to light their innermost thoughts at times of great stress and conflict but they also give us an insight into all aspects of their life, from their hardships when man-hauling sledges in deep snow to their admiration for their dogs. We read of their thoughts of home and of their dreams while on the Great Ice Barrier. We see the different way each man handles crises and how they react when pushed to the limit. They describe their joyous early days in Antarctica and then later the misery of their final days when they wondered if they would survive. We are privy to an insider's view; a vivid picture of how six men lived and worked together as they strived to achieve their goal of laying supply depots, which they believed were critical for Shackleton's survival.

Although it is not always clear from their diaries, distance measurements would appear to be in geographical miles, not statute miles, which is the measurement we normally use, on road signs and maps for example. A geographical mile is one-sixtieth of a degree of a great circle of the earth. Geographical miles are multiplied by approximately 1.14 to obtain the statute miles. For example, between Hut Point and Cape Evans the distance was given as 13 (geographical) miles, which is 15 statute miles. (For kilo-metres, the metric equivalent of miles, multiply the miles figure by 1.853. The distance out to Mount Hope is usually quoted as 360 miles and that is 670 kilometres.)

Heights were recorded in feet, for example Mount Erebus was stated by the men to be about 13,000 feet high, and that is 3,962 metres. (To convert feet to metres, multiply by 0.3048.)

Temperatures were always in Fahrenheit. (To convert to centigrade, sub-tract thirty-two and then multiply by five-ninths. For example: 32°F is 0°C, 20°F is -7°C, 0°F is -18°C, -20°F is -29°C, -40°F is -40°C.)

Weights were recorded in imperial measures.

The metric and centigrade equivalents are not shown in parenthesis throughout the book because there are so many references, especially to distances and temperatures.

The diary quotes are shown exactly as they were written at the time.

In preparation for this book, not all the repetitive routine of the early days of sledging is included and some irrelevant or inexplicable quotations are not shown, but no important event has been omitted. The diary pages published here are unedited and in the main are shown indented. The spelling, punctuation, abbreviations and grammar are left intact as they add to the charm of the words. The men used rounded brackets in their diaries – any square brackets indicate a word edited in.

The maps are stylised and three-dimensional to give the reader some feeling for the topography of the Antarctic landscape. They are not drawn to scale but give a clearer picture of the distance travelled than would be obtained from a traditional two-dimensional map.

As a starting point, and to put the diaries in perspective, we begin with background information of the men of the Mount Hope Party, their recruit-ment in England and Australia and then their voyage to Antarctica. Diaries were issued to the men when they arrived. Most of the six men started their diaries immediately and continued recording notes right through to the end. The vast majority of the book covers the period from when they first set foot on Antarctica, in January 1915, up to the time they finish their depot-laying work in May 1916.

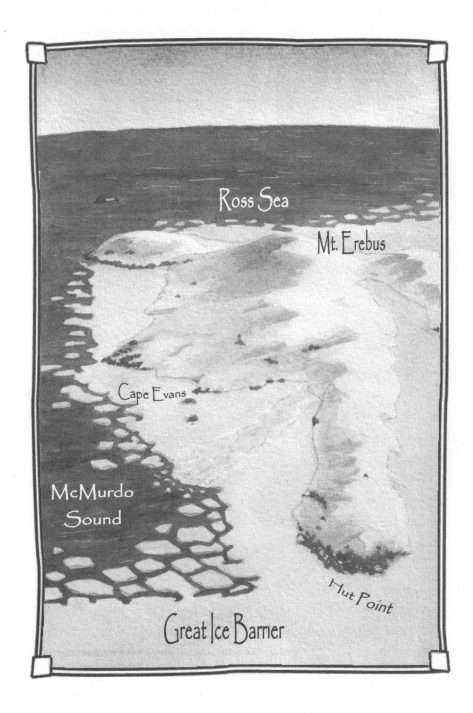

Chapter 1

'I HAD NOT ANTICIPATED THAT THE WORK WOULD PRESENT ANY GREAT DIFFICULTIES'

Shackleton in the Antarctic before 1914

EARLIER BRITISH EXPEDITIONS to Antarctica had a marked influence on how Sir Ernest Shackleton organised his Mount Hope support party. There were three in particular: Captain Scott's National Antarctic *Discovery* Expedition of 1901–04, Shackleton's own Antarctic *Nimrod* Expedition of 1907–09 and Scott's Antarctic *Terra Nova* Expedition of 1910–13.

These expeditions were all based in McMurdo Sound in the Ross Sea. The southerly tip of the sound is the closest part of Antarctica to the South Pole reachable by ship so it was the logical place for previous expeditions to establish base, and for Shackleton to locate his 1914–17 support party.

McMurdo Sound is an inlet about 30 miles long by 20 miles wide pointing towards the South Pole. At its most southerly shore is Cape Armitage and nearby is a 750-foot high hill, Observation Hill, named for its use as a lookout for returning sledges in Scott's *Discovery* Expedition.[1] The eastern shore of McMurdo Sound is Ross Island and the active volcano Mount Erebus (12,448 feet) dominates the region. Also on Ross Island are three other (extinct) volcanoes: Mount Bird (5,900 feet) at the northerly end, Mount Terra Nova (6,988 feet) and Mount Terror (10,700 feet).

Two significant landmarks on Ross Island are Hut Point, a rocky peninsula at the base of McMurdo Sound, and Cape Evans, a sheltered inlet to the north of Hut Point. These landmarks would become highly significant for the Mount Hope Party. Huts had been built at each of these two places, which were only 13 miles apart, but to travel between these two locations was difficult.

Icebound rocky cliffs and impassable glaciers follow the coastline from Hut Point round to Cape Evans and make it almost impossible to travel between the huts via that route. Travel between the two locations by ship is only possible for a few weeks in February, when there is water at the base of McMurdo Sound. At that time strong southerly winds push the ice in the sound northward into the Ross Sea, leaving open water or very thin sea-ice in the southerly tip, but only for a limited time. For the other eleven months of the year McMurdo Sound is largely frozen over with sea-ice. This means that for the majority of the year there is only one practical way to travel between Cape Evans and Hut Point, and that is on foot over the sea-ice. Only in the winter months of June or July when the sound completely freezes over with sea-ice about 10 feet thick is it a safe journey. In addition, any trek is made somewhat arduous and difficult by a floating 100-foot-high glacier, Glacier Tongue, which blocks the direct route between these two locations. This mile-wide glacier is surrounded by sea-ice and extends out into the sound for more than 5 miles. These conditions had a huge impact on the Mount Hope Party, who had to travel frequently between Cape Evans and Hut Point.

A second feature of Shackleton's planning was for the *Aurora* to be win-
tered at McMurdo Sound, as Scott had with the *Discovery* in 1901–03. The
ship would serve as living quarters and in addition his Mount Hope Party
would also make use of huts that had been built by previous expeditions.
However, it eventuated that the men did not live on the ship. They used
two huts, one at Hut Point and the other at Cape Evans.

In Scott's 1901–04 expedition, *Discovery* hut was erected on the location designated as Hut Point.[2] The hut was essentially a wooden shell,
prefabricated in Sydney, Australia with an open veranda surrounding it
on three sides. It was built entirely from Douglas fir and Scots pine with a
pyramid-shaped roof. Unfortunately the hut was too hard to heat and was
never used as a base; only as a storeroom, a shelter, for recording scientific observations and for 'theatrical performances' by Scott's men. They
lived on board their ship, which was frozen into the sea-ice. *Discovery* hut
was to become a refuge of safety for the Mount Hope Party when returning from their depot-laying journeys in 1915 and 1916.

On Scott's second expedition, the *Terra Nova* Expedition, he set up their
base at Cape Evans and the hut built there was far more substantial than the one
at Hut Point. It was 50 feet by 25 feet in size, with Ruberoid on the roof, floor,
walls and ceiling for insulation. Additional insulation, finely shredded seaweed
known as Gibson quilting, was placed on the walls. Lighting was by acetylene
gas, and heating from coal-burning stoves.[3] Shackleton's support party would
use this Cape Evans hut as their main base. There is also a third hut at Cape
Royds, about 5 miles to the north of Cape Evans, which Shackleton built on
his *Nimrod* Expedition. This hut was not lived in by the Mount Hope Party.

A third aspect of Shackleton's planning was that his support party would
lay depots out to Mount Hope on the same route that he and others had
pioneered on previous expeditions.

A ship cannot go south beyond Hut Point, the southerly tip of McMurdo
Sound, because of the Ross Ice Shelf (also called the Great Ice Barrier or
simply the Barrier).[4] The Barrier is a permanent sheet of ice, 160 to 200
feet above the water and about 1,100 feet thick, that spreads southward
from near the foot of McMurdo Sound to the Trans-Antarctic Mountains.
It is attached to land and is constantly fed by glaciers.[5]

On the *Discovery* Expedition, Scott, Edward Wilson and Shackleton took a journey south onto the Barrier and they reached a position approximately 260 miles to the south of Hut Point before turning back north. They saw and named Mount Discovery (8,794 feet) on the Trans-Antarctic Mountain range and Minna Bluff, a 3-mile-wide peninsula that extends into the Ross Ice Shelf from Mount Discovery. Scott named it 'Minna' in honour of the wife of Sir Clements Markham, who was then President of the Royal Geographical Society. These landmarks would be used by the Mount Hope Party some fifteen years later. They used Mount Discovery as a reference point and at Minna Bluff they would place a large food depot, which became instrumental in saving their lives.

A more significant southerly expedition was Shackleton's *Nimrod* Expedition of 1907–09. Shackleton, in his quest to reach the South Pole, had hoped the pole would be located on the Barrier. He initially described the Barrier as 'level as a billiard table, with no sign of any undulation or rise'[6] but as his party went further south, now some 300 miles from Hut Point, they saw mountains, well over 10,000 feet high, that had been to the west but slowly curved to cut straight across their path. As the days wore on, mountain after mountain came into view but Shackleton was hopeful that they 'may find some strait' that would enable them to go through them and continue further south. When they reached the mountains they found them entirely clear of snow, with vertical sides and not less than 9,000 feet in height. After following the mountain range for two days they saw a red hill about 3,000 feet in height which they climbed so as to gain a view of the surrounding country. They named the hill Mount Hope and from the top of a ridge they saw their way forward, to the south. Shackleton wrote in his diary: 'There burst upon our view an open road to the south, for there stretched before us a great glacier running almost south and north.'[7] Adjacent to Mount Hope they found a snow-filled pass flanked by great granite pillars at least 2,000 feet in height which they called the Gap; a gap through the mountains to the glacier, later named the Beardmore Glacier (after a sponsor). It would be at this gap that the Mount Hope Party planned to lay their final depot for Shackleton in 1916 so that it would be visible by the party descending the glacier.

Shackleton was able to recruit two men who had been on these past expeditions. Ernest Joyce was a member of the supporting parties that laid food and fuel depots for Scott, Wilson and Shackleton to use on their trek back to Hut Point on the *Discovery* Expedition. A few years later Joyce was a member of the shore party on Shackleton's *Nimrod* Expedition. Also on the *Nimrod* was a man who would later be appointed leader of Shackleton's 1914–17 support party, Lieutenant Aeneas Mackintosh.

The final aspect of Shackleton's planning for the Mount Hope Party was to copy the methods of depot-laying used on previous expeditions. Small teams of men would work together, sharing a tent, food and equipment, and they would be able to travel quite independently of other parties. Dogs were taken, not ponies; no doubt as a result of the success Amundsen had over Scott in their race for the South Pole. Their food and clothing remained virtually unchanged from previous British expeditions. Teams of men would lay food and fuel depots out to the south so a final southbound party would not have to carry supplies for the whole journey, a system Shackleton had used before. For example, while his team was on their southern journey on the *Nimrod* Expedition, Joyce was in charge of a party which included Mackintosh. This party was responsible for laying support depots for Shackleton's return and a major depot was located near Minna Bluff, 70 miles from Hut Point. Supplies would be laid at the same Minna Bluff location by the Mount Hope Party in 1915 and 1916.

Shackleton had his Mount Hope Party travel to McMurdo Sound and use the huts at Cape Evans and Hut Point. They would base themselves at Cape Evans hut but also use *Discovery* hut at Hut Point, initially as a place to store supplies, but it ended up being lived in for many winter months. They were to lay food depots along the same route Shackleton had used, all the way out to the Beardmore Glacier. Depots were to be placed about a week's travel apart, at each degree of latitude, which is close to 70 miles apart.

According to Shackleton: 'This programme would involve some heavy sledging, but the ground to be covered was familiar, and I had not anticipated that the work would present any great difficulties.'[8]

Instead, what transpired was one of the most harrowing and torturous feats of courage in the history of polar exploration. The men of the Mount Hope Party travelled over 1,500 miles, with few dogs, poor equipment, insufficient food and tattered clothing to lay the depots for Shackleton.

The men of the Mount Hope Party

The six men of the Mount Hope Party appear to be an ill-assorted lot. There were five Englishmen and one Australian and only two had any experience in Antarctica. Their backgrounds and education were quite varied; a padre, a clerk from London, a school teacher from Australia and navy men, two of which were lower-deck sailors, from a different stratum to their captain.

AENEAS LIONEL ACTON MACKINTOSH

- Aeneas Mackintosh was the leader of the party. From photographs, he was clearly a handsome man, although not tall, possibly only a few inches over 5 ft. His privileged early upbringing in India and his commissioned officer rank would have set him apart from the two non-commissioned navy men, Joyce and Wild, as would his manner of speaking in what A. P. Spencer-Smith termed an 'Oxford' voice.[9] The other men often referred to him as Captain, O.M. (Old Man), Mack or Skipper in their diaries.

- He was born in India to British parents in 1879.[10] The Mackintosh family papers show that his father was an 'Indigo Planter' and that his mother Annie left India with her six young children, moving to Bedfordshire in England when Aeneas was a young boy. His father had Bright's disease and remained in India. Aeneas never saw his father again but remained fond of him, writing regularly; his father kept every letter but sadly they were found unopened when his father died.[11] As a young teenager in the 1890s Mackintosh lived with his mother and his younger brothers and sister in England. He attended Bedford Modern School, an independent school in Bedfordshire, from 1891 to 1894.[12]

- In 1895, at fifteen years of age, he left school to go to sea to become a commissioned officer in the Merchant Navy, serving as an apprentice on the full-rigged sailing ship *Cromdale*. (The Merchant Navy deals with mostly cargo and civilian transports.) His naval papers state that he joined the Peninsular and Oriental Steam Navigation Company (P&O), a British commercial shipping company, in 1900.[13]

- In 1907 Mackintosh's Antarctic experience commenced when he was recruited by Shackleton as second officer on the British Antarctic (*Nimrod*) Expedition of 1907–09.[14] On this expedition he lost his right eye. In January 1908 the *Nimrod* arrived in Antarctica but while unloading stores at Cape Royds a crate hook attached to a barrel swung across and struck him on the face. Ernest Joyce, also on the *Nimrod* Expedition, happened to be there at the time helping with the unloading. After the accident Mackintosh was sent back to New Zealand in the *Nimrod*, but twelve months later he returned, with a glass eye, and helped to lay depots out on the Great Ice Barrier.

- After the *Nimrod* Expedition, Mackintosh was given clerical duties in England because the loss of his eye precluded him from being appointed to any of the P&O Company's ships.[15] He remained on-shore until he joined Shackleton's expedition in 1914. His naval records show that after the *Nimrod* Expedition he held the rank of 3rd Officer, which is below a normal captain's ranking. However, as the officer in command of the *Aurora*, he held the higher rank of Captain, being in charge of the ship, and his men, including Shackleton, referred to him as Captain Mackintosh.

- He was the only married man of the Mount Hope Party, having married Gladys Campbell at Holy Trinity Church in Bedford, England. His best man was Dr Eric Marshall, one of the doctors who operated on his eye in the Antarctic. The Mackintoshes' first daughter, Pamela, was born in 1912 and Gladys, their second, in 1914.[16]

- We have Mackintosh's personal diary from late 1914 to January 1915 and his 1915 sledging diary, up to September 1915. Every day he writes up an accurate recording of events and on many days he pens 300 to 400 words. He includes meticulous notes on a myriad of issues with odd comments interspersed within his daily log. Examples of his 'unusual comments' include one on the health hazard of carbon fumes emanating from seal blubber burning in a stove and another, on more than one occasion, of the number of days since he last washed. He writes often on the unpleasant aspects of sledging and the difficulties of living, cooking and sleeping in a tent on the Great Ice Barrier in freezing conditions. It is an enlightening document.

ERNEST EDWARD MILLS JOYCE

- Joyce was the oldest member of the Mount Hope Party, and the man with the most experience in Antarctica. He was a short, stocky man, only 5 ft 7½ in. in height, with dark brown hair, blue eyes, a tattoo on his left forearm and a scar on his right cheek.

- His naval records show that he was born at Feltham, Sussex in southern England in 1875, making him four years older than Mackintosh. Joyce's father was a former naval rating and after his father's death, Joyce was sent to the Greenwich Royal Hospital School in London, founded in

1712 to educate boys for service in the Royal Navy. (Unlike the Merchant
Navy, in which Mackintosh was employed, the Royal Navy is a branch
of the British armed forces.)

- His naval records also disclose that, as a twelve-year-old, he joined the
  navy as a Boy 2nd Class Seaman, on the ship *St Vincent*, in 1891. From
  1891 to 1901 Joyce progressed through the ranks as an Ordinary Seaman to Able Seaman, gaining a character rating of 'Very Good' on many
  of his reports.[17]

- In 1901 Joyce was serving on HMS *Gibraltar* at Simon's Town, Cape
  Town in South Africa when Scott's expedition ship *Discovery* stopped
  there on the way to the Antarctic. He was chosen to join the *Discovery* Expedition and on this trip Joyce was allocated tasks that were to
  stand him in good stead for his work as a member of the Mount Hope
  Party. He assisted in the laying of the supply depots, gaining experience in sledging, dog-driving and Antarctic conditions, but he suffered
  severely from frostbite. In September of 1903 the mercury in the thermometer sank to below -67° F when Joyce was out on the Barrier. He
  found one of his feet white to the ankle and it took over an hour before
  his tent-mates could get any sign of life in his foot, by taking it in turns
  'to nurse the frozen member in their breasts'.[18] Joyce was promoted to
  Petty Officer 1st Class on 10 September 1904 in recognition of his service in the *Discovery* Expedition.[19]

- In 1907 he was discharged from the Royal Navy to form one of the crew
  of the *Nimrod* on Shackleton's 1907 expedition to Antarctica. On this
  expedition we learn from Shackleton of Joyce's fondness for dogs. He
  tells us Joyce enjoyed running them when on-shore, giving them steam-
  ing hot feeds and working at training them to pull a sledge.[20] To the
  other men on the *Nimrod* Expedition Joyce 'had charge of them, fed
  them, and taught them sledging'.[21] We will see from Joyce's Mount Hope
  diary records that he realises the value of dogs. Joyce was not chosen
  to be on Shackleton's main southbound party – he had suffered badly

from frostbite and the doctor (Marshall) diagnosed a damaged liver due to excess drinking, and a weak heart.[22] However, he was a member of a support party that initially accompanied the southern team and he led a team to lay supplies at Minna Bluff for the return of the southern party. In late February 1909, Shackleton's party was struggling back north towards this Minna Bluff depot, after turning back less than 100 miles from the South Pole. Shackleton tells us that they were at the end of their supplies, except for some scraps of meat scraped off the bones of one of their horses that died on the trek south. Shackleton had faith in Joyce and had no doubt that the Bluff depot would have been laid correctly because, in his words, 'Joyce knows his work well'.[23]

• Joyce did not return to the Royal Navy after the *Nimrod* Expedition but worked in Australia, at one time managing a lodging house in Kent Street, Sydney.[24] He gained some notoriety in 1911 when he was charged with assaulting a policeman but a testimonial from Shackleton was read to the court which, a newspaper claimed, stated that Joyce bore an excellent character.[25]

• Joyce's written notes on the Mount Hope Party are in three documents. There is his original blubber-oil-stained field diary where he recorded what happened during and at the end of each day. He rarely misses a daily entry from January 1915 until May 1916 and this field diary forms the bulk of Joyce's words that are included here. He writes short cryptic notes and he is very straightforward with his opinion of people, particularly in naming those who, in his eyes, are malingering or not contributing. We see the picture as it was for Joyce, warts and all. He clearly did not expect this field diary to be used by others because he created a second set of notes, a transcript of his field diary that he made with Richards's help, when recuperating at Cape Evans at the end of the expedition. Many of the harsher criticisms of the other men are not carried forward into the transcripts and only a handful of transcript notes are reproduced here. Finally we have Joyce's book, *The South Polar Trail*. The book is excellent from the point of providing us with a day-by-day account of the expedition, but it differs in too many ways from his actual field diary to be of more than a limited value. His field diary notes reproduced here are as they appear in his diary, even though there are many sentences with no structure and sometimes only a few words are used to explain an event. His grammar is often non-existent and there are spelling mistakes. He uses words like 'weigh' and 'shew' which, until the 1920s, were not considered as incorrect spelling. He uses symbols, such as 'S' for Mackintosh (the Skipper) and abbreviations like 'Provi' for 'Providence'. This is understandable, however, when one considers Joyce's education and the situation he was in. Like all the men, he was usually writing up his diary in miserable circumstances; sometimes in the dark, in his sleeping bag, in a tent, in freezing conditions and after a day's work hauling a sledge.

- His portrait, taken from a photograph after Joyce had returned from Antarctica, shows a rugged weather-beaten face, a shock of hair, and beard. He appears to have an almost quizzical look in his eye, or possibly a disdain for someone in higher authority; a character trait that surfaces many times in his diary concerning his relationship with Mackintosh.

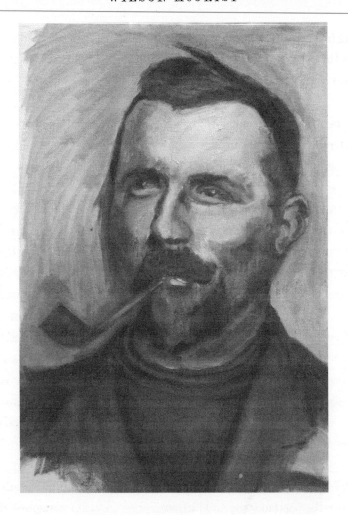

HARRY ERNEST WILD

• Harry Ernest Wild was a navy man, serving an uninterrupted twenty
  years on ships before joining Shackleton's expedition in 1914. He was
  born in 1879 at Nettleton, Lincolnshire in England, the third son of Mary
  and Benjamin Wild and one of thirteen children.[26] [27] In 1885 the Wild
  family moved to Eversholt in Bedfordshire, a tiny village which even
  today consists of little more than a small number of homes, a cricket
  green, the St John the Baptist church and a pub, The Green Man. As
  a boy, Ernest was in the church choir. Later he reputedly developed a
  good tenor voice and became known as a person who could sing a comic

song heartily.[28] From diary records of the Mount Hope Party it appears
that Ernest Wild's singing helped maintain the good spirits of his tent-
mates at crucial times.

- His brother was Frank Wild, who had been on the *Discovery* and the
  Nimrod expeditions and he was Shackleton's second in command on
  the *Endurance* Expedition.

- In 1894, at fifteen years of age, Wild entered the Royal Navy and his
  naval records show he was barely 5 ft tall at that time, and that he only
  grew another 3 inches. He started as a Boy 2nd Class in HMS *Boscawen*,
  a boys' training ship at Portland. He served with a number of ships,
  advancing to Able Seaman on 1 May 1898, still aged only eighteen. Like
  Joyce, Wild was stationed in South Africa in 1901 when Scott's HMS
  Discovery called at Simon's Town. In 1905 Wild was promoted to Petty
  Officer 1st Class.[29] His naval service record shows that he was awarded
  a Good Conduct badge in 1904, which was taken from him a year later,
  but restored in 1906. This process was repeated in 1909, then again in
  1911, showing a character trait that personnel at the Naval Historical
  Branch have described as 'Wild by name, wild by nature'.[30]

- Wild's diary entries vary considerably in length. At times he obviously
  felt predisposed to write and he pens paragraph after paragraph describing what had gone on over the previous few days, or weeks. At other
  times he would hardly make a diary entry for a month, apart from a very
  brief note with no more than a sentence or two to mention one feature
  of his day. He was the only man of the Mount Hope Party to write with
  any humour. Others mention occasional events that make them laugh
  or that they found amusing, but Wild seemed to have the ability to look
  at the lighter side of life when writing up his diary notes. This was even
  after struggling all day hauling a heavy sledge, lying in the tent eking out
  diminishing food rations, or when he had severe frostbite in his toes –
  even when he was in a life-threatening situation. Wild was very direct in
  what he wrote and was not afraid to say what he thought, particularly in

regard to Mackintosh's behaviour. He was a navy man of many years but Wild did not swear in his diary at all, the closest being when he would write 'h__l' and 'd___d' for 'hell' and 'damned'.

- His nickname was 'Tubby', which had come about because he was short and looked heavy. He became the most popular man of the Mount Hope Party team, seen by Richards and the others as 'an uncomplicated soul, always cheery and willing to help at all times'.[31]

- The portrait of Wild is from a photo taken after his rescue, on the *Aurora* returning to New Zealand. Knowing through his diary how much Wild misses his 'bacco' on the Mount Hope journey, one can almost feel the happiness and contentment emanating from his face as he smokes his pipe.

ARNOLD PATRICK SPENCER-SMITH

• Arnold Patrick (called A. P., 'Smithy' or 'Padre' by the other men) Spencer-Smith was born at Streatham, London on 17 March 1883. He was one of seven children.[32] When he was thirteen his father Charles applied for Arnold to be admitted to a boys' boarding school, Woodbridge Grammar School in Suffolk. Arnold studied classics at Woodbridge for six years, and the school magazine shows that he was also much involved in sport, excelling in cricket, football, fives and gymnastics. His later interest in travelling to Antarctica may have been kindled at an 1899 school lecture given by a W. W. Mumford on 'Arctic Travel and Adventure'. The lecture touched on the travels of explorers in the Arctic regions, some who perished in their attempts to reach the North Pole and others who lost their lives searching for the North-West Passage. Spencer-Smith wrote a report of the lecture for his school magazine.[33]

- He passed First Class London University Matriculation Examinations and then attended King's College, London and Queen's College, Cambridge where he read history. In 1907 Spencer-Smith was appointed Master at Merchiston Castle Preparatory School, Edinburgh, a boys' boarding school, where he taught French and mathematics. He was elected a Fellow of the Royal Historical Society in 1913 and ordained as an Anglican priest five days before he left London for Antarctica.[34]

- Spencer-Smith's character and occupation as a priest come out in his diary. He clearly enjoys friendly discussions and arguments, singing hymns at times of celebration (Mid-Winter's Day, for example) and reading. There are many Latin quotes, references to sermons and almost daily quotes from the Bible. He tells us of the hard graft of man-hauling, of running low on food and of his faltering health, but there is no trace of bitterness, no complaint and no person is blamed. He writes up his diary almost every day, often musing on his dreams or events of his past. When facing the possibility of dying, he remains positive and is confident that all will be well at the end – his strength appears to come from his faith in God. He writes a wonderfully eloquent diary.

- In all group photographs of the Mount Hope men Spencer-Smith stands out. He was the tallest man in the party; around 6 ft 4 in. in height, and, unlike the other men, he was of slim build. When he was a student at Queen's College in Cambridge, an article described him as 'slight but bony'. Another article gives us a clearer picture of the man: 'His lithe and lengthy form, studious stoop, pallid brow, neatly-groomed head, mediaeval raiment, decadent pumps, and inevitable Woodbine,* are familiar in the courts (of the College). It has been said that he has charming manners.'[35]

---

*   Woodbine was a brand of cigarettes.

VICTOR GEORGE HAYWARD

- Victor ('Vic') Hayward was born at Harlesden, London in 1887 into a very large family, having five brothers and eight sisters.[36] There are few records to be found of his early schooling or his childhood. Like Spencer-Smith, Hayward's desire to visit the polar regions may also have been with him since he was a boy. At Christ Church Sunday School in Willesden, London, when he was ten years old, he chose as a prize Ballantyne's book *The World of Ice*.[37] It is easy to imagine a young boy being entranced by Ballantyne's tale of men in the Arctic, such as when he describes two teams of men, with their dogs and sledges, setting out – with the romance of the 'sharp, dry, crunching sound' of the men as they walked along in the snow.[38]

- Hayward was educated at St Mark's College, Chelsea, before gaining employment with a large firm of stockbrokers in the City of London.[39] He was attracted to a life with some adventure, however, because at the age of twenty he left London to experience life in colder climates – working in the northern regions of Canada. He was employed on a ranch, gaining experience working with dogs and there he learnt to be a good dog driver before returning to England in November of 1907.[40] His parents only married in 1908, after the birth of the last of their thirteen children, and by 1914 his father had retired. At that time Victor was living at home and employed as a produce clerk in London.[41]

- A Londoner in his mid-twenties, Victor Hayward was the 'romantic' man of the Mount Hope Party. In August of 1914 he had become engaged to a Miss Ethel Bridson, whose family also lived in the inner north-west suburbs of London. Apart from Mackintosh, who made occasional diary references to his wife, Hayward is the only other member of the Mount Hope team who mentions a lady friend in his diary. The two navy men, Joyce and Wild, are twelve and eight years older than Hayward, but they make no reference to a sweetheart or loved one in any of their diary notes.

- Hayward's diary is fascinating because he writes most of the time for his fiancée. He pens over 24,000 words in a day-by-day record of his stay in Antarctica, in exquisite detail at times, and in a style that is quite unique. Where the other five men of the Mount Hope Party appear to be recording their diaries for anyone to read, Hayward's diary is very personal. Not only does his love for his fiancée come through, but he exposes his innermost thoughts, especially in the early stages of his time in Antarctica. He tells her of what happens almost every day, on the march, in the tent and in the hut, so we have a wonderful picture from his diary of what he and the others experienced. His diary pages are also brightened by occasional sketches. Some are of his fiancée, and others of the scenery, the *Aurora* and penguins. There are even images unrelated to Antarctica: horses, a Canadian Mountie on horseback, a man with a monocle in his left eye, looking resplendent in a top hat and formal attire, and other men with different hats. His education and upbringing shows through in some of the phrases and words he uses. He describes his life at times as a 'ducky life', calls a short sleep 'forty winks', uses the term 'by jingo' to express his surprise at something, calls an argument a 'roar' and often describes something as 'jolly nice'. He uses the phrase 'the bally thing didn't budge' when trying to move a sledge, whereas Wild would write 'd___d hard work' and Joyce in his untutored grammar would make a note: 'We struggled on + on'. Hayward's diary even contains a thirty-line poem that he and his tent-mates made up. He includes quotes from the book *Lorna Doone* and a full menu of two 'champagne suppers' he plans to have with his fiancée when he returns. However, as Hayward weakens with scurvy, his 400 and 500-word daily diary entries in his first sledging season dry up. In 1916, as he struggles back to Hut Point, his diary note each day is often nothing more than a few numbers; of the distance covered in the day, and the number of miles remaining to reach Hut Point.

- He was 5 ft 8 or 9 in. in height, a heavy, solid man.

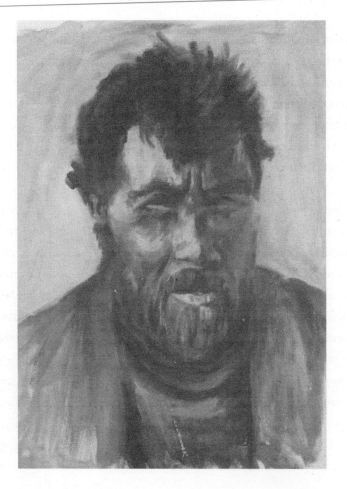

RICHARD 'DICK' WALTER RICHARDS

- The only Australian in the Mount Hope Party, Dick Richards, was interviewed on more than one occasion on his memories of Antarctica. From these interviews we glean some details of his early life, his education and his work prior to joining Shackleton's 1914 expedition.

- Richards was born in 1893 at Long Gully, a small country town near Bendigo in Victoria, Australia. He had two brothers and two sisters. His friends and family called him 'Wally' but to the men of the Mount Hope Party he was 'Dick' or 'Richy'.[42] Richards makes the point in one of his interviews that as a youth he walked to school every day, about

3 miles, and he was glad he did as he felt it stood him in good stead for his time in Antarctica. He said that his knees and legs were the strongest part of his body, and believed this helped delay the onset of scurvy when returning from Mount Hope.[43] At the age of sixteen he went to Melbourne University, where he completed work in natural philosophy (physics and mathematics). He then spent a number of years teaching in rural Victoria.

- Richards was in Antarctica from January 1915 until January 1917 but he made a diary entry on only forty days. Most of these entries were made in the early months of 1916 when he and the others were held up by a blizzard for days and it looked like they might not even survive. Like Joyce, Richards wrote a book (*The Ross Sea Shore Party*), but he was different to all the other men of the Mount Hope Party in that he was interviewed a number of times in later years. At these interviews he was able to elaborate on events even further. He also responded to any letters with detailed and blunt replies. These letters were written and these interviews conducted fifty and sixty years after, but Richards's memory seems crystal clear. His thoughts and words do not vary from one interview to another, or in his letters and, together with his diary, give us a deep insight into what happened to the Mount Hope Party – and why.

- He was the youngest man in the Mount Hope Party, being twenty-two years old when he left Australia. His portrait, from a photograph taken soon after he was picked up from Cape Evans at the end of his time in Antarctica, shows a handsome, rugged young man. He was 5 ft 9 in. tall and weighed almost 12 stone.[44] He looks older than a man in his early twenties, and we will see as the Mount Hope story unfolds that Richards acts far beyond his age.[45]

Chapter 2

'BUT SURELY, SIR ERNEST, THIS ISN'T GOING TO FIZZLE OUT INTO A PICNIC'

The Englishmen join Shackleton's Expedition

SHACKLETON STARTED PREPARATIONS for his Imperial Trans-Antarctic Expedition in the middle of 1913, but no public announcement was made until January 1914. For the last six months of 1913 he was engaged in the necessary preliminaries; 'solid mule work' were his words. It was an extensive expedition that had to have his ship, the *Endurance*, on one side of the Antarctic continent and the support ship, the *Aurora*, on the other, with a land journey of 1,800 miles to be made. In January 1914 he received nearly 5,000 applications to join his expedition, from what he described as all classes of the community.[1]

His first appointment for his support party was Mackintosh, as its leader. At the time, Mackintosh was working for the Imperial Merchant Service Guild in Liverpool and he had written to a colleague from his *Nimrod* days that he was dissatisfied with safe, routine work. His *Nimrod*

Expedition had left him unfulfilled. He told his colleague he was 'only existing at this job, stuck in a dirty office. I always feel I never completed my first initiation – so would like to have one final wallow, for good or bad!'[2]

Shackleton knew Mackintosh from their time together on the *Nimrod* Expedition, so he clearly had some understanding of Mackintosh's abilities and leadership skills. Mackintosh had gained sledging experience as a member of a party that laid support depots for Shackleton on that expedition. Shackleton placed Mackintosh in command of his support party despite knowing that Mackintosh had been involved in two ill-planned and risky actions in 1909. On one of these Mackintosh made a decision to camp on sea-ice, and he and a colleague almost lost their lives. The other involved Mackintosh and the colleague becoming lost and it was the latter, a non-commissioned sailor, who took over the leadership role.[3] Shackleton may have appointed him to lead because of Mackintosh's eye loss on the *Nimrod* Expedition. Richards believed this to be the case, writing later that Shackleton promised Mackintosh that if he could ever do anything for him he would, and Mackintosh held him to his promise in 1914.[4]

Shackleton issued written instructions to Mackintosh. He was to use his own discretion as to who went on the Mount Hope depot-laying party and if he went himself he must have full reliance on his Chief Officer.[5] Joseph Stenhouse was later appointed Chief Officer. He would be captain of the ship when Mackintosh was on shore.

In early 1914 Ernest Joyce was working for the Sydney Harbour Trust in Australia and Shackleton sent him a cablegram confirming his appointment. Joyce tells us in his book *The South Polar Trail* that Shackleton placed him in charge of the dogs, stores and sledging equipment and that Mackintosh would be in command of the ship.[6] However, Joyce's actual invitation of appointment from Shackleton stated that an officer would be in command of the shore party, not Joyce.[7] Why Joyce misrepresented the facts when he wrote his book, over ten years after the events, is unclear. Joyce may have wanted to give the impression to his readers that he was leading the shore party, a supposition that is supported by the fact that there is no reference in his book to Mackintosh being in charge. However, through the diaries of Richards, Spencer-Smith and Hayward it is very clear that Mackintosh was the leader of the shore party, until he fell ill with scurvy in 1916.[8] [9] [10]

Joyce's invitation from Shackleton was written up in the Australian newspapers and the article also stated that Joyce 'knows perhaps more of the transport and stores side of a polar expedition than anybody else', which we could assume are Joyce's words to the journalist writing the article. The article gave some additional information on the dogs to be used:

> They are to be secured by the Hudson Bay Company, and are expected to weigh between 70 and 80 pounds each. They are really the most efficient mode of traction for such expeditions, as each one draws a load of over 100 pounds, and eats only 1lb of food a day. This is in the form of biscuits,* with cod-liver oil forming a big part. They are fed once a day after halting at night.[11]

Three other men of the Mount Hope Party were also recruited by Shackleton in England: A. P. Spencer-Smith, Ernest Wild and Victor Hayward.

Spencer-Smith submitted a successful application to join as the chaplain and photographer. At the time he was teaching at Merchiston Castle in Edinburgh. A reference from the headmaster described him as a 'man of culture, of good practical sense and of pleasing personality'.[12] There is no record of why he was accepted but he was a photographer and Shackleton knew the value in visual images for later publicity and promotional purposes – he had the Australian photographer Frank Hurley in his own party travelling to the Weddell Sea. Unfortunately, very few quality outdoor photographs by Spencer-Smith have survived.

Wild was thirty-five years old and serving on the *Pembroke* in 1914 when the Navy approved for him to be lent for service with the Imperial

---

* Biscuits were made of flour mixed with Plasmon powder. The biscuits were hard – usually eaten by being broken into small pieces and then softened by putting them in hot chocolate or tea.

Trans-Antarctic Expedition.[13] His brother Frank had served with Shackleton in two expeditions to Antarctica and he may have influenced him to apply. Being Frank's brother would have almost certainly placed him at the top of the list of suitable applicants in Shackleton's eyes.

Hayward was working as a clerk in London when he applied and he received a letter of confirmation from Shackleton dated 28 August 1914.[14] Hayward's experience with dogs and sledge work in Canada would have been a significant contributing factor in him being accepted. His appointment was even reported in his local newspaper, the *Willesden Chronicle*, with the note: 'We feel sure that Mr. Hayward's many local friends will wish him good luck and a safe return.'[15]

In September 1914 Hayward and his parents met Shackleton before departing and Shackleton remarked to Mrs Hayward: 'I'm not going to give your son much hard work to do.' To which Hayward replied: 'But surely, Sir Ernest, this isn't going to fizzle out into a picnic – I could get that at home.'[16]

Others taken on in England who would be involved with the men of the Mount Hope Party were: Joseph Stenhouse, the Chief Officer of the *Aurora*; Alexander Stevens, a geologist and the chief scientist; John Cope, a biologist, who was also the party's medical officer; and Aubrey Ninnis, a motor engineer responsible for a motor tractor taken.

In spite of thousands of applicants, not all positions were filled from England. It appears that Shackleton did not have the time, leaving it to Mackintosh to recruit additional men in Australia. Shackleton admitted he was 'rather tired', having managed in only eight months to get his expedition ready, but he felt he had the 'complement of the *Aurora* practically complete' and he was sure it would eventually be right.[17]

The men recruited in England arrived in Sydney in November 1914 after Wild, Ninnis and the dogs had been dropped off in Hobart, for the dogs to be quarantined.[18] Mackintosh had not travelled to Australia with the other men. He went to Hobart earlier to arrange for the *Aurora* to be taken to Sydney, the ship having been idle since Douglas Mawson's Australasian Antarctic Expedition of 1911–14.

The Aurora in Sydney

The *Aurora* had been built in Dundee in 1876 and designed for navigation in northern seas. The hulls were wood, for greater elasticity when pressed by ice, with hardwood sheathing to minimise abrasion when in contact with jagged ice floes.[19] The ship had been bought from Mawson by Shackleton for £3,200 and was similar in all respects to the *Terra Nova*, of Scott's last expedition. She was registered with the Royal Yacht Squadron, which meant she could evade all loading restrictions when she left port – essential for the *Aurora* given her decks were covered with cargo when she left Australia.[20]

The Australian newspapers proudly reported the arrival of the *Aurora* in Sydney, adding that Mackintosh hoped to take several young Australian scientists as well. He had room for a physicist and a surgeon, and one or two others.[21] Hayward had an interview with Mackintosh and he was appointed as the secretary to the expedition, on account of his office experience.[22]

The *Aurora* underwent an overhaul at Cockatoo Dock in Sydney and Mackintosh, Spencer-Smith, Joyce, Hayward and others stayed at the Australia Hotel there. Hayward sent a card to his family and Spencer-Smith sent letters to his parents and a menu card from the hotel, signed by Mackintosh, and others. [23] [24] In one letter Spencer-Smith tells his parents: 'In the hut I shall probably sleep in my dark room, like Ponting did.'* He also makes reference to a visit from Irvine Gaze, his cousin: 'Googs has turned up from Melbourne looking very handsome and fit. He will possibly come with us.'

Mackintosh and Spencer-Smith appear to have developed a close and friendly relationship from the outset, with Spencer-Smith including in the letter to his parents:

> Captain M met us on the quay & I got a snap of him exchanging compliments with
> Stenhouse. He's an absolute 'dear' – such a neat wee chap, with a gold eyeglass in
> his one remaining eye, and an 'Oxford' voice: a glutton for work and very cheery.
> We are all, staff & man, absolutely in love with him!

---

* H. G. Ponting was the expedition photographer on Scott's *Terra Nova* Expedition.

In Sydney, Mackintosh asked the padre to say grace at meals, much to Spencer-Smith's delight.[25] This bond of respect and friendship between these two men continued throughout their time in the Antarctic.

The Australian Dick Richards joins the expedition

In late 1914 Richards saw an advertisement in the Australian papers for a physicist who was wanted for an Antarctic expedition. Why he applied he was not sure, although he saw himself as a 'sort of restless chap' and he was 'pretty fed up' with teaching at that time.[26]

He wrote to Mackintosh saying that he had completed two years' work in natural philosophy, pure mathematics and applied mathematics at Melbourne University. He gave his age as twenty-two, told him he was engaged as a teacher at the Junior Technical School in Ballarat and that he was 'anxious not to lose chance' to be on the expedition.[27] [28] [29]

In his book Richards tells how he went to Sydney, where he met Mackintosh, Spencer-Smith and Stevens. He must have impressed the three men because at the end of the interview he was told to get his gear together and rejoin the ship in Hobart. Richards could not remember any salary being offered, and he did not expect any.[30] He tells us they simply said: 'Alright we will take you, meet us in Hobart; make your own way there.'[31]

At that time Richards signed the standard agreement, which all members of the Imperial Trans-Antarctic Expedition were required to do. The agreement was between Shackleton and Richards and it stated a salary, £52 per annum, and included normal conditions for such an enterprise, particularly that he must obey all commands and not publish anything without consent.[32] (When Richards was in Antarctica, Mackintosh made him sign another agreement, with very similar content.)

In Sydney Mackintosh recruited three other Australians who were to be involved with the Mount Hope Party. They were Irvine Gaze (Spencer-Smith's cousin), who was listed as a Commissariat Officer (general assistant), scientist Keith Jack, and Lionel Hooke as the wireless operator.

The *Aurora* left Sydney on 14 December 1914 with Hobart her first port of call, and Richards joined the expedition there. In his book he tells us that the ship was overladen, with a heavy deck cargo of coal and cases of petrol stacked on the top of the cook's galley and on deck.[33]

The Aurora leaves Australia

The Hobart newspaper *The Mercury* reported that the Ross Sea members of Shackleton's expedition made their departure from Hobart in 'the auxiliary barquentine *Aurora*' at 6.30 a.m. on Thursday 24 December 1914. Spencer-Smith sent home a brief cablegram: 'Blessed Xmas. Strictly Private.'[34] The ship took on Ernest Wild (and Ninnis) and eighteen dogs at the Quarantine Station. Then, after clearing land, Spencer-Smith held a Christmas service and that night they celebrated the start of their voyage south, obviously with a number of drinks as Richards thought they 'dined perhaps less wisely than well'.[35]

The six men who would form the Mount Hope Party were now on board, and together for the first time: the ship's captain and expedition leader, 36-year-old Lieutenant Mackintosh; forty-year-old Antarctic veteran Ernest Joyce; fellow Petty Officer Ernest Wild, who was the same age as Mackintosh; thirty-year-old Reverend A. P. Spencer-Smith; Vic Hayward at twenty-eight years of age; and Dick Richards, the Australian and youngest member, at only twenty-two years old. The *Aurora* would take more than two weeks to reach Antarctica, a voyage of 2,500 miles, from Hobart at latitude of 42° 88´S to McMurdo Sound in the Ross Sea at latitude of 77° 84´S.

On the voyage south Mackintosh worked on the sledging arrangements for his Mount Hope Party and the other five men helped with various deckhand duties. These duties included being a lookout, helping with the setting and taking in of the canvas sails, meteorological readings, shifting coal on deck and emptying ashes from the boiler room.[36] [37]

When the men assisted with hauling on the canvas sails, Richards tells us that he was fascinated by the sailors singing sea shanties for pulling in time on the sail ropes. He explained that the sailors would know on which shanty beat to start pulling, 'O Shenandoah! I LONG to hear you, O Shenandoah, I LOVE your daughter', and they would all pull on those words. He realised that a 1-2-3 call would be nowhere near as effective as a shanty.[38] In Antarctica the men would often sing shanties, both in celebratory times (Mid-Winter's Day for example) and to keep their spirits up in difficult times.

The *Aurora*'s only stop en route to Antarctica was at Macquarie Island, 950 miles from Hobart, which was reached on 30 December. A meteorological station had been established there during the Australian Mawson's expedition a year or two earlier, and they were to land stores for the staff.[39] This was the last chance for the men to send messages home. Hayward sent a radio telegram to his fiancée and letter to his father, telling the latter he expected to be back home in March 1916.[40] Mackintosh sent a letter to his wife telling her that his men were a 'real good lot of fellows' and it was a 'treat' to be with them.[41]

At Macquarie Island Spencer-Smith and Richards (and possibly Wild and Hayward) were introduced to seal meat. This would become the only fresh meat that the men of the Mount Hope Party would eat for many months at a time in the following two years. Joyce and Wild killed a number of seals for dog food and also for the men, as some parts of the seal – its liver, kidney and heart in particular – were considered delicacies. Joyce in his book tells us that some men who were unaccustomed to seal and penguin meat found them unappetising at first. But, in Joyce's words, seal was similar to beef and 'penguin breasts compare favourably with wild duck'.[42]

After leaving Macquarie Island the weather turned colder and the seas became wilder, although Mackintosh made a note in his personal diary that the *Aurora* was 'behaving admirably and proving her worth as a ship'.[43] He noted that the air was becoming 'decidedly cooler' and warmer clothing was issued – outer woollen clothing made by the London firm Jaeger. He also recorded the ship was lurching about a good deal and that his cabin had been wet twice by seas breaking over the stern of the ship.[44] This was Mackintosh's first note on unpleasant living conditions and such references are common throughout his diary.

As the *Aurora* travelled further south, Mackintosh often thought of his family and wished for news from home, to know how his loved ones were faring. To Mackintosh, that was the only drawback to the position he held and the task he was undertaking.[45] He wanted his wife Gladys with him so she could see the sights – one day there were beautiful clouds that 'show like some gigantic drop scene, only so delicately outlined that it would make an artist's mouth water to view'. He wrote in his diary that if she was with him, then he 'would consider everything complete'.[46]

The voyage to Antarctica through the Southern Ocean was rough and wild but relatively uneventful. Richards, in his book, tells us that the sleeping and living conditions for the men were severe. Their bunks were a narrow slot-like region, about two feet high extending across the width of the stern. Three men slept side by side and the man whose bunk was farthest astern had to get in first. The *Aurora* would roll like a cork at times, sometimes 30 degrees to each side, and moving around the ship was difficult, especially at night outside as there were no lights on the decks. Richards also tells us of other difficulties, such as the steward attempting to bring food to the dining room when the ship was rolling. Also the open lavatories, which became very unpleasant when the ship was rolling – waves would wash over him as the ship was no more than three or four feet above the water line. [47]

In addition to helping with deck-hand duties, the men were involved in an essential task: making new footwear for their use in Antarctica. Boots had been ordered but did not arrive before they left England so Mackintosh had the men work at making some, using sennit (a braided cord) for the soles. The navy men Joyce and Wild did the sewing and cutting out while the others made the sennit.[48] They had purchased boots in Australia to replace the ones that were missing but everyone was suffering with them. Mackintosh described them as 'wretched sea boots' which kept their feet constantly wet. He wrote that it was 'a pity the maker was not here wearing them himself'.[49]

Mackintosh was uncomfortable with the conditions under which the dogs travelled to Antarctica, writing that they 'look objects of abject pity and look appealing at us for consolation in their discomfort, but we are not able to do anything'.[50] Joyce in his book wrote that the 'dogs looked miserable, drenched through'.[51] Richards remembered the dogs' plight, including a sentence in his book: 'The dogs were wet and miserable.'[52]

Shackleton's instructions to Mackintosh

On the *Aurora*, Mackintosh worked out the sledging programme and he found it very difficult to decide on the quantity of sledging foods that were required to be carried, and where the depots should be laid.[53] [54] He was naturally focused on the task of laying the depots as he felt Shackleton was 100 per cent dependent on them. In his final letter of instructions (of September 1914) Shackleton had reminded him that the main object of his support party was to set up depots to assist his Trans-Continental Party coming across from the Weddell Sea.[55]

However, Mackintosh must have been confused by the written instructions he had received from Shackleton. On one hand he was told that it was of 'supreme importance' to have the depots laid; that is, Shackleton was completely dependent on these depots. On the other, Shackleton told Mackintosh he would be carrying 'sufficient provisions and equipment' to cross Antarctica to McMurdo Sound. Shackleton told Mackintosh that he made this second statement about carrying sufficient provisions 'in case some very serious accident' incapacitated the depot-laying. He wanted Mackintosh not to 'have the anxiety of feeling' that his party was absolutely dependent on the depots that Mackintosh was meant to lay.[56]

In spite of this, Mackintosh always gives the strong impression that his party *had* to lay the depots. He makes no reference to the notion of Shackleton carrying sufficient provisions, hence making their depot-laying superfluous. To the contrary, he writes in his diary later that he is worried they may not be able to relieve Shackleton,[57] and what a weight it will be off his mind when they do meet him.[58]

There is another interesting instruction from Shackleton to Mackintosh; one that is not common knowledge. Mackintosh was told to leave a fully equipped emergency lifeboat at McMurdo Sound, if Shackleton did not come across from the Weddell Sea. He was told not to discuss this with anybody. He was to leave the lifeboat with the 'foreport decked over with canvas, or even decked halfway along with a canvas cover and framework', with a good mast and sail. If Shackleton were to arrive at McMurdo Sound after the *Aurora* had gone, he would be able to go north in the lifeboat and make for Macquarie Island.[59]

From this we learn that this type of boat journey, to escape from Antarctica in a small lifeboat, was clearly on Shackleton's mind in 1914, well
before he actually made such a journey in the *James Caird* in his escape
from Elephant Island in 1916. The decision to deck out the *James Caird*
was not an impromptu one. The 1914 specifications for an emergency lifeboat match those he implemented in 1916, from the covering for the boat
using lids of cases, sledge runners and canvas, through to taking sextant,
charts and even 'some blubber-oil in an oil-bag'.[60]

McMurdo Sound, Antarctica

After battling huge seas and exceptionally strong winds past latitudes 50°S
and 60°S of the Southern Ocean, the *Aurora* reached the calm waters of the
Ross Sea on 1 January 1915. Ahead they could see the pack ice at McMurdo
Sound. Mackintosh noted in his log that the pack was as 'thick as a hedge'
and 'as far as he could see'. He had no option but to order the ship to push
its way through.[61]

The Ross Sea by the Antarctic continent is known as the 'silent sea'
because of the solitude of the vast expanse of open water that is met after
coming down through the wild seas of the Southern Ocean. The men on
the *Aurora* experienced an eerie stillness and silence as their ship passed
icebergs and ice floes moving up from the south. They found the silence
was particularly striking, and weird, after days of being battered by bitter
winds. The only noise was that of floes grinding against the ship's side and
the soft, deep sound of the ship's engines. On days where the wind died
away a dull light in the sky seemed to reflect from the white surface of the
thickening pack ice.

The *Aurora* worked her way steadily through the pack ice. The men
noticed that the streams of ice thickened as they advanced south, and they
passed many icebergs, some tubular and others worn down by the wind. On
4 January land was reported 'off the port beam', which caused considerable
excitement as no land was marked on their sea charts, but as they neared
the 'land' turned out to be a huge iceberg close to 300 feet high and 5 miles

long. The shadows falling off three high peaks had given the appearance of land. They saw clouds of many forms with varying light and shade and the sun would appear through the cloud breaks illuminating some part of the ice pack, an iceberg or a patch of the bluest sea. There was now little or no swell and the ship was on an even keel, steady except for the occasional shocks when it struck the ice.

Joyce wrote in his book that the men were entranced by the wildlife. They saw the Antarctic petrel and snowy petrel. They stared in wonder at Weddell seals, crab-eater seals, Adelie penguins and emperor penguins on the pack ice next to the ship. They could see whales, hundreds of them, some estimated at 25 to 30 feet long, and they occasionally rose close to the ship.[62]

In the early afternoon of 7 January the fog was less dense than in the morning but no sign of land could be seen. Then they saw two or three dark patches, which at first were mistaken for a detached cloud until the patches gradually assumed a more definite shape. Then they clearly saw gently rising snow slopes followed by even steeper broken slopes of snow, and as the clouds cleared they could see land, without any doubt. It was the first sighting of Antarctica for four men of the Mount Hope Party: Wild, Spencer-Smith, Hayward and Richards.

As the *Aurora* edged its way towards the bottom of McMurdo Sound they noticed an extensive expanse of land at Cape Bird on Ross Island, which was off to the east. There were black rocks exposed, showing up in sharp contrast to the white snow and the white ice. The whole environment was seemingly devoid of any colour except black, white and shades of grey. In early January there was 24-hour daylight with the sun circling low on the horizon at midnight. At that time the low light turned the surrounding sea-ice into a softer, almost milky blue colour while giving the mountain tops and the glaciers a soft orange tinge.

The landscape was mesmerising. Gigantic snow slopes gradually descended into the sea and all around were ice-covered mountains with black and brown foothills. They could see the blue outline of the majestic peaks of the Trans-Antarctic Mountains, an imposing range running roughly south and north for about 1,000 miles and rising in places to upwards of 15,000 ft. The range flanks the western shores of the Ross Sea for about

500 miles and then continues southward and in 1914 Richards tells us it was usually referred to as the 'Western Mountains'.[63]

On 9 January 1915 the men on the *Aurora* could see Mount Erebus, visible at about 80 miles distance, but a cloud hung over the peak. Mackintosh wrote that a stream of smoke was coming from its crater and he could see 'peaceful snow-covered slopes and rock protrusions from the steep perpendicular cliffs at the sea edge'.[64] Richards described Mount Erebus as 'a magnificent sight rising steeply some 13,000 ft. from sea level'.[65] It dominates the area and, in Richards's opinion, is probably one of the most spectacular mountains in the world as it rises up straight from the sea, completely covered in snow and ice. At times, the emission would climb to 20,000 feet, which was useful for the men of the Mount Hope Party when weather forecasting as the smoke flumes would show different currents above the summit. In winter, when it was dark, occasionally a pink glow would reflect from the smoke.[66]

Mackintosh recorded that, on a day of beautiful, clear weather, 'the whole scene was majestic'. He added: 'All the new comers stood amazed at the splendour of the scene.'[67] Thousands of penguins could be seen and when the men climbed to the crow's nest they could look over the 60-foot cliffs of the Barrier. They even played gramophone records on the stern and for Richards the sound of Caruso's voice ringing out in the stillness was 'unforgettable'.[68] Spencer-Smith held a service, and Mackintosh informs us that most of the men attended. 'They felt at least a thanksgiving was due, for the safe journey that had been granted them.'[69]

They had reached Antarctica. Their adventure was about to start.

Chapter 3

'I AM GOING TO WRITE
A DAILY ACCOUNT OF
MY DOINGS TO YOU'

January 1915

ON 10 JANUARY, the *Aurora* was stopped by thick sea-ice, deep in McMurdo Sound, about 4 miles to the south of Cape Evans, and 9 miles north of Hut Point. The ship was tied up to the ice edge.[1]

It was a calm day and the ship became motionless and eerily quiet once the engines had stopped. The air was crisp and clear, almost breathlessly still, and Mount Erebus with its plume piling straight up into the sky dominated the view.[2] The men on the *Aurora*'s deck looking south would see a flat expanse of dazzling white sea-ice stretching away as far as they could see, towards Hut Point.

Some of the men went out on the ice floes and tried their skills at skiing. In this Mackintosh thought that Wild proved the best whereas his own attempts were amateurish.[3] They also skied across the ice to visit the Cape Evans hut, located on a rocky cape. The wooden hut was on a beach of coarse gravel, facing north-west and well protected by Mount Erebus and numerous small hills behind. Joyce saw 'hundreds of wooden cases, most of which contain provisions' around the hut.[4] Mackintosh's first impression was on the neatness of the area. He noted there were little compact heaps of store cases surrounding the hut itself – sledges, snow houses, huts – and 'electrical wire like cast off spider's webs seemed to litter the place'.[5] The Cape Evans hut would be their main base, especially over the winter months of 1915 and for the months from July 1916 to January 1917.

On the voyage to Antarctica from Australia, Mackintosh had worked out his programme. The first season's depot-laying would be carried out in the months of February and March of 1915 and the second and main season of sledging would be from October 1915 to March 1916.

For the first season he planned for teams to take provisions from the *Aurora* to Hut Point, and then onto the Barrier further south from there. The depots on the Barrier would start with one called Safety Camp, at the start of the Barrier, about 20 miles from Hut Point. Then three smaller depots would be laid, which would be called Cope No. 1, 2 and 3 depots. These would end up being approximately 25, 32 and 40 miles south of Hut Point. The next depot would be a large one at Minna Bluff, location 79°S, 70 miles out. The last depot to be laid in the first season would be at 80°S, 140 miles to the south of Hut Point.

In the second season Mackintosh planned for teams to restock the depots laid in the first season, particularly the Minna Bluff depot, and then place new depots out to 81°S, 82°S and 83°S, with the final one at Mount Hope at 83° 30´S, 360 miles from Hut Point.

On 24 January, stores were on the decks ready to be unloaded so that Mackintosh could arrange for sledging to start immediately. He did not allow any time for the men or the dogs to become fit for travel because he was already a month behind the timetable Shackleton had set for him: 'Sail from Hobart about 1st Dec or in sufficient time to enable you to reach McMurdo Sound about the 1st of January'.[6]

Sledging was to be conducted by parties of three men. Mackintosh would be in charge of one team, Joyce another, and these two teams would carry out the bulk of the sledging in the first two months. Two other teams would lay depots close to Hut Point while Mackintosh and Joyce's teams were placing depots further out on the Barrier. Stenhouse would remain on the *Aurora* and be in command of the ship.

24 January 1915

Gold-titled and embossed leather-bound diaries were distributed, but Joyce commenced his note-taking by writing on loose-leaf pages, waiting until October 1915 before using his diary. In his first entry, on 24 January 1915, he records his disagreement with two of Mackintosh's decisions – both would have serious ramifications later on. The first was Mackintosh's plan to use the dogs for hauling sledges before they were fit. The second was not sending the ship back to New Zealand for the winter.

Richards later wrote that at this stage of the expedition Mackintosh was in charge and Joyce loyally obeyed his instructions.[7] But Joyce was the most experienced and expected some weight to be attached to his views. In his note he clearly felt that the dogs were not acclimatised (owing to the small amount of space they had had for exercising on the ship and the continual soakings they had from the sea water). However, Mackintosh was determined to have a depot laid at 80°S before winter so he decided to take the dogs sledging straight away.

Joyce was back in familiar territory, working around Hut Point, Observation Hill and Cape Armitage at the base of McMurdo Sound as he had in this area with Scott in 1901–04 and with Shackleton in 1907–09. Joyce's main concern was the thickness of the sea-ice between Hut Point and the Ice Barrier to the south.

The dogs were clearly an important part of Joyce's Antarctic life. Throughout his diary he made constant reference to them; how they prevented the men feeling lonely, how the dogs were always pleased to see the men and how he felt for them when they were short of food or dying.

Joyce starts his diary notes. (He occasionally used verbose or flowery phrases, for example, here he uses the term 'the inner man' – meaning he fed himself and the other men.)

Joyce:

Sledging Jan 24

Jan 24. After breakfast Skipper + I discussed several details. I could not get him to see that we were jeopardizing the dogs + I cannot quite understand why Shacks should alter his plan of campaign. As for wintering the ship – this to my mind is the silliest damn rot that could have possibly occurred. The wintering of the *Discovery* was quite alright in its way, but then we had no experience of Antarctic conditions. If I had Shacks here I would make him see my way of arguing.

Anyway Mack is my Boss + I must uphold him until I find that he is not fit to carry out the hard tedious work that is in front of us. Having one eye will play merry hell with him in the extreme temperatures. As he will not take my advice about the dogs I must let him have his way.

I gave a lecture to the parties on sledging. With the exception of Mack who accompanied me on a short journey in 1909 no one has any experience. I related to them some experience, advising them on different subjects such as avalanches, frostbite, snow blindness etc.

As I am laying the course to the Bluff I am marking same by cairns + flags as one is liable to find crevasses. As this is my 7th journey to the Bluff my experience will help them through.

After lunch packed sledge on the ice – the weight over 1200 lbs. Harnessed the dog team after a struggle they wanted to get right away. Their names are Nigger (leader), Dasher, Tug, Pat, Briton, Scotty and Hector. The average weight of the team about 80 lbs – a good heafty lot. My sledging mates are Gaze + Jack.

With many cheers we proceeded on our course south.

Arrived at Hut Point about 5 o'clock.

Tethered the dogs and viewed the sea-ice from Observation Hill. The ice around Cape Armitage seems very thin so will have to steer well out.

Fed the dogs + then the inner man. Turned in early in readiness for an early start in the morning.

During the night heard the dogs barking. On going out to find the cause – found some of them adrift. They had bitten through their harness. Were in a fighting mood, and before I could separate them one was killed. Unfortunately they have very sharp teeth + I suppose they have some old time feud to settle. Moral – see them properly secured.

   I have seen one big dog fight here in about the same spot in 1902 when several were killed before we could get to them. This breed of dog requires studying – with the wolf strain they are almost human in their likes + dislikes.[8]

The dogs were given no shelter, but simply tied up by chains, suitably spaced, to a long steel cable, giving them a radius of movement of a few yards. They were usually very eager for work, and rushed up to the men and tried to insert their heads into the loop of harness being carried. The men noticed that dogs lived by incident; monotony was a dearth to them. After a night's sleeping they would watch the tent as the men were making arrangements to start, yelping all the time at their companions with a general eagerness to be off. They would gallop gloriously for the first half-mile or so, when the sledge seemed to weigh nothing to them, but then the excitement began to pall, especially if there was nothing ahead to see, or smell. One man would often walk ahead when the going was very heavy, which would raise the spirits of the dogs – they would have something to see. If they saw a mirage up ahead the dogs would cock their ears and their footsteps would quicken. The men thought the dogs would see the mirage as a penguin or a seal.[9]

   Mackintosh had been keeping a daily log, but his first diary note in Antarctica, on 24 January 1915, describes the dogs of Joyce's team as they left the ship for Hut Point. Wild starts his diary when he and a few men from the *Aurora* skied across the sea-ice to Hut Point. His dry sense of humour comes through as he describes the destination not being any closer after each hour's skiing. In his laconic way, Wild explained what happened

when they reached the hut, with a backhanded compliment to the two
Scotsmen in his group.

Mackintosh:

> Nigger made a splendid leader and as soon as he was traced on the sledge, was all
> ready, legs spread out in the orthodox fashion … when once the order was given
> to start they made a wild dash, ran into each other and furiously bit their partners
> which brought the sledge to a standstill.
>
> Another try was then made after adjusting the tangle they had put themselves
> into. The method was then tried of each man leading a dog, which went well at
> first: but again, a bundle of dogs fighting in their keenness to be off again occurred.
>
> A third & fourth try and then at last with three men sitting on the sledge they
> went off fairly respectfully. A parting shout and three cheers, and they gradually
> were specks in the distance.[10]

Wild:

> I must go back to Hobart now. We got the dogs ashore there on 31st of Oct 14. Nin-
> nis & I stopped there with them until the ship came round from Sydney. We made
> a rough sledge & used to exercise the dogs whenever possible making three good
> teams. The ship came to Hobart on the 20th December & we went aboard with the
> dogs on the 24th. The Aurora leaving on the same day calling at Macquarie Island on
> the 29th to land stores. I went ashore & shot three seals for dog meat. We killed our
> first penguin there & had some of it for dinner. Everyone pronounced it excellent.
>
> Since then, up to now, we have been trying to get to Hut Point. A party of six,
> myself included, left the ship last Monday to go to Hut Point. We went on ski &
> took a sledge with tent, food, etc. It took us eight & a half hours to get there & the
> last five hours it was only half a mile away at the end of every hour. The Skipper
> said it was 12 miles but we reckoned it was twenty.
>
> Two others in the party fell into a crack in the ice and got wet feet and legs and
> a third fell into the water up to his neck, shivering so much when he got out that it
> made them all shiver so they dashed to the hut at Hut Point.
>
> There was a blubber stove in there so we lit it & put some blubber on, drove
> everybody except Stenhouse & Stevens out; they are Scotch so they could stick

it. There were only two sleeping bags there, so we had to take it in turns to have a sleep. It was too cold anywhere else. That was my first sledging experience.[11]

25 January 1915

The first team led by Joyce had departed on 24 January. The second sledging party of Mackintosh, Spencer-Smith and Wild, with a team of nine dogs, left the ship on 25 January, also aiming for Hut Point. These three men shared the one tent, cooked, and travelled together for the vast majority of their sledging. There was no explanation from Mackintosh as to why he chose Spencer-Smith and Wild to be in his team.

Spencer-Smith's first diary note was made that night, 25 January. It was after his initial foray into sledging, but he had no complaints.

Wild made a few notes that evening. He mentions 'Oates', who was Captain Lawrence Oates, a member of Scott's polar party. He had frostbitten feet and was unable to keep up with the others on their return journey. He is best known for sacrificing himself with the words 'just going outside and may be some time', found within Scott's journal. The date was 17 March 1912 and Oates was also born on 17 March, in 1880. In a remarkable coincidence, Spencer-Smith too was born on this date, in 1883.

The sledge for each three-man party carried their equipment (tent, sleeping bags, etc.), their own food requirements and provisions that had to be left at depots for Shackleton. In his diary Wild listed the equipment they carried on each sledge for the three-man team.

Mackintosh described their departure from the ship but they did not reach Hut Point that day and camping on the ice worried Mackintosh. He may have remembered a narrow escape from floating sea-ice he had back in 1909 on the *Nimrod* Expedition. Then, he and a companion had camped on sea-ice and overnight conditions changed and the next morning they found open water between their tent and the land. Fortunately they were able to escape before the floating ice went out to sea.

Mackintosh seemed to enjoy his first night away from the ship. He mentions 'hoosh', which was the name for their regular meal, eaten at breakfast, lunch and dinner. It was pemmican, the staple food for Antarctic explorers of the day, which was a mixture of dried beef and fat, usually boiled up with crushed biscuits.

In the morning Mackintosh would give out a call to action and they would throw their sleeping bags open and jerk up into a sitting position. When they shook the side of the tent, down would come a shower of frost rime which had formed during the night, from their breathing and the previous night's cooking. Some of the rime would fall down their neck and they would start the day with a cold damp collar and jersey. The dogs could just be seen, their noses only visible out of the snow but, to Mackintosh, they appeared quite comfortable sleeping that way.[12]

He had shaped a course where he imagined Hut Point to be, but even after a second day's travel the sledge-meter showed 13 miles, and this was 4 miles in excess of the distance from the ship to Hut Point. So he decided to halt and camp again.

Mackintosh:

> All day we have been busy on the ship getting prepared, prior to starting off – which we intend to do by the evening. At 7pm all was ready and shortly we started off. All hands came on to the ice to see us away, and lend a hand at the last lashings on the sledge, adjust the dogs' harness and keep them also from fighting.
>
> My companions consist of Smith (the Padre) and Wild; the dogs are nine in number. When all was prepared a parting handshake all around, a shout and we were off – the dogs went splendidly for a while at least. We found it necessary at first for one to sit on the sledge, so eager were the dogs. As we started a cheer went up from those of the ship's party.
>
> All went well until about ½ mile had been traversed when Pompey* felt he had had enough of this rapid mode of progression, so he turned back and headed for the ship. This naturally caused a mix up, the result of which was a riot, such a mix up one could hardly conceive – a mass of rolling, struggling fur and fury. It took all our beating to separate them which after a tussle we managed.
>
> We proceeded as hard as we could, hoping to get to Hut Point by that night.

---

*   Pompey – one of the dogs in Mackintosh's team.

In this direction our luck was out for we had not gone more than 5½ miles when it commenced to snow and everything became obscured. We were then forced to camp. It was against my wish to do this as I did not like the idea of a 'pitch' on sea-ice, especially at this season when there is a danger of the ice breaking out.

However we were not disappointed for, being out of training, the excuse for a rest and a meal was welcome. We very soon heard the hum of the primus and our first hoosh was shortly going down our throat followed by a good brew of tea.[13]

Spencer-Smith:

The dogs at once snuggled into the snow and slept, while we unpacked the sledge, pitched the tent, with snow shovelled all around, got the Primus working and the hoosh water on the go.

The hoosh was very thin, but quite acceptable as we have had no food since lunch at 1pm. Also had tea and several smokes and are now in sleeping bags about to fall off for eight hours. Everything is very cosy: temperatures 28° F and snow falling.

We don't know where we are.[14]

Wild:

We have travelled 13 miles now by our meter, & we are still not at Hut Point. It's blowing a bit of a blizzard, & are not going to leave until we can see where we are going. We have got one of the new tents & are very pleased with it. It is easier to put up than the pole tents. Dogs have been pulling very well today & no scraps. Poor beggars, they have only had two biscuits for 48 hours.

Smith told us something else. i.e. Oates was born & died on his birthday. I forgot to say that the Skipper, Smith & myself form the party with nine dogs.[15]

Primus Box

1 Primus

1 spare parts

Toilet paper

1 medical bag

1 repair bag & spares

1 cooker

3 mugs & spoons

1 Alpine rope

1 Ice axe

1 shovel

3 sleeping bags

1 tent

3 skis & sticks

spare bamboo, lashings & bunting

2 pr sox

2 pr sleeping s[*]

1 extra mits

2 pr finnesko

safety pins

senna grass

broom

matches

knife.[16]

Mitts, which Wild spelt as 'mits', were made of fur and usually hung around their shoulders by a lamp-wick.

Finnesko, sometimes spelt as finneskoe or finnesco, were their Antarctic boots, made from reindeer-skin with the fur on the outside. When short of boots in the winter of 1915 they made more out of an old horse rug.

Sennegrass, which Wild spelt as senna grass, is Norwegian dried hay with insulation and moisture-absorbing properties. It was placed inside their finnesko.

For three men their personal clothing weighed around 15 lb; tent and poles, 30 lb; sleeping bags, 30 lb; shovel, 12 lb; ice axe, 9 lb; flags and bamboo, 4 lb; alpine rope, 4 lb; a medical case, 5 lb; a repair bag, 3 lb; the primus cooker, 6 lb; senna grass, 4 lb; and the sledge, 60 lb. This was a total weight of 182 lb.[17]

Their food allowance was packed in lots for three men. A daily ration (for three men) was weighed and put into a linen bag, and seven of these

---

*   sleeping s – sleeping socks.

were placed in a canvas 'tank', called the food bag. Each food bag weighed 44 lb 10 oz. This would be the ration for a three-man unit for one week and under all circumstances had to be made to last a week. Food was rationed by the week because depots, such as those to be laid at 79°S, 80°S, 81°S etc. were about 68 miles apart. The men would normally expect to march this distance in a week. In addition to their food ration, a little methylated spirits and a gallon of kerosene were allowed each week for lighting and running the primus stove.[18]

27 January 1915

Mackintosh, Spencer-Smith and Wild reached Hut Point on 27 January, joining Joyce's party. Spencer-Smith described the *Discovery* hut as 'not nearly as nice as the one at Cape Evans and is in a horrible condition of dirt and untidiness'.[19]

The next step was to place two depots on the Great Ice Barrier, the first near the Minna Bluff location 70 miles out, and the second another 70 miles further south, at 80°S. Their route from Hut Point would run south for about a mile then turn east for 5 or 6 miles, at which point the ascent was made from the sea-ice to the ice shelf, the Great Ice Barrier.[20] The Ice Barrier is where the sea-ice joins up to the land-ice and is 15 to 40 feet high.[21]

Joyce's party was first away from the hut and he makes a couple of diary entries for the three days it took his team to reach the Barrier. There is only a passing mention of any difficulties, such as falling through the sea-ice, or relaying heavy loads. In his book, *The South Polar Trail*, Joyce gives us some general information about their sledging routine, which he did not record in his diary. He says they wake at 5 a.m. and, except for the cook, have breakfast in their sleeping bags – a mug of pemmican with biscuits and a mug of tea. They extract their socks which had been placed inside their clothing (to stop them from freezing overnight) and then work at putting on their frozen boots, their finneskoe. After packing up, securing the sledges and harnessing the dogs, they are away, stopping every half-hour for a three-minute rest. He writes that sledging is a 'hungry and starving game' and after five hours pulling the leader calls out 'Luncho' and up goes the tent where they have their lunch of tea, biscuits and chocolate. Their afternoon went through to around 6.30 p.m., when they again put up the tent and feed the dogs – who then simply coil up in the snow to sleep. Joyce says that it was useless building them any shelter as they would not use it. [22]

To erect their tent, six bamboo poles had to be slotted into a heavy canvas pole cap, and this was only possible if they took off their outer mitts. The poles had to be quickly put in position then the canvas skin of the tent had to be placed over the poles and then weighed down. Two men hauled the tent over the frame of poles while the other man raced around placing blocks of ice or snow on the skirting of the tent, before the wind lifted the canvas up and off the frame. [23]

Joyce:

27th – Under weigh. Found the going very sticky + slushy. Altered course to the W. At about 2 miles off Cape Armitage I fell through although the ice looks firm it is badly undercut + it is only snow covered. I carried on until firm ice was struck. Changed my wet clothes we managed to find enough for a shift. [24]

30th – The haul was very heavy so decided to relay. Makes the work easier. Although it doubles the journey. [25]

28 January 1915

Mackintosh, Spencer-Smith and Wild followed Joyce's team south from Hut Point but by the end of their day the three men were disappointed. For Spencer-Smith and Wild this was their first sledging experience and like Mackintosh they found relaying to be irksome. Through their diaries we can see these three men found sledge-hauling much harder than they had anticipated. However, from Joyce's diary it appears he did not find hauling particularly unpleasant. He had taken loaded sledges out onto the Barrier a number of times (with Scott in 1902–1903 and with Shackleton in 1908–1909) so it was probably all in a day's work for him. He makes one diary entry for the eight days as his team went from the edge of the Barrier out to where the Minna Bluff depot was laid.

Wild:

> We left Hut Point in grand form for about 40 yards then it took us 8 hours to go 400 yards. We stopped then & had some tea & then started again & have come four or five miles.
>
> We got here at 3.0 AM so of course it is Friday now. The dogs have had about 10 scraps today & my arms are aching with banging & pulling them. About 4.0 AM now. Pack up, sleep.[26]
>
> Woke up with a blizzard blowing, had breakfast & turned in again. Woke up again, nice & fine, had tea & biscuits, and got under 'weigh', or tried to but couldn't budge the sledge.
>
> Unloaded half & the Skipper & I went on with it for about 600 yds. The dogs couldn't or wouldn't go on, so unloaded & went back for the other half. Got it along about 80 yds past the first half & pitched tent.
>
> Smithy got dinner ready, while we went & brought the other lot up. We are going to have another go tonight. Can't say much for the travelling, 680 yds., snow nearly up to our knees all the time.
>
> Relay work no good makes one swear.[27]

Spencer-Smith:

> We now know what utter exhaustion is! We could only do short spells, halting at hard spots and hard spots seemed very few and far between; I was too done to pray for them!
>
> We had come only about four miles, though it seemed like twenty. At last the sledge nearly capsized and stuck in a deep place, and Mac, very disappointed, decided to camp. It was 3 am and felt like it.[28]
>
> After the first 100 yards we, dogs and men, found it absolutely impossible to move the sledge. We tried again and again. 'Team. Come along then! What about it today? Getty-up!!!' And she hasn't moved an inch.
>
> We used the boot, the whip, words and blandishment, but it was all in vain, and Mac had to give in to Fate, and order a relay.[29]

Mackintosh:

> Try as we would, no movement could be produced. Reluctantly we unloaded and began the tedious task of relaying. The work, in spite of the lighter load on the sledge, proved terrific for ourselves and for the dogs. We struggled for four hours, and then set camp to await the evening, when the sun would not be so fierce and the surface might be better.
>
> On waking this afternoon at 5 pm found it drifting, all land shut out! Therefore nothing to do but remain in our bags and await the God of Blizzard's orders.
>
> It's a curious sensation remaining silently in the bags, with just the sound of gentle snow pattering on the tent, the great sense of comfort one finds in the bag, our keen sense of any untoward noise such as the ceasing of the snow or any sign of clearing weather. We are quietly reading in our bags, a jet of steam coming out of our openings – What a weird situation when you come to think of it – what on earth are we so keen about?
>
> I must say I feel somewhat despondent, as we are not getting on as well as I expected, nor do we find it as easy as one would gather from reading.[30]

Joyce:

> From the 31st of Jan until I picked up the Bluff Depot on Feb 9th was very hard work and took us over 16 days to trek the last 100 miles. We built up the depot to about 12 feet high put up flag poles making it about 24ft all told – A splendid mark. Gaze + Jack are two splendid tent mates. The dogs behaved splendidly.[31]

30 January 1915

Mackintosh, Spencer-Smith and Wild, even with their team of dogs, struggled to start the sledge moving at times. All the men wore a harness that consisted of a broad waistband of double canvas. It was pierced at the back and fitted with an eye, through which passed the alpine rope leading back to the sledge. All the weight was taken by the waistband but the harness was suspended from the shoulders by a light canvas and leather shoulder straps attached to a buckle fixed on the main belt.[32]

By this day, 30 January, only a few days since they had started out,

Mackintosh had ailments to which Spencer-Smith attended. He mentions Borofax, a weak acidic hydrate of boric oxide with mild antiseptic. They see a 'motor car' which presumably was one of the three motor sledges that Scott took on his *Terra Nova* Expedition. Mention is also made of one of their dogs, Towser, who twelve months later would be one of the four dogs crucial in helping them return safely from Mount Hope.

Spencer-Smith:

It was cruelly hard work. Wild went in front. Mac and I harnessed up, but of course could not have our ski on as we both had to be pulling.

The heartbreaking part is the preliminary 'hoicking'. Mac and I swing the sledge to get a smooth starting place and to break the frozen runners: then I heave back the team with one hand ('Team'), keeping up the swinging with the other: then 'Getty-up' and a mighty heave from both of us to get a slight move on (it usually takes three repetitions of the above) and then we get a strain on our trace – starting breathless, of course – and plug on through the yielding snow, until our combined energies, dogs and men's give out.

It is the most quaint sight in the world to see a stout seal lying luxuriously on his side, and idly scratching with the upper most flipper.

Wild killed a young seal with the ice-axe, and I helped him skin him, our weapons being (1) a shoemaker's knife belonging to Wild (2) a table knife. It was a grisly and greasy job!

Temp 31° 'tonight' – a very sudden change: this morning all the metal work was sticky with the cold. I can see that cooking will be a delicate operation when we touch the minus temperatures.

Festering sores on Mac's right hand. Bathed place & sterilised instruments in Hyd. Pot. Iod. Lanced places & freed pus. Applied Boris wool and Borofax and bandaged. Gave tonic.[33]

Wild:

Smithy & I killed & skinned a seal. We gave the dogs a feed & depoted the remainder.

I fell down a small crevasse with one leg only. It was only about a foot wide but went down a long way.

Came across one of Scott's depots & found dog biscuits, sack of oats, a couple of weeks provisions, seal meat & blubber & last of all a motor car.[34]

Mackintosh:

Our throats are hoarse as soon as one dog appears to slacken his name is yelled out, they are doing their best poor brutes, Towser a great fat hulking animal is a fool and a great nuisance always getting tied up in his harness, with the result we had to stop the sledge.[35]

31 January 1915

Mackintosh, Spencer-Smith and Wild finally reached the Great Ice Barrier with Wild noting they had 'to climb a steep hill to get onto it'.[36] Ahead they could see nothing but a featureless landscape, a gigantic land of snow stretching hundreds of miles to the south where, at the horizon, the snowy wasteland met the sky. At this point, at the start of the Barrier, there were no mountains in the background and as far as they could see there was nothing but a straight or smooth level plain sweeping away to the south.

Spencer-Smith was the only one of the Mount Hope Party to comment on seeing the Barrier. He was so impressed he described the scene as 'covered with diamonds', and he was taken in by the solitude, the absolute silence. This comment was unusual in that he gives us a (brief) description of the landscape, but he, and others of the Mount Hope Party, usually focussed diary notes on the events of the day, hardships, the distances travelled, food and the surface they were travelling over.

On the Barrier the surface became harder so they attempted to haul the total load instead of relaying.

Mackintosh:

Of all the back-breaking jobs, ye that have not done such a thing, this is absolute perfection. The great trouble is to get the sledge started. The method is: with one hand we catch hold of the line to which the dogs are attached; this is drawn in, then with the other a wiggle is given in the bow of the sledge, shouting 'getty up' to the dogs at the same time.

Sometimes they start – more often they don't. So again and again this is repeated! Should a move be made we jump aside in case our sledge harness gets entangled and then we pull for all we are worth. This is alright if it only happened once in a way but after 30 shots in an hour one begins to weary!

We managed a direct mile. This is even better than relaying.[37]

Personally I feel just done up. Smith I am sure who was taking turns with me must have felt the same. When one thinks of it we have to shove 1100 lbs and after doing this about a dozen times you begin to wish the sledge in Kingdom Come.

Sledging I have come to the conclusion is no joke. But such hard, hard work. But we are getting along. Each day one day less.

In the tent Wild is repairing our broken ski sticks which have come to grief on the poor dogs! That made Smith say to me 'I do feel sorry but we have to get on and as persuasion has no effect this is the last resort'.

All kinds of subjects are discussed from meals we'd like to be eating to quandaries as to what's happening at the front, religion, seeing we have a parson, politics, in fact there's precious little that is not turned over in our conversation by one or other of us.[38]

Spencer-Smith wrote of the Barrier:

A vast wall surrounding an immense snow plain bediamonded by the sun. All the old questionings seem to come up for answer in this quiet place: but one is able to think more quietly than in civilisation.[39]

Had a long talk with Wild after supper tonight. He seems to have been everywhere during his service in the Navy. He talked mainly of Jerusalem & Egypt tonight – very interesting.[40]

Late January

The third sledging team, led by Cope and including Hayward and Richards, started their sledging from the ship to Hut Point three days after the others, on 31 January 1915. This team started with a motor sledge but it broke down near Hut Point and was not used again. The six men did not use dogs even though Hayward had experience with sledging with dogs in Canada. Their task over the two months of summer 1915 was to take stores to Hut Point and to lay three depots on the Barrier quite close to Hut Point. After the motor sledge broke down the team worked in two three-man parties; Hayward, Richards and Ninnis pulling one sledge and sharing a tent, Cope, Stevens and Hooke with a second sledge and tent.

Their sledging efforts in this first season were not particularly significant or admirable, but they did put down three depots, named Cope No. 1, 2 and 3 depots, which were all located within 40 miles of Hut Point. These three Cope depots would all be needed by the Mount Hope Party when they returned from Mount Hope in 1916.

Richards's initial diary entry, at the end of their first day of man-hauling, was one of only a dozen diary notes he made for all of 1915. By contrast, Hayward was writing a prolific diary, for his fiancée, Ethel Bridson, and it started as a daily record. He acknowledges the work makes him both hungry and tired but his description of having to relay was pragmatic. He tells his Ethel all the details of his sledging and how often she was on his mind. He mentions the *Ionic*, which was the ship that took Hayward and others from England to Australia.

Richards: 'Hauled 1100 lb with 4 men to Hut Point ... snow soft – heavy going (on sea-ice) – no sleep for 24 hours ... Last pace a crawl ... Turned into bunk 9 a.m. – awakened 8 p.m.'[41]

Hayward:

I am going to write a daily account of my doings to you as I promised you. I must tell you that I think of you all the time, on the march, in my sleeping bag, & on all conceivable occasions & find the process a great help & comfort.

Decided to stow everything on 2 sledges & haul by relaying, that is haul 1 sledge 1 mile & return for the 2nd & so on, we got under way, & by 6 o/c AM Monday morning had advanced 4 miles in this way, this of course means that we had traversed a total distance of 12 miles.

On the way the Mirage effects were wonderful the Great Ice Barrier seeming close at hand, at times I ought to mention that we have arranged to sleep during the day & get the advantage of the warmer atmosphere & travel during the night when it is colder & therefore more conducive to work.

It is now 5 o/c pm (Mon) & we shall get away again about 6. I am looking forward to the hoosh this morning but am now just going to have another 40 winks, while I have the opportunity. This work makes me both hungry & tired. It is hard to say which most.

Of course I am in my bag writing this & you would be surprised how comfy & warm it is. (10 minutes later) The 40 winks is not a success there is nothing doing, no sleep left in my bag I find. I have been thinking of you & shall just have a little tête à ... on the strength of it.

Right away down here ducky life develops on much different lines to those which prevail at home it is a hard life, to say nothing else & one continual struggle with conditions & the elements & in the ordinary way there is very little room for sentiment, as far as I am concerned however I think of you, more than anything else & am quite content, much more so than was the case when slacking about coming over on the *Ionic* & during the 7 weeks I spent in Sydney as here I have the satisfaction of knowing that I am actually engaged in the thing I am so anxious to complete satisfactorily.

I wonder if you understand what all this means to me, coming down here away from you & everything I live for with only my hopes & future plans as an incentive, of course I find it easier, when as you know my hopes & future plans are centred in you & you only, this of course would make anything possible as far as I am concerned.

Well the hoosh is underway & when disposed of it will be a case of stow sledges, 'up & at it', so, so long.

Yesterday we tried skiing after the first 2 miles & found it a great advantage, it is quite good fun, 6 men hauling a sledge on skis all in time.[42]

Within a week of arrival at McMurdo Sound Joyce's team and Mackintosh's team had reached the Barrier. They were to then push on south, to place a depot at Minna Bluff at latitude 79°S, and another 70 miles further on, at 80°S. Hayward and Richards had started sledging supplies out, closer to Hut Point.

Chapter 4

'THE OTHER TWO ARE SNORING PEACEFULLY ALONGSIDE OF ME'

February – The trek to Minna Bluff

OUT ON THE Barrier, Mackintosh's and Joyce's team travelled near to each other, with Joyce travelling by daytime hours and Mackintosh travelling at night. They found the surface much better than the sea-ice surface between Hut Point and the Barrier and Mackintosh even challenged Joyce's team to a race to Minna Bluff.

At times they travelled over a surface they called 'the Barrier Hush'. This occurred when a surface crust lay over softer snow and the weight of the sledging party would break the crust and the air from underneath it was expelled in a long 'hush-sh'. The noise began sharply and then slowly and eerily died away in the distance.[1] Another type of surface they commented on was sastrugi, which, in his book *The Ross Sea Shore Party*, Richards described this way: 'Large hard parallel furrows running south-east and north-west, called sastrugi, are sculptured by the blizzards which blow with great regularity in these fixed directions.'[2] To Spencer-Smith, sastrugi looked like a frozen sea.

There was no undressing at night. They turned in fully clothed. Their wet socks were taken off and sometimes hung up so they would lose some moisture, but in the morning they would be stiff as a board. To put them on then required beating and bending and tugging, all of which took time. If they put their wet socks in their sleeping bags they would stay wet and soft but they found them a horror to put on that way in the morning.

Their boots were wet and would freeze overnight so they had to be shaped carefully so they could get the tips of their toes inside the opening. First of all they would roll up their sleeping bags and sit on these while wrestling with their boots – pushing and pulling until their foot was completely inside.[3]

Mackintosh: 'Smith wrote facetious messages in the snow for Joyce's party to read: BUCK UP. SHIP WILL CATCH YOU UP YOU CRIPPLES. Wild added by way of encouragement: PUB AHEAD.'[4]

2 February 1915

Sledging with the dogs was now quite enjoyable at times for Spencer-Smith and he compared the yelling to being at a football game at Merchiston. Wild was looking forward to the day when they made 12 miles.

Spencer-Smith:

Joyce and co. came by at 4.15pm. The barking of our team woke us; and we found that our Jock had joined them and that they had their full load and were proceeding merrily. We passed Joyce a little before lunchtime, amidst a tremendous howling of the combined teams. Our lot made a great spurt as we drew near and were much disappointed when we turned aside to go on.

There was quite a good crust on top of the snow, and the dogs went well: also Mac and I were able to get into our harness and do useful work on the ski. The surface was undulating and we soon found it necessary to haul like demons up the slopes, with plenty of 'getty-up' at the critical moment: the snow was inclined to be soft, on the slope.

Three or four times we were stuck in these drifts and had to dig to get the sledge on an even keel for starting. We had 3 good sprints – 2 mile, 1 mile, 1 mile and are fairly satisfied with the work done. Given such a surface, we ought soon to be doing our daily 12 miles, or perhaps more.

Apart from the 'hoicking' and the sprint to catch up after it, this pulling on a good surface is great fun, though the continual shouting rather takes one's breath – compare a very long football match at Merchiston.[5]

Wild:

Joyce passed us while we were turned in. We passed him again to-day & have left him five miles behind. He travels when we are asleep & we travel while his party sleeps so when we wake up I expect he will have passed us again. Seven miles today, we are bucking up.

When we do 12 miles in one day, we are going to splice the main-brace (with brandy) so I hope it will be tomorrow.[6]

3 February 1915

After checking the food supply Spencer-Smith found out that he, Mackintosh and Wild had been underfeeding themselves. The biscuits, although they were hard, had what has been described as 'a flavour a combination of nuttiness, meatiness and plain fillingess'.[7] The most satisfactory aspect of the biscuits for the men was that they took a long time to eat.

Spencer-Smith: 'In future the tea is to be stronger and the hoosh more abundant both in oatmeal & pemmican. We have decided to have butter (which is extra) only at lunch, so that our 4 or 5 lbs may be made to spin out the 7 weeks.'[8]

Mackintosh was again critical of Towser:

When we started off again Towser would keep stopping the team; also committing the heinous offence of getting out of his harness, so he had a good beating as his crime was premeditated we are sure. We had to wait some considerable time for him whilst he was wandering about, but he thought the devil he knew was preferable.[9]

4 February 1915

Mackintosh was encouraged by words from a book he was carrying, *Being and Doing* (a 1897 book on life studies), so much so he added a poem from the book, one by Ralph Waldo Emerson, into his diary.

> *So nigh is grandeur to our dust,*
> *So near is God to man,*
> *When duty whispers well I must,*
> *The Youth replies 'I can!'*[10]

5 February 1915

Spencer-Smith:

The low temperature helped us greatly: the Minimum Thermometer touched -22 F today but we did not notice the cold until the wind set in, when our beards etc (which are always thick with frost) stiffened into ice in a moment. It was quite painful once I opened my mouth rather wide to shout – and every hair on my face seemed to be tearing out at the roots.

The range of temperatures is amazing. -22 to +20 in 12 hours. So one has burns from the cooker when hot and burns from the cooker when cold, and it's all in the game.

The whole plain looks as if a vast sea, slightly troubled, had frozen in an instant, the tops of waves are smooth and slippery and one has to be careful on the ski.[11]

6 February 1915

Spencer-Smith created a special hoosh, diarising the ingredients.

> Recipe for Hoosh deluxe, for 3 men:
>
> 1 mug Pemmican (¾ lb)
>
> 6 lumps sugar
>
> ¾ spoonful salt
>
> 9 spoonful oatmeal
>
> (6 crushed biscuit) extra
>
> Tea for 3 men.
>
> 3 spoonful Glaxo*
>
> 3 spoonful Tea
>
> 24 lumps sugar (at lunch 30 lumps)
>
> The pemmican is only taken at Bkft & Supper. Lunch consist of Tea, Biscuit, Chocolate (1 stick each) and Butter (if any).
>
> Each man gets 2 Biscuits at Brft & Supper and 3 at lunch.
>
> A hard day. 11 miles 25 yards. It is to be noted that these miles are all geographical miles (2028 yards) which makes a considerable difference to one accustomed to statute miles.[12]

7 February 1915

Mackintosh gives us an outline of their normal morning ritual. (The 'cooker' he refers to was a Nansen cooker, designed by the Norwegian Arctic explorer. It was made up of five parts. There was a shallow dish in which a primus stove stood. Then there were two pots in which water was heated and meals cooked with one lid covering both pots. One pot sat inside the other and the meal was cooked in the inner one. This allowed food to be cooked and snow melted simultaneously. An outer cover was lowered gently over the whole apparatus in order to keep in as much heat

---

* Glaxo, like Plasmon, is a dried milk powder.

as possible. The primus stove burnt paraffin, after being started with methylated spirits. A small amount of spirit was poured into a cup at the base of
the stove, lit and when it was almost burnt up an air-valve was screwed up
and a few tentative pumps made. If the paraffin in the pipes was not heated
sufficiently pure paraffin would come through the stove jets, which was a
bright yellow flame of 2 or 3 feet long. But with patience, they could have
the right mixture of paraffin vapour and air rushing up and then a blue
flame would start from under the top of the burner. They would increase
the air pressure with more pumping and the burner would then be surrounded by a halo of intensely hot bluish flame. Many explorers of the era
made notes of the 'cheery hum of the primus'.)

He also explains their method of dividing up the food, a game that
ensured a fair distribution. One man, the cook, would divide up or pour
out roughly equal portions into each bowl and then turn his back to the
food; another would point to a bowl and say 'whose?', and the cook
would say one of their names, and so on. (Shackleton is said to have
made up the game on the *Nimrod* Expedition when he noted that the
men stared at each other's portions as if one had deliberately received
a bigger portion.)

Mackintosh:

> I am usually good at waking myself, the order of things go: I wake, get out watch
> usually hitting the correct hour, shake self out of bag, call the others, Smith usually
> gets out first, I go out, fill up cooker and pass it in. By this time, Wild is up, Smith
> gets the primus going during this time I build a cairn, – breakfast we always find
> our longest period.
>
> We always try to hustle but so far have not succeeded to an ideal routine. Today
> for instance. Temp +3 for us quite 'nippy'. Hoosh does not take long and once
> down a fine tingle passes over one. – then the struggle, boots as hard as iron, this
> operation takes the longest, after this the rest of the gear, bags folded, sledge packed.
>
> Wild attends dogs I attend sledge lashings. Smith takes tent down. With this
> completed 2½ hours have gone.
>
> Played the sledge game of Shut Eye for our portion of butter which we have
> brought a small portion of as a luxury.

He added:

Tested time it takes primus to melt snow which is as follows:

Snow melts: 15 mins

Water boils: 20 mins

Total: 35 mins.[13]

8 February 1915

Mackintosh on Towser, again: 'A fool, morose skulker, yellow and dashed with white; lazy and fat, always has to be hustled, gets plenty of beatings, never yelps or barks – quite hopeless for this task. Has absolutely no brains or energy.'[14]

9 February 1915

Mackintosh: 'I had a weird dream, something about an operation, and I had just been wheeled to the tent and would not be able to proceed any further as a warm bed awaited me. I was soon disillusioned however on waking.'[15]

10 February 1915

From Mackintosh's words we can visualise the three men waking up and having their morning breakfast – a cup of hoosh. Note: after less than two weeks of sledging, scurvy was on their minds.

Mackintosh:

Greeted on wakening by the pattering off drift against the tent and hissing of wind outside! Smith is making some hoosh, which as we are unable to proceed, are going to have in our bags.

A little later – we have just finished sitting in bag both hands clasped round the mug as to lose no warmth; then when hands get nicely warmed, the biscuit is broken into the hoosh by cracking it up first with our teeth – then the first spoonful gives a delicious glowing tingle right through the body. When this is over a cup of tea which is the end of the meal – but we are nicely warmed up again.[16]

Spencer-Smith: 'Dressed Mac's finger: his right ear seems affected in a similar way and the gland beneath is also swollen. We must start the lime juice tonight. I feel sure that my toes and his hand are missing vegetables.'[17]

11 February 1915

The two parties at Minna Bluff

Joyce's party had reached a point near Minna Bluff – where the depot was established – on 9 February. It was about 70 miles south from Hut Point. Two days later Mackintosh's party joined them and the parties were then rearranged. The three navy men, Mackintosh, Joyce and Wild, and the majority of the dogs, continued on south to lay another depot 70 miles further on, and Spencer-Smith returned to Hut Point – with Jack, Gaze and a few of the dogs.

At this depot point, Mackintosh wrote a letter of instruction for Spencer-Smith.

Letter from Captain A. E. Mackintosh to Spencer-Smith

11 February 1915.

... it is with deep regret that I have to part with your company as a sledging companion for it has been through your ready aid and shoulders that we have enabled to reach so far on our journey.

I now depute to you the charge of the Bluff depot laying party, as I consider by your tact, discretion and character you are a fit person to take over this responsible position.[18]

Spencer-Smith returns to Hut Point

Spencer-Smith's trek back to Hut Point was uneventful, but he made occasional notes in his diary. His charitable nature shows through by the way he writes about one of the dogs he names as 'Gunboat'. This dog (called Gunboat here but he was usually called Gunner) survived the first sledging season and was one of the four dogs that went out to Mount Hope in 1916.

14 February 1915

Spencer-Smith:

> There is, of course, practically no incident to record on these marches. But one's thoughts go in curious cycles. First one's orations and a certain amount of meditation: as cairns and other definite points draw near one makes guesses of the number of paces and starts counting, and often continuously mechanically long after the spot is passed.
>
> As meal-camps draw near, food is the predominate thought – I incline usually towards sardines, jam and chocolate (all of which we shall find at Hut Point in due course). The other two are more ambitious. Jack wants oyster soup & Irvine salmon, poached eggs and grilled steak.[19]

16 February 1915

Spencer-Smith includes a quote from a Robert Browning poem, 'Andrea del Sarto', and in a portent of what was to come, he mentions a pain in his chest.

> Poor old 'Gunboat' saw a fragment of dog biscuit on the track – grabbed at it and missed it – and for the next 2 or 3 minutes sulked and refuse to pull.
>
> Thoughtlessly I let them see the biscuits I was carrying for lunch today, and it was painful to see them look piteously at them as I passed.

Ah, but a man's reach should exceed his grasp. Or what's heaven for?

People at home are just finishing their after-church supper. One wonders if they are thinking of us at all – and how the war is proceeding.[20]

I am a little strained on the left side intercostals, I hope not heart, and shall have to be careful. Put a few Kola Compds in my pocket and think them very useful.[21]

Most annoying – snapped a gold tooth clean off at supper time tonight, the nearest dentist being in New Zealand.[22]

18 February 1915

On the way back to Hut Point, Spencer-Smith, Jack and Gaze met Hayward's team, who were laying depots near the edge of the Barrier.
Hayward:

We made out a camp about 2 miles ahead, this we took to be Joyce & his party returning. We could see somebody skiing over the track towards us & Cope & I set out to meet him on skis. We were surprised to find it was A. P. S-Smith, but nevertheless very pleased to see him.

Smith has with him, more out of kindness than any other consideration Gunboat & Towser.

It appears that the Skipper is not up to the mark, some sort of skin disease, probably scurvy manifesting itself, but as I always thought he is a 'game one' & I hope he is soon better.

They are absolutely out of provisions & we have given them a week's supply, they ought to get back to the Hut in that time as they are travelling light & can average 15 miles a day.

One could not realise how jolly nice it is to meet these chaps here, as to us it seems ages since we last saw them, & they of course are equally delighted. I rather envy them in a way & under the circumstances, as they have only another week to go & they will have the comparative comfort of the Hut whereas we have 3 weeks to go before we can hope to reach the depot & at least another fortnight on the return journey & I must confess that my inner man shouts hard for something square to eat already, still it's got to be done & there you are.[23]

22 February 1915

Apart from the creature comforts, Spencer-Smith was not looking forward to the icy interior of *Discovery* hut at Hut Point but on arrival he recorded their splendid meal. He had brought back safely two dogs, Gunboat (Gunner) and Towser, who would be two of the four dogs to be used in the following sledging season to Mount Hope. There are no diary notes at this time on the other two dogs that would also be used, Oscar and Con.

Spencer-Smith:

> – glorious porridge, made with oatmeal, Plasmon,* butter and salt, and eaten with Trumilk† and golden syrup (Lyle's). Then scones, butter and strawberry jam thickly spread.
>
> Gunboat has given us a lot of trouble this morning; he does not seem to be ill in any way (good appetite, cold nose, etc) so I gave him a good thrashing in the middle of the morning, not without effect.[24]

Mid-February 1915 – Mackintosh, Joyce and Wild continue south

After Spencer-Smith's team had turned back to the north, Mackintosh, Joyce and Wild went on to lay a depot at 80°S before winter set in. Beyond Minna Bluff they started to feel very alone and almost lost on the great open plain. They had some fine days with sunshine where they could clearly see Mount Erebus throwing out 'huge columns of steam' and on other days they had overcast skies. The surface of the snow presented a bewildering variety of surfaces where sometimes they encountered very soft snow and at other times a smooth, almost marble-type surface on which their sledge runners made no impression.[25]

They simply plodded along, putting in ten hours a day, averaging 5 miles

---

* Plasmon is a dried milk powder with gluten.

† Trumilk is also a milk powder.

a day. There was nothing to break the monotony and little for the men to write about although Mackintosh continued to record events, particularly on the uncomfortable conditions in their tent, something Joyce and Wild rarely mentioned in their diaries. Joyce clearly did not want the dogs to be taken on and Wild gives us an interesting take on his own ailments – using cryptic naval terms.

They laid their southerly depot (at 80°S) on 20 February. The day before they had covered 12 miles and received a reward, which Joyce missed out on. Mackintosh had previously said: 'If we do 12 miles a peg of brandy out of the medical comforts.'[26]

They called the depot 'Rocky Mountain Depot', spending a number of days building it up so it could be easily seen. They also put up cairns to the east and west with flags and directions to reach the depot.

After setting up the depot they were held up by a blizzard for a day. They were careful to pile enough snow on the skirting of the tent to keep it secure or else by morning they might find themselves lying in a snow drift, unable to see the tent, or each other. In a strong blizzard the tent would billow wildly and threaten to take off at times. With frozen fingers they would all clutch at the skirting and attempt to keep it down until they could sit on it or hold it down against the wind. At those times they just had to not let go. If they left even a small portion of the skirting showing the blizzard would find it and use it as a lever to work its way under and into the tent, filling the interior with a thick powdery drift that covered everything.[27]

11 February 1915

Joyce:

> Spencer Smith, Jack + Gaze with 5 dogs returned to Hut Pt.
>
> Mack, Wild + self + 9 dogs to go to 80°. The sledges were repacked.
>
> Spencer Smith party taking 1 week's provisions turned N + we went on our weary way south. Camped 7 o'clock.

I had him one side & tried to persuade him not to take the dogs any further south as they were feeling the effects of the hard sledging and were not acclimatised.

However he decided otherwise. I could see his point that the depot must be laid at 80° as Shackleton may come across this year & expect to find food there.[28]

14 February 1915

Wild: 'Port lug & Starboard toe slightly frost-bitten.'[29]

15 February 1915

Mackintosh:

Got into a most peculiar surface, it showed in the distance in distinct contrast to what we were travelling on, being in a kind of glassy state whenever we were in a snow crusted surface. When we got onto it the sledge glided along smoothly. I wonder if it is due to the clouds being over this part thereby keeping it harder frozen than the rest where the sun would shine.

Anniversary of my wedding day – thoughts turn back 4 years and what a change! What on earth am I doing here? That's what I ask myself and such thoughts wish me back at Home to the dear ones, waiting so patiently.[30]

17 February 1915

Mackintosh:

Experiencing cold nights. The steam from the cooker and I suppose our breath freezing onto the tent, our bags as well are all ice, as soon as we turn out in the morning and we should happen to touch the tent the whole mass comes over us like a shower. After a restless night this does not encourage one's feelings![31]

18 February 1915

Mackintosh:

Spent a rotten night, cold in spite of being right inside the bag, the cold & draught seem to get all around me. It was a pleasure to get out in the morning. The sun does not shine which is still very bad light for travelling.

Attempted to steer by compass, and taking a cloud ahead to steer by, in this fashion we kept going, Joyce went ahead and I stayed behind the sledge with a compass & steered him by shouting 'right' or 'left'.

Joyce is complaining about his fingers which he finds 'going' frequently. My own ears are getting better, Middle second fingers still very bad which is a great inconvenience.

Wild, ever jolly, cheerful, an optimist, keen and ever ready to take up anything, very humorous with a large vocabulary of naval expressions, fairly tough, and plucky as any Britisher.

Joyce, a different character, quite alright while humoured, when he is willing, and would do anything for any one, but he has no stability; alright while all goes well, not very hard, feels the cold very easily but always sticks it out. [32]

19 February 1915

Mackintosh:

Had a better night last night, but these days never get more than two hours consecutive sleep; if I can do this I consider myself fortunate – the bag freezes every night now, thawing out when we are in, that is the parts armed by where our body may be lying. On colder days no thaw will take place so we remain in a frozen chest the whole time.

Taking the time today as a test to see how long it takes us to get off from the time we get up in the morning until we are away. These times I took without warning to the others.

Rose 5am.

Hoosh ready 5.30

Finished 6.15

Foot gear on 7.40

Sledge packed & dogs harnessed 8.30

Camped 12.30 Lunch

Finished 1.30

Packed 2pm away.[33]

20 February 1915

Mackintosh:

Very cold wind playing on the nose, which waters and then a thick coating of ice hangs down from that protuberance.

Had been awakened by a policeman who had been moving me off from the side of the tent I was lying on and was struggling in the bag to get to the other, when on coming in contact with Joyce's bag I realised I was not in Piccadilly![34]

Mackintosh, Joyce and Wild reach 80°S

Wild: 'Hooray 12 miles today. Just had that lot. We are making our Southern Depot here for this year – Rocky Mountain Depot.

Joyce set fire to his brandy when he was trying to warm it. Excitement reigned supreme (I don't think).'[35]

21–22 February 1915

Joyce:

After breakfast Wild + I trekked with dog team making a course due East. The other flag 5 Miles + 15 feet high. We left directions where to find the main depot.

On our return after 5 hours out we built the main depot – a base of 10 feet with 15 feet bamboos 3 flags 25ft high. On a clear day this depot could be sighted at a distance of 12 miles and almost impossible to miss coming from the South.[36]

Mackintosh:

As soon as breakfast was over, Joyce and Wild went off with a light sledge and the dogs to lay out the cairns and place flags to the eastward, building them at every mile. The outer cairn had a large flag and a note indicating the position of the depot.

I have remained behind to get angles and fix our position with the theodolite. The temperature was very low this morning, and handling the theodolite was not too warm a job for the fingers. The arc and the view getting frozen over with the moisture from one's breath. This I had to clear or rather thaw out before I could get a reading. My whiskers froze to the metal while I was taking a sight.

After five hours the others arrived back. They had covered ten miles, five miles out and five miles back. During the afternoon we finished the cairn, which we have built to a height of 8 feet. It is a solid square erection which ought to stand a good deal of weathering, and on top we have placed a bamboo pole with a flag, making the total height 25 feet.

Building the cairn was a fine warming job, but the ice on our whiskers often took some ten minutes thawing out.

I write this sitting up in my bag, while the primus is going as an extra luxury the heat from this keeps the interior quite warm but we shall suffer in the morning owing to the freezing of the condensed water in the tent. Minus 8 degrees outside. We are snug and warm inside though, in fact hot![37]

22 February 1915

Mackintosh:

Except for an occasional peep at the howling 'pea soup' weather outside we really have to hibernate & it is extraordinary how we sleep the time away. – whilst it remains warm. It's a great feeling of security to be sheltered here, It's wonderful too to consider that only a thin sheet of cloth separates us from all that is misery and worse to safety and comfort.

The other two are snoring peacefully alongside of me. When not doing this I lie down again, toggle up, and then court sleep which eventually comes, in waking you build castles, go through your whole life – past, present and future, and then probably drift off to sleep again, all this while the bag remains dry, fortunately now it is.[38]

The first part of their mission had been accomplished – two depots had been laid, at Minna Bluff (79°S) and the Rocky Mountain Depot (80°S). Mackintosh, Joyce and Wild and their dogs were now on their way back to Hut Point. Cope's team (including Hayward and Richards) was still to finish depot-laying near to the edge of the Barrier.

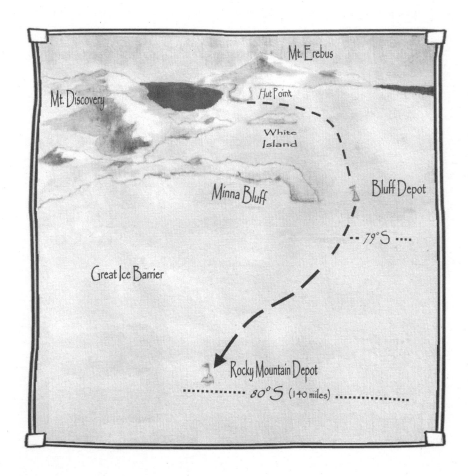

Chapter 5

'ON POLAR JOURNEYS THE DOGS ARE ALMOST HUMAN'

24 February 1915

THE BLIZZARD EASED after two days and on 24 February Mackintosh, Joyce and Wild set off north from the 80°S depot. They were 140 miles from Hut Point; however, another blizzard soon stopped their progress. Mackintosh:

> The poor dogs are feeling hungry; they eat their harness or any straps that may be about. We can give them nothing beyond their allowance of three biscuits each as we are on bare rations ourselves; but I feel sure they require more than one pound a day. That is what they are getting now.
>
> The dogs are feeling the pangs of hunger and devouring everything they see. They will eat anything except rope. If we had not wasted those three days we might have been able to give them a good feed at the Bluff depot, but now that is impossible. It is snowing hard.

Wild is having a weekly clean of pots & pans. We sit & talk over all kinds of subjects.

Reading 'Riddle of the Sands' by Erskine Childers. Finished 'Soldiers of Fortune'.[1]

25 February 1915

Tent bound by the blizzard, Mackintosh wrote up extensive diary notes. Joyce commented on the state of the dogs, blaming Mackintosh. However, the dogs were trained by Wild and Ninnis when at Hobart, so the problem may have been their diet. The diaries do not indicate who was responsible for allocating the food ration for the dogs.

Mackintosh:

Whilst lying here thought I would write up a description of the scene.

Our time is principally occupied by reading which we do holding the book as close as possible to the bag so the hands won't get cold for of course we are lying down as sitting up we would get too cold. While we read sleep often comes on then we toggle up, the book falls in the bag and we doze off; it's remarkable the amount of sleep that is put in this business.

Outside is a scene of chaos. The snow, whirling along with the wind, obliterates everything. The dogs are completely buried, and only a mound with a ski sticking up indicates where the sledge is. We long to be off, but the howl of the wind shows how impossible it is. The sleeping-bags are damp and sticky, so are our clothes. Fortunately, the temperature is fairly high and they do not freeze.

One of the dogs gave a bark and Joyce went out to investigate. He found that Major, feeling hungry, had dragged his way to Joyce's ski and eaten off the leather binding. Another dog has eaten all his harness, canvas, rope, leather, brass, and rivets. I am afraid the dogs will not pull through; they all look thin and these blizzards do not improve matters.

We have a week's provisions and one hundred and sixty miles to travel. It appears that we will have to get another week's provisions from the depot, but don't wish it. Will see what luck to-morrow. Of course, at Bluff we can replenish.[2]

Food was the predominate issue.

> We have been discussing how some nice chops, sauce, chipped potatoes and coffee would 'go down'. Meal and what we would eat take up a deal of our time – mine is frizzled bacon and eggs, porridge, toast and butter, coffee which must be in plenty.
>
> Got out of bag, looked out, found horizon visible, had tea and biscuits and hope to make a start. A little later. It never happened! Scarcely had I written this when I looked out and found snow falling. All obscured. What a place, still, what else can we expect? It's all happened before and we knew it would be so before we came so we must grin and bear it.[3]

Joyce:

> Trekking out of the question, the blizzard a fury. We are now on ½ rations. Dug out the dogs. My heart aches for them.
>
> I don't know how I refrain from giving Mack a bit of my mind, will have to keep that in until we get back. We will have enough to think about before we get to Hut Point.
>
> Fed the dogs they seem very weak. The temp is very high. Our sleeping bags are wet through, clothes in a similar condition.[4]

26 February 1915

Joyce's diary note was again on the dogs – he could not understand their sleeping behaviour:

> The blizzard still raging. Went outside to feed the dogs. The wind a great force almost possible to lean against it. It is a miracle the tent stands the strain. The dogs were completely buried. I could not find them, so had to take directions from the sledge mast. After an hour I dug them out + gave them extra biscuits. They seemed very weak.[5]
>
> When they are out in a blizzard they coil around the drift covers them after a time they are completely buried with no chance whatever of freeing themselves. This

is against the laws of nature. If human aid was not at their assistance where would they be? With the temp well below zero, the snow compact, so what chance have they of freeing themselves?[6]

27 February 1915

They found that, the day after they had been out in the blizzard for an hour or two, either an ear, the nose tip, a fingertip or one cheek was a bit tender, but there was nothing to show. However, a longer frostbite, particularly on the face, would appear in a day or two as a brownish blotch, which took a week or two to disappear by peeling.[7]

Still held up the blizzard, they moved onto reduced rations. Mackintosh:

We have now reduced to one meal in the 24 hours trusting for sleep to feed us the remainder of the time. Of course this going without meals keeps us colder there's no doubt food is the fuel herein more ways than one.

Hours pass, we roll round in bags, build castles, sleep, read and hope. The bags are now getting so damp that we try and look out for dry patches where to lie – lucky there are no rheumaticky people here.

On one occasion when I woke up this morning I found poor Wild rubbing his bare feet in an attempt to bring his big toe round which has 'gone'.* He is always suffering from one or the other of his feet. But he takes it philosophically and is very amusing when he gets up to say 'It's the left foot now, presently it may have been the right'. He says he has scarcely any feeling in them for the past 24 hours. I felt them and gave them a bit of a rub. Indeed they were cold.

Joyce too is affected. The only time I get it is when I have been without hoosh for some time. My feet get cold but if the hoosh is there I am quite alright and have no trouble whatsoever.

It's most annoying that while this wind is in our faces the tears from our eyes run down our faces and freezes on to our goggles; of course we wear these religiously

---

*   'Gone' was a term used to describe a part of their body that was completely frozen.

and so far none of us have been affected by snow-blindness. This light we are travelling in is just the kind that would affect one for there is a dull grey sameness with no contrast between the horizon and surface.[8]

1 March 1915

The blizzard finally broke and they started their trek back.

Joyce: 'I have had a bad attack of snow blindness. I have been rather fortunate in that respect as I have been steering since we left the ship.'[9]

Mackintosh:

> Wild, whose big toe has been suffering ever since the day he went out, last night found it frostbitten. Joyce has been getting it round – it is blue all over. It looks as if there is an in growing nail, but I doubt it would cause the whole toe to go black, as this is.
>
> Joyce has suffered from colic.
>
> I found my legs cold on account of the one pair of drawers I have on not being sufficient.[10]

2 March 1915

Then, tragically, their dogs started to die. They simply gave up and lay down in the snow to sleep, where their body cooled down to such an extent they died of hypothermia. Joyce and Wild write on the dogs dying but Mackintosh confined his diary notes to his own agonies, and occasionally the beauty of their surroundings.

Joyce:

> Poor Nigger the leader of the pack gave in after lunch. I unharnessed him, his legs refusing to support him. The strange feature about the dogs is they lie down, coil themselves around + go to sleep. Scotty + Pompey collapsed in the afternoon. Pinkey out of harness following the sledge.
>
> The Southerly is still with us. So sail is helping us along at a fair speed.[11]

Wild:

Nine miles & all dogs chucked their hands, except Major. Pat stopped behind so I expect he is done for.

Very pretty sunset tonight. Can't explain it but I have never seen such a one before.

We made sail today which helped a lot. Wind on our Port quarter. Very cold.[12]

Couldn't write last night, too cold, but anyway we did 7½ miles. Poor old Shacks fell out, we had to leave him. Today we did 4 miles. First Nigger, then Pompey, Major & Scottie fell out so now we have only got Pinky left. He has had a good feed tonight. We shall have to call this the Dead Dog Trail.

The Skipper fell over & the sledge ran over him happily doing no damage.[13]

Mackintosh:

Set sail for which we use the floor cloth of the tent, this is lashed to a bamboo, used as a yard, then at the centre of this yard is placed the halyards which we trice the whole to the mast another bamboo, lashed on the sledge; the sail and yard are then guyed up and we are ready to be off.

While writing here – lunch hour – found myself dropping off to sleep while writing. Have had very little this past week, feel weary.

Very chilly on march, we all have a thick growth of beard now – this is a great hindrance in low temperatures as the breath freezes onto the whiskers gradually increasing in bulk until you have about a pound weight to carry, to say nothing of the coldness of the ice against the face, this particularly catches the tip of my nose especially if the wind plays on it. Giving several 'bites' to that member.

Another glorious sunset. Golden colours illuminate the sky, moon casting gorgeous rays in combination with the more vivid one from the dipping sun. If all was as beautiful as the scene we could consider ourselves in some paradise. But to come down to our position it's more like a cold hell![14]

3 March 1915

The loss of the dogs, the cold, the lack of food and sleep and their ailments made for trying times, but there was a rare light moment this day.
Wild:

> Started with great hopes this morning & found we couldn't move the sledge, so we took the double runners off, doing which I broke my knife. Then we made another attempt. Joyce forgot to hitch his harness on & while the Skipper & I were struggling away he went saying 'By Gollams, this is better already'. I shouted out to him & he came back & hitched on & then we couldn't move the sledge so we off ski & pulled that way.
>
> By the way we didn't see the humour of this till night-time, & then we laughed until we cried talking about it.[15]

Mackintosh:

> To our horror we found Joyce gaily marching off without us saying out loud 'Why that was what the trouble was' while Wild and I were struggling along. Joyce quite thought he had found out the cause, but was surprised when he looked back to find us behind with the sledge. Sledging has its humorous incidents after all.[16]

6 March 1915

They had pushed on, now with only one dog. They were warmer when actually on the march, although steering was not easy.
Mackintosh:

> The starting off is the cold job, for after getting nicely warmed up in the tent and with the lunch we get chilled down, especially now when we have a blizzard blowing about us, rigging the sail with bare hands, drift snow blowing all over you, temperatures below zero – no enviable position – once we get started and our frost-bitten members restored, we feel more or less comfortable.
>
> At times the sledge going along by itself but we found steering difficult as at times

the sledge would broach to and capsize. We adopted various methods for steering which proved the only thing that hindered us taking advantage of the propelling force. We are still using our ski, so these we took off and one of us harnessed up to a quarter of the sledge and thus regulated the direction by pulling or otherwise but even now as we passed over an extra large mass of sastrugi, the sledge would skid, nearly run over one of us and we were continually falling in our tracks.[17]

Joyce:

The Southerly once more sprang up. Sail set. The sledge overhauling us. With our feet frostbitten + our strength fading it is hard going to keep pace.

Wild + Pinkey the dog having a busman's holiday riding on the sledge, but a cold one. Essential for one to keep on the move, the temp about 20- below zero.

Our last dog collapsed in the afternoon. I am more than sad about it. This could have been avoided, if common sense had been shown from the time we were at the Bluff. On Polar journeys the dogs are almost human. One never feels lonely when they are around.[18]

7–14 March 1915

The three men struggled on towards the Minna Bluff depot. In their diaries they made occasional reference to personal aspects of their daily life as they were now starting to develop serious complaints (even a severe toothache). Their faces were a mass of scabs and sores, their fingers and toes were badly frostbitten and gangrene was setting in to Wild's toes.

In the low temperatures their fingers were apt to go even when fastening or unfastening buttons or ropes, because they had to remove their mitts. In a wind with snow drift, even at -20°F, they could not expose their hands for a minute or two, even if they were otherwise quite warm, without getting the fingertips frozen. They found their fingers recovered in five minutes or so, if their gloves were warm and they would then have no side effects, except a little tenderness, which lasted for three or four days. However, if the fingers took longer than a few minutes to recover they would blister and be very sore for a week or more, after which all the skin would peel off.[19] They found that if frostbite reached below the surface tissue of the hand or foot the result was a water blister, like in a bad burn. If the frostbite became deep seated the blood vessels would not recover and it would lead to gangrene.[20]

Mackintosh:

10 Mar: Just prior to starting Joyce had a look thro glasses and was fortunate in spotting the flag he laid on the outward journey when the stores had been depoted. We are now going to fetch in this load taking a light sledge. After a hard 4 hours pull over a rough surface we got to the depot flag and found it and the cairn intact.

We loaded the sledge with the stores and proceeded back to our tent which by now was of course out of sight – indeed it was not wise to come out as we have without tent or bag but we have taken that chance and the weather promised fine, yet that is no criterion in these parts.[21]

(The last paragraph by Mackintosh is significant. It shows that he knew about the fickle weather, how it could change quickly, and how foolish it would be to go out at any stage without a tent and sleeping bag. Twelve months later, Mackintosh (with Hayward) would attempt to trek from Hut Point to Cape Evans, without a tent or sleeping bags.)

12 Mar: We use our bodies for drying socks and such-like clothing, which we place inside our jerseys and produce when required. Wild carries a regular wardrobe in this position, and it is amusing to see him searching round the back of his clothes for a pair of socks.[22]

13 Mar: Wild slept like a top; he is a remarkable little fellow, always merry & bright; as soon as he lays down he starts snoring, he has been reading a book in which there has been 3 murders and he expects several more.

Have just dreamt I was strolling about outside when a paperboy came rushing to tell me to say Erebus was in eruption 1,000 lives lost. Smoke was coming out of Castle Rock! I woke to find myself in this wet clothing and dampness all round.[23]

14 Mar: All our clothes have a dampness about them which as we get out in the air freeze hard. I won't be sorry when this trip is over. Turned out of the bag while having our hoosh we found on our return a stiff hard board. In it we had to get however, the hard lid was placed over our head, on top of which we wear our caps, at first nothing occurs., in a little time lumps of ice fall on you as the breath may thaw some off, this you place at one side or perhaps let it thaw into water and so absorb into one's clothes.

In this state we lie twisting and turning, during the morning as the temperature gets lower we find the whole bag frozen again. Then you find one or other of us groaning and cussing trying to bring back a frozen toe or rub some part of the body that has been cooled.

After a long while in bags and missing a meal makes a tremendous difference to the attack of the cold. I have always noticed that after I have been in the bag for 8 hours; first my feet show signs of cold and gradually work upward so for me after 8 hours (in a sleeping bag) food is required.[24]

Joyce:

12 Mar: Mack never ought to have left the ship, his eye is very painful. Blizzard-ing. Wild's feet in bad condition. One big blister + badly frostbitten brought them around with my warm hands. Later I suffered with the same complaint. Our cir-culation must be at a very low ebb for frost bites to occur in our sleeping bags.[25]

14 Mar: Wild in agony with frostbites, difficulty treking on hard ice with raw feet.[26]

15 Mar: Another heartbreaking night. The temp down below 50°-. Heard Mack groaning during the night. I emerged from my sleeping bag to find him in agony with toothache. In the medical case there was naught to ease him.

My thoughts could only think of methylated spirits a bottle of which we kept for starting the Primmus. This I passed to him together with cotton wool. During the evolution* of putting the spirit on the cotton wool his fingers went.

He placed the cotton wool on the tooth, a second elapsed + then a yell. The

---

* 'evolution' – a Navy term used for an event.

sound of which must have penetrated to Cape Evans. The toothache was cured, the inside of the mouth raw. The temp of the spirit was the same temperature as the air 82 deg of frost* it had the same effect as boiling liquid.[27]

Mackintosh:

15 Mar: Last night was one of the worst I have ever experienced. To cap everything, I developed toothache, presumably as a result of frost-bitten cheek. I was in positive agony. I groaned and moaned, got the medicine-chest, but could find nothing there to stop the pain.

Joyce, who had wakened up, suggested methylated spirit, so I damped some cotton-wool, then placed it in the tooth, with the result that I burnt the inside of my mouth. All this time my fingers, being exposed (it must have been at least 50 deg. below zero), were continually having to be brought back.

After putting on the methylated spirit I went back to the bag, which, of course, was frozen stiff. I wriggled and moaned till morning brought relief by enabling me to turn out.

I swear this place, once I return home, will never see me again! The skin has peeled off the inside of my mouth, exposing a raw sore, as the result of the methylated spirit. My tooth is better though.[28]

15 March 1915

On 15 March they reached the Minna Bluff depot, about 70 miles from Hut Point. To Joyce the trek from 80°S to the Bluff depot had been an 'abominable long struggle'.[29]

Mackintosh often recorded details of the temperature, wind and other readings and his notes for 15 March are shown below.

Their next target would be the Safety Camp depot, near the edge of the Barrier, approximately 50 miles to the north of the Minna Bluff depot, and

---

* 'deg of frost' means the degree of temperature below the freezing point of water. 82 deg of frost meant the air temperature was -50°F.

only 20 miles from Hut Point. The three men left the Minna Bluff depot on 16 March and slowly edged their way north.

Joyce:

> Our progress ominously slow. For Wild each step a ball of fire.
>
> Our food bag dangerously light. We are on half rations. No sleep + we are on the verge of extreme exhaustion. After a day's hard march our dinner consisted of half a cup of pemmican + a biscuit. Our human machine is truly wonderful in supporting us in our task.[30]

Mackintosh:

> After lunch we travelled well, but the distance for the day was only 7 miles 400 yds. We are blaming our sledge-meter for the slow rate of progress. It is extraordinary that on the days when we consider we are making good speed we do no more than on days when we have a tussle.[31]
>
> 8pm: Readings. Ane 29.62.[*] Ther (sling) +2.[†] Wind nil. Wisps of whaleback clouds over Castle Rock.[‡] Cum banked to North about Cape Crozier,[§] light strands of cir s to south.[¶]

18 March 1915

Mackintosh:

> All of us bear marks of our tramp. Wild takes first place. His nose is a picture for

---

[*]   Ane: Aneroid barometer – an instrument for measuring atmospheric pressure. 29.62 meant the air pressure, measured in 'inches of mercury'.

[†]   Ther (sling): is the temperature using a sling thermometer. Before it was read the thermometer was briskly swung round at the end of a string about half a yard long. The swinging brought the thermometer in contact with a great volume of air, and it therefore gave the real temperature of the air. The reading that day of +2 meant thirty degrees below freezing; freezing being 32° Fahrenheit.

[‡]   Castle Rock is located close to Hut Point.

[§]   Cape Crozier is on the north side of Ross Island.

[¶]   Abbreviations were commonly used – Cum for cumulus clouds, Cir for cirrus clouds.

Punch to be jealous of; his ears, too, are sore, and one big toe is a black sore. Joyce has a good nose and many minor sores. My jaw is swollen from the frost-bite I got on the cheek, and I also have a bit of nose... [32]

(Wild's frostbitten big toe had to be amputated a month later.)

Very snappy breeze in face during march. Our beards and moustaches are a mass of ice. I will take care I am clean-shaven next time I come out. The frozen moustache makes the lobes of the nose freeze more easily than they would if there was no ice alongside them.

What on earth one comes to these parts of the earth? I ask myself – is it worth the candle?* Here we are frostbitten in the day, frozen at nights, no sleep, what a life! [33]

22 March 1915

Mackintosh: 'This morning's hoosh (or what was supposed to be) we demurely asked if it was tea? It certainly was no thicker.' [34]

(One of the worst calamities for one of the men was when they dropped their hoosh, which occasionally happened when it was being served out from the cooker pot. To the man whose meal was spilt it was a catastrophe, that would, in their words, rank with 'the fall of the British Empire'. When it happened everything was scraped up off the floor cloth; a mix of pemmican, crumbs and finneskoe reindeer hairs. The heat of the meal was immediately lost and the flavour never improved. [35])

23 March 1915

On 23 March a blizzard again stopped their slow progress north.
Mackintosh:

---

*   Is it worth the candle? – is it worth the effort?

No sooner had we camped last night than a blizzard with drift came on and has continued ever since. This morning finds us prisoners. The drift is lashing into the sides of the tent and everything outside is obscured. This weather is rather alarming, for if it continues we are in a bad way.

We have just had a meal, cocoa mixed with biscuit crumbs; this has warmed us a little, but the cold on empty stomachs is penetrating.

All kinds of gloomy thoughts come to one lying in bag. How one longs to be out of this infernal region – the dear ones at home what are they doing? After this meal we have a sing-song which has cheered us up. But food is our one thought, what will we eat when we get back? Even dog biscuits now would be a luxury.[36]

Joyce: 'Our food biscuit crumbs + cocoa. The temp well below 50.'[37]

24 March 1915

However, the next day, 24 March, the blizzard stopped and they managed to reach the Safety Camp depot where Wild ran into more problems.

After leaving the depot they went onto the edge of the Great Ice Barrier but the final step, from the edge of the Barrier to Hut Point, was not straightforward. The direct route was across sea-ice but if the ice was not strong they would have to take a longer and more circuitous route around the edge of the Barrier. This would involve climbing up pressure ridges and ice cliffs and camping for one or two nights. Unfortunately they could not take the direct route.

Mackintosh:

We have some biscuit-crumbs in the bag and that is all. Our start was made under most bitter circumstances, all of us being attacked by frost-bites. It was an effort to bare hands for an instant. After much rubbing and 'bringing back' of extremities we started. Wild is a mass of bites, and we are all in a bad way.

We plugged on, but warmth would not come into our bodies. We had been pulling about two hours when Joyce's smart eyes picked up a flag. We shoved on for all we were worth, and as we got closer, sure enough, the cases of provisions loomed up. Then what feeds we promised to give ourselves.

While Wild was getting the Primus lighted he called out to us that he believed his ear had gone. This was the last piece of his face left whole — nose, cheeks, and neck all having bites. I went into the tent and had a look. The ear was a pale green. I quickly put the palm of my hand to it and brought it round.

Then his fingers went, and to stop this and bring back the circulation he put them over the lighted Primus, a terrible thing to do. As a result he was in agony.

It was not long before we were putting our gastronomic capabilities to the test. Pemmican was brought down from the depot, with oatmeal to thicken it, as well as sugar. We felt like new beings. We simply ate till we were full, mug after mug.[38]

Joyce:

At the physiological moment Provi.* gave us a chance.

The 1st mug of pemmican had the machine pumping the blood through our veins the 2nd we began to feel the thrill of warmth. It was essential to be cautious in regard to the amount of food we consumed after starvation diet. Still a starving man has little conscience when the cross roads meet.

After our meal, a banquet to us, we got under weigh with the sufficiencies of the glories of the Great Ice Barrier for a time.[39]

Mackintosh:

When we got to the Barrier-edge we found the ice-cliff on to the newly formed sea-ice not safe enough to bear us, so we had to make a detour along the Barrier-edge and, if the sea-ice was not negotiable, find a way up by Castle Rock.

At 7 p.m., not having found any suitable place to descend to the sea-ice we camped. To-night we have the Primus going and warming our frozen selves. I hope to make Hut Point to-morrow.[40]

---

* 'Provi', that is 'Providence', was a word Joyce used at times, as did Scott and others on expeditions of that era. There is no indication that Joyce was a religious man, and his references to Providence indicate that it was possibly a term he used for luck, or good fortune, rather than calling on God.

A day out from the hut, Joyce jotted down a Browning poem, 'By the Fire-Side':

> *The little more + how much it is*
> *The little less + how far away – Br.*[41]

Other depots were also laid, closer to Hut Point

Meanwhile, while Mackintosh, Joyce and Wild were out on the Barrier, Richards and Hayward, with Cope, Ninnis, Jack and Hooke, had been laying depots closer to Hut Point. (Stevens had returned to Hut Point with Spencer-Smith and Jack had taken his place.)

    Richards wrote in later years that the loads were far too heavy and in his opinion Cope was the last man in the world to be in charge. He tells us that he regarded this particular part of his experience in Antarctica as a good comic opera, but he does admit that they learnt a good deal from it.[42] Hayward, Richards and Ninnis were critical and mocking of the other three-man team – of Cope, Jack and Hooke. They even wrote their own 'poem' at one stage, when complaining about the speed and efforts of the others. Hayward called it a 'little ditty' entitled 'What the Hell' and the first few lines are shown below.

9 February 1915

Hayward:

> Myself supported by Richards, Ninnis, raised a protest on the slow progress we are
> making, due to the way the other three potter about, having spells for breathers &
> 'nibbles'. Last night for instance we spent an hour & a half over the midday meal
> & consequently had to march well over routine.[43]

10 February 1915

Hayward: 'Eventually the 2nd sledge was hauled up to the first & by this time 2 of the other party nicknamed Tanglefoot owing to his acrobatic feats to retain his equilibrium for Skis & Sparrow Knees owing to the decided affection his knees show for one another, were walloped.'[44]

Richards: 'Marched 3¼ miles in (with) one relay. Bandsmen held their own. (For some rediculous [sic] reason we in our tent called ourselves the Bandsmen. We rather looked down on the pulling capabilities of the other tent and fancied ourselves as sort of supermen!)'[45]

Hayward:

I am sorry to say that I have had occasion to do a roar to-night, which was heartily endorsed by Ninnis & Richards my fellow 'tenties' & their opinions are the only ones worth having, as the others have no experience of cold weather travel & conditions & are moreover hopelessly inefficient & incapable of even pulling their pound.

Really they are the biggest messrs humbugs that it has been my misfortune to be up against & instead of realizing that we have a duty to perform and hard work in front of us they think it is a bally afternoon tea party, they will certainly be shaken up by us before we are through.[46]

A Penguin sat upon the Barrier Edge
Singing what have you been doing all the day?
Six great men a tiny little sledge
You must have been stopping on the way
What the Hell? What the Hell? What the Hell is it all about?
You've got to put your back to it
Before you can do a shout.[47]

12 February 1915

Richards:

> My rupture is a bit painful tonight and we are all fairly tired … Most of the party
> are not taking too kindly to their rations – especially pemmican … Sledging is
> monotonous. Very often too short of wind to talk and travel for hours without
> a word spoken. The bunk at night on the hard snow is relished as much as any
> feather bed.[48]

In a note added later he said:

> The rupture had been sustained at football the previous season and under
> medical advice at the time I used a truss. I cannot imagine how incredibly fool-
> ish I was to conceal this disability which could have had disastrous results had
> things gone wrong badly with me the following year. In the upshot I threw the
> truss away when discarding everything possible in our retreat from Mt. Hope
> the following year.[49]

Early diary entries
of Hayward

As well as making comments about the other sledging team, Hayward often
mused in his diary, always with his fiancée Ethel on his mind – he had a picture of her which he kept in his diary. He is reading *Lorna Doone*, an 1869
romantic novel, by Richard Doddridge Blackmore and he wistfully writes
about a man who was in love but this love was not returned. He even tran-
scribes a paragraph or two from *Lorna Doone* into his diary. In two long
and convoluted (but intriguing) sentences he describes a time when they
had a quarrel, and he pens two 'champagne supper' menus they would
have on his return. At this stage, through his diary, he is in a conversation
with his loved one.

12 February 1915

You ought really to see me now in my bag writing this to you thinking sweet thoughts of you & feasting my eyes on your dear picture, which by the way, I have fastened on to the fly leaf of this note-book.[50]

14 February 1915

We have just finished our Hoosh & tea & I am just beginning to feel comparatively warm once more. I have brought with me on this trip my old favourite *Lorna Doone* & am about to have a rasp of it. Did you ever read it? I have an idea that I got it for you, to do so, but somehow think that you said you could not tackle it. When I come back I am going to insist upon you reading it, but in case you defy me, I will insist upon reading it to you.

At last we are on the move again, very hot day travelling, have had to divest myself of quite a lot of sweaters & things. Relayed 2 sledges 1½ miles. I have had a piece of rotten luck to-day.

When we were ready to haul up 2nd sledge, we found it was stuck in the loose snow & after Ninnis had had several unsuccessful attempts to start her up I got hold of the thing & gave a terrific wrench to get it out, the bally thing didn't budge & I strained my back pretty badly, it has been very painful hauling.[51]

15 February 1915

I am sorry to find that my back is awfully stiff this morning and I know it means a rough passage for me for a few days at least. Camped for midday meal, the cold made it very comfortless & we were glad to get going again 4 o/c pm.

We tried an experiment for tea – had Pemmican, Plasmon, Biscuit Hoosh & found it quite a success, it will certainly become a frequent addition to the menu.

The total distance covered today is barely 4 miles not much result for so much real hard work.

Anyhow this I do know & I want you when you read this to see that it is carried out. Just you and I are going to have 2 champagne suppers. 1) At the Crown Stanmore & 2) At 'Ye Old Cheshire Cheese' Fleet St.

Menus suggested by me are

1) Thick gravy soup

Salmon mayonnaise

Spring chicken in aspic

Roast Rib Beef & Yorkshire Pudding Sauté Potatoes

Black Currant boiled Jam Roll

Stewed mixed Fruits

Gorgonzola Cheese (Ripe)

Black Coffee & Kummel

& for me a Pkt of Wills Gold Flake Cigs

2) Real Turtle Soup (Thick)

Braised Gosling & Red Currant Jelly

Pigeon Pie

The Pudding (Beef, Steak, Lark & Oyster)

Some other dish optional

Toasted Cheshire Cheese

Black Coffee &c

Now please do not forget to remind me of this, not that I think it will be necessary. Marching along here, with a lot on one's mind & very little in ones 'innards' I feel like breaking something when I think of it just your dear little self and myself making veritable 'gormandizers' of ourselves. By jingo would it be good.

I am in my bag at present it is about 1 o/c Tuesday aft. Writing this occasionally lending the others a hand, to prepare our frugal breakfast. Half a mug of Skilly oatmeal, a Pannikin of tea, 10 lumps of sugar & 2 very Hard biscuits.

However it's all in the game & I can keep on thinking of the good times to come eh!

However in my bag & reading *Lorna Doone* does me alright, but I cannot help feeling that there is too much pottering going on this trip which is by no means satisfactory. The following strikes me as being a jolly nice expression of thought

& sentiment by the Girt Jan Ridd the strong man in love with the sweet Lorna Doone, but whose love at this time is not reciprocated don't you think it nice. He had promised not to try see her again till a month had passed & during this time was working on his farm, thinking naturally more of Lorna than of the work he was engaged upon so:–

'Perhaps it is needless for me to say, that all this time while my month was running or rather crawling, for never month went so slow as that with me, neither weed nor seed, nor cattle, nor my own mothers anxiety, nor any care for my sister, kept me from looking once every day & even twice on Sunday for any sign of Lorna … All the beauty of the Spring went for happy men to think of, all the increase of the year was for other eyes to mark, not a sign of any Sunrise for me, from my fount of life: not a breath to stir the dead leaves fallen on my hearts spring.'

Ethel I can appreciate all this fully & even if I could not write it so beautifully I can at any rate substituting you for Lorna Doone remember when I have thought exactly similar thoughts. In any case I am sure you will understand how, down here, where everything breathes of the unknown & appears so vast & limitless, how nice it is to be reminded in such a nice way of other & more pleasant scenes, even though certain of them are bitter-sweet.

I have been thinking of those lovely times of which I have such a vivid recollection, those times which we have spent together at Pinner, Stanmore, Chorleywood & Woldingham & really I find it difficult to find any one occasion which appeals more strongly to me than another, in fact I would not detract from the merit of either by trying to do so, they are all such sweet episodes, full of interest & delight & this applies none the less to those times when no doubt we have both experienced the 'bitter sweetness' of a combat of wills, or indeed when this has developed into open conflict, it has always been sufficient for me to just have been with you & under all circumstances I have been so satisfied.

Nevertheless as you will understand some episodes retain their freshness with us more than others naturally & I have been thinking particularly of that Sunday when it was raining hard & we went to Chorleywood this was after a few days of silence between us, & I shall never forget the sweet, gentle way in which you accepted my, obvious & apparent efforts to fix things up which of course were successful. I wonder if you can call to mind what took place, with the same accuracy as I can.[52]

Richards, a man of twenty-two years of age, with no romantic connections we know of, writes matter-of-fact notes.

Richards:

It turned very cool towards evening and when I came to take my boots off socks were frozen hard to the boots and were with difficulty removed without damage. The sleeping bag was frozen. On running my hand inside I could feel ice all over the bottom. However, notwithstanding managed to get through a fairly comfortable night. I am changing my footwear for today's march. In place of boots which freeze as hard as boards and are very cold I shall wear pair of finneskoe.[53]

17 February 1915

Smoking, of cigarettes or a pipe, was the luxury all the men enjoyed.

Hayward:

Am now just having a nice smoke. For some time I have been making my cigarettes with tissue paper from the biscuit tins, but just now I am in clover, as yesterday I swapped a black silk navy neckerchief with Ninnis for 20 Virginian cigarettes & consider I made a good bargain, anyway I am enjoying one immensely just at present especially as my sleeping bag is nice & warm & DRY.[54]

18 February 1915

Hayward:

I have had a desperate time, trying to get comfortable in my bag, & when I tell you that the temperature dropped to 50 degrees below freezing point* you will understand why.

You can have no idea what this means every breath one takes condenses in

---

* 50 degrees below freezing point is -28°F, or -33°C.

the atmosphere of the tent & makes everything damp for the time, this then freezes up, then when we get the cooker going as we just have for the Pemmican, all this thaws out & down drops the moisture all over one, wetting one through, then to complete the operation this freezes hard & cold, when the cooker is turned off.[55]

19 February 1915

Hayward:

Spent a very comfortable night, the most comfortable since starting as a matter of fact we placed our bags close together & of course had the benefit of our combined warmth.

Have had breakfast, very good too, by Jingo, a man feels good after his pannikin of Porridge & Hut Tea, he is ready to push Mount Erebus over, the only thing preventing him is that although it looks quite close it is something like 60 miles off & therefore quite safe.

We have had a regular gorge to-night, Pemmican & oatmeal Hoosh thick, & a pannikin of tea with 20 lumps of sugar in it each it was a feed for the Gods & I have the most comfortable feeling inside that I have known for some time. It is going to be very cold to-night in fact even now I can hardly hold the pencil I am writing with & shall have to chuck it, till it gets warmer.[56]

Richards: 'We are getting thinner. (Seems as though we were getting a wee bit sorry for ourselves too).'[57]

Hayward and Richards, with Cope, Ninnis, Hooke and Jack put down their first depot of supplies on the Great Ice Barrier, approximately 25 miles from Hut Point. This was known as Cope No. 1 depot.

21 February 1915

Hayward continues his detailed diary, including his feelings when visited by the men of the other team (Cope, Jack and Hooke).

Hayward:

This morning we have been laying a depôt here, & making up our load on the one sledge according to arrangement made yesterday. Depot consists of, 1 sledge 1 Case Biscuits 1 Box provisions 1 Pr ski, 2 Coils Rope 1 Kit Box, 3 tins Kerosene & Sundries. Sledge buried at the bows to amidships Cairn erected & surmounted by flag. Sledge to go on weighs 1200 lb.

The weather to-day has been delightful, it has been possible to potter around with no hat or mitts & to feel quite warm, whilst lying here smoking we actually have the tent door open as it is quite unbearable inside without.

I meant to make reference to the remarkable phenomenon noticed yesterday with regard to the sun, over & under the sun appeared two small concave patches of rainbow effect & on the outsides two converse patches of a similar kind, whilst the sun itself shone with a quite white light.

This was distinctly visible for about 1 hour & a half, from 9 AM till 10.30., when it gradually disappeared. Nobody of our party which includes two meteorologists have seen or heard of anything like it & it must be quite unique.

Several of us are suffering from frost bite, my neck & cheeks are quite stiff & swollen & it is quite painful to turn round or laugh. In my case I suppose I must not be surprised as even in the coldest winds I have marched without my hat on & as I left the ship with my hair closely clipped & have continued to keep my beard also clipped (on account of the beastly mess one face gets in, if one favours a beard, when it freezes up & icicles form on it).

I have had no very great protection, although not finding it cold at the time, in my case these little things are undoubtedly sent to try us & without them to contend with, I expect one would almost feel out of place, I am pleased to say that I have now got the better of my strained back & shall no doubt get the better of frost bite without having to force the growth of a protective 'face fungus'.

You would not realise the terrible silence & monotony which exists here. & when on the march one thinks & thinks & thinks & only thinks & pulls & pulls & thinks, he thinks no doubt because he has not sufficient breath to converse with, but more particularly because he can think of things which take him out of the present surroundings to other & more homely & pleasing ones.

We were surprised shortly afterwards at being invaded by the other three, bringing with them all the snow they could possibly accommodate on their enormous feet into our tent, of which we are always careful, even changing our footgear for the purpose of leaving the snow outside.

They were also armed with a big Thermos flask & it was evident that something important was toward. It turned out to be another re-arrangement of plans, to be discussed immediately everybody had partaken of hot tea from the flask. In course of this process, two of our visitors Cope, Hooke, managed to upset the contents of their mugs over Richards & myself respectively & in consequence the meeting was nearly broken up, peace & order was eventually restored however & the discussion duly took place.

We had a lovely gorge to-night before turning in, we always celebrate occasions of this sort in this way, we had 4 biscuits each, an extra whack of sugar 20 lumps each & half a bar of chocolate. First we had a nice drop of Pemmican & Oatmeal mixed, then we each crushed 2 biscuits put them together with enough water, added 1 spoonful of Glaxo, & 1 of Plasmon, brought to the boil & wolfed it, it was great, followed by a nice mug of tea. I turned in & remember nothing more till now.[58]

23 February 1915

A few days after laying the Cope No. 1 depot, they put down another, named Cope No. 2, less than 10 miles further south.

The men found it took time to become accustomed to sleeping with their head inside their sleeping bag, without any fresh air to speak of. It was impossible to sleep with their head exposed with the temperatures always below zero.[59]

Hayward:

Had a very funny experience during the night, being so cold I put fur mitts on & did all the toggles of my bag up, somehow or other I dreamt during the night, woke up suddenly I could not imagine where I was, only that I was absolutely helpless & suffocating.

Of course I lashed out pretty freely & having fur mitts on I could feel nothing.

However very soon Richards & Ninnis undid the toggles & I sprang out like a Jack in the Box, they say the awful language & the struggle going on inside my bag had been too much for them in spite of their being so utterly tired. I can tell you I was glad to get some fresh air as it was a most uncanny feeling inside that bag.[60]

After laying the second depot, Cope, Hayward, and Jack continued on south to lay a third depot while Richards, Ninnis and Hooke returned to Hut Point.

Hayward:

Naturally, Richards & myself are quite cut up on our separation, as on a trip of the sort we have been engaged on, one makes fast friends (or otherwise) of one's companions. We have been jolly good comrades all through never having a difference of any sort & always showing a most unselfish spirit towards one another.

To-night I have been most touched by the good fellowship they have shown to me, Ninnis with the best spirit in the world, giving me his last & treasured 40 cigarettes which of course I only accepted after much insistence on his part.

Richards too pressed a supply of tobacco on me with equally warm & friendly feelings & although we have been together for only 3 weeks I am feeling quite hurt at the prospect of our parting in the morning with positive regret & although I should feel honoured at being chosen to go on, I cannot feel the slightest joy about it, although of course I cannot help feeling some satisfaction, in doing so.

I honestly feel very sorry for them. In any case they will not have to undergo the hardships we shall have to face completing our journey as it is getting colder daily & we shall be out very nearly a month yet, whereas they should reach the Hut inside 10 days. [61]

24 February 1915

Hayward, now with Cope and Jack, set off south to lay their last depot, called Cope No. 3, less than 10 more miles onto the Great Ice Barrier but any 'fun' of sledging appears to have disappeared.

Hayward:

Last night I had an extra long & lingering look at your dear picture & I feel quite homesick & rotten this morning. More so than I have felt for some time, as I have purposely refrained from looking too long for some time, as the last time I did it, I experienced the same feelings.

I wish I could tell you here what I should like, but you will realise that I must be content with thinking things only & of course I am satisfied, especially as I believe you will understand what I should write if I expressed my thoughts, if you do not I will explain in detail & with the pleasure, as far as this instance is concerned, and the many instances where I have omitted similar explanations for similar reasons previously & so frequently.[62]

25 February 1915

Hayward may have been unhappy to part with Richards but he enjoyed his new tent-mates: 'Tent companions & I are all very comfortable & jolly together & comprise a happy little party. Jack is an exceedingly nice chap. We have spent the day more or less in our bags, talking of things past, present & future, reading & smoking.'[63]

26 February 1915

Hayward:

8 o/c pm. We have been lying here all day, the snowstorm which held us up this morning having developed into a bad blizzard, & it is very disheartening in view of the delays we have already had to contend with & the good going we were making of it this morning.

In any case I have managed to get nice & warm in my bag & have plenty of nice things about you to think of. I must say that I am very glad, that there is so much to occupy ones energies & attention, that so far the time has not seemed to drag; it would be unbearable if this was not the case. We have been able to start again to-day & are just about to have some grub & make ourselves comfortable for the night, as we are quite resigned to the fact that it will be some time before the weather clears sufficiently to make further progress possible.[64]

28 February 1915

Hayward:

Lying in my bag with just one toggle undone to enable me to come up for air when necessary.

I cannot help thinking what extraordinary things take place in the course of a man's otherwise ordinary existence, here am I at the uttermost ends of the earth, parted from you, for whom I would give my life, working for the furtherance of an undertaking with an object of Worlds interest from a Scientific Point of view for its goal, lying in a fur bag, inside a little tent, with 2 other chaps, with a wind at 40 miles an hour & a temperature of 50 below outside, when I ought to be sitting in front of the fire at home & keeping warm & yet in spite of all this can look upon my present occupation with utter fortitude & 'matter of factness' & I know that it is only my hopes & thoughts of you which make this possible, you will understand I know what I mean even if I fail to put it down as clearly as might be.

Before turning in proposed & carried unan.* the old Antarctic toast Sweethearts & Wives done in brandy from the Medical Comforts.[65]

3 March 1915

Hayward, after a freezing night (-62°F):

God I hope we have a better night when we camp to-day (might mention temperature 94° below freezing last night).

Funny thing I laughed with a sort of feeling of insult when on getting out of my bag at 5 o/c to get breakfast, I found I had 'pins & needles' in my arm, think of it a damn paltry little thing like 'pins & needles' in the morning, after the agony I had endured all night.[66]

---

*   'unan.' – unanimously

6 March 1915

On 6 March, after laying the Cope No. 3 depot, approximately 40 miles from Hut Point, Hayward, Cope and Jack turned around and headed back north. Hayward mentioned their major concern: 'We are all absolutely stumped for tobacco this is the worst blow of all.'[67]

7 March 1915

Conditions were now deteriorating for these three men.
   Hayward:

> Now very tired indeed but unfortunately cannot look forward to turning in bag with any degree of pleasure as the lateness of the season & the suddenness with which the cold weather has set in renders them practically uninhabitable, it is as much as we can do to get into them, as they are absolutely frozen hard.
>
>   After having succeeded in forcing an entrance the frost naturally thaws out & the result is best left to the imagination, anyhow I begin to dread the time for turning in & however tired I may feel would prefer to keep going.[68]

By early March, Richards (with Ninnis and Hooke) had already arrived back at Hut Point. Spencer-Smith (with Stevens and Gaze) was already there and these six men would soon be picked up by the *Aurora* and taken to Cape Evans. Hayward (with Cope and Jack) was on his way back to Hut Point but still out on Barrier. Mackintosh, Joyce and Wild were further out, also heading for Hut Point.

Chapter 6

'I WENT ON BOARD TO FETCH A PLUM-DUFF PRESENTED BY THE COOK'

At Discovery *hut*

ON 12 MARCH the *Aurora* picked up Spencer-Smith, Richards, Stevens, Gaze, Ninnis and Hooke from Hut Point and the ship went north to Cape Evans.

The day before Hayward, Cope and Jack had arrived at Safety Camp, on the edge of the Barrier, only 20 miles from Hut Point. The sea-ice between the Barrier and Hut Point was not firm so Hayward's party had to trek 5 miles through the hills, and he wrote a full description of their four-day march. Their trek, in bitterly cold conditions, was difficult and dangerous, and included camping one night on a ledge, on a steep slope of Observation Hill.

11 March 1915

Hayward:

On our arrival here we have found that all the sea-ice has gone out & we are unable therefore to get round to the Hut by that route. Jack & I skied 4 miles along Barrier Edge roped together hoping to find track across the Hills, but snow-storm coming up we were forced to return hurriedly.[1]

12 March 1915

Hayward:

Have decided when weather permits to travel parallel to the Barrier Edge to the foot of Observation Hill where Scott's cross is erected & work south making the ascent at the first available point.

I have been 3 hours collecting every scrap of tobacco I could find amongst my personal gear, the net result after removing bits of biscuit, sleeping bag hairs &c &c was just about enough for one cigarette, however I enjoyed it more than any gold tipped, jewelled in every hole sort of thing, I ever smoked.[2]

13 March 1915

Hayward:

To-day has been a day crowded with incident not to mention danger & writing this now camped for the night I cannot help feeling thankful that we are safe.

We carried out the plan agreed upon yesterday but when within ¼ a mile of Observation Hill we came upon enormous crevasses running parallel to the land (as opposite) & certain death to anybody attempting to cross them, this was a sad disappointment as of course it meant working inland out to get round them and eventually we had to travel 5 miles off our course for this purpose.

Close here we passed an enormous bunch of seals, thousands of them & I have no doubt this must have been their breeding ground.

After safely crossing 2 small cracks we pulled our sledge just up the incline & camped for lunch. Immediately after lunch we resumed operations re-stowed & loaded the sledge, putting our skis on it, the first effort hauled us 100 yards, when we were all blown, by sticking to it we reached a point ½ a mile up the gradient to this point being 1 foot in 5 think of it dragging a 410 lb sledge with us.

Anyway here it was absolutely impossible to proceed further in this way & relaying had to be resorted to, so having dumped half our stuff which by the way we had to stick firmly into the snow to prevent it rolling down the incline and had another shot & how we succeeded in getting the sledge up to the first ledge I do not know, this ledge was ¼ mile further off. Returning with the empty sledge for our remaining load, we had the utmost difficulty in controlling it, we were all very pleased when at last we succeeded in getting the 2nd half of our load safely up & camped for the night.

It might be interesting to give you some idea as to the temperature we have been experiencing, immediately on taking off my Burberry* blouse it freezes so hard that I can within ½ a minute hold it out by one (wristband) then if one touches metal with bare fingers all the skin is taken off & left attached to it.[3]

Hayward's team arrive at Hut Point

On 14 March the three men reached Hut Point, but they found nobody there. A letter from Stenhouse told them the *Aurora* had picked up the others two days ago. For ten days Hayward, Cope and Jack were at Hut Point on their own, before being joined by Mackintosh, Joyce and Wild. They found *Discovery* hut a reasonable place to live, compared to sledging on the Barrier.

Hayward:

---

* Outside all their garments 'Burberry' was worn, a woven fabric that breathed – an essential in Antarctica with its low humidity and low temperatures – to stop sweat building up, and freezing, on or inside the clothing. The Burberry helmet completely enclosed the head except for the face, which remained uncovered at the bottom of a funnel stiffened by a ring of copper-wire.

14 Mar: We set out after breakfast this morning roped after Alpine fashion & after looking round realised that the ascent was too steep to even consider attempting to haul up the sledge, we therefore decided to continue in the direction of Hut Point with all speed & after 5 hours precarious going we were rewarded by making the Hut safely, which I can honestly say I at times hardly expected, as without exaggeration we were several times as near to fatal accident as it is comfortable to be, & I am exceedingly thankful at our safety.

We have missed her by just 2 days.

We must now prepare ourselves for a sojourn here until the sea is sufficiently frozen to enable us to sledge to Cape Evans where the ship will winter, this will probably be 3 months.[4]

Hayward:

15 Mar: By Jingo, what a joy to sleep in something dry. I feel quite young again. Had a busy day straightening things up, a sort of Spring clean without the nuisance of soap & water, a shovel pick-axe & broom & a little effort has made the Hut far more comfortable than it was.[5]

Hayward: '21 Mar: Weather as usual rotten, heavy drift & driving wind. Temperatures these days average somewhere about 70° below, somewhat parky I tell you & makes the Hut seem very nice although it isn't really.'[6]

Hayward:

22 Mar: Weather continues bad. Pottered about Hut making candlesticks out of Syrup tins & spoons out of wire, as although the ship so kindly left us any amount of Corned Beef & sardines, they very kindly omitted to leave us anything to tackle them with, we would use our fingers, only the tips are so badly sore through frost-bite.[7]

Mackintosh, Joyce and Wild arrive at Hut Point

After an uncomfortable night in the hills near Hut Point on 24 March, Mackintosh, Joyce and Wild left their sledge (with their sleeping bags) and risked sliding down the hills; a gamble which paid off as they landed safely, only a short distance from Hut Point. Hayward and Jack were out walking and were surprised when they heard their voices from inside the hut.

Cope, although a biologist, was the party's doctor and he attended to Mackintosh, Joyce and Wild's sores and injuries. Wild made no mention of his frostbite ailments, or the amputation of his toe.

Before long Mackintosh started to compare living in *Discovery* hut to being on the march, and then after only a few days at the hut his thoughts turned to the 13-mile trek north, to Cape Evans. They found a small quantity of meat at the hut, and Hayward had an unusual interpretation of 'fresh'.

Joyce:

> 25 Mar: A woe begotten night. Feet + hands throbbing through the blisters. Made breakfast + proceeded towards the hut. We are on the trail of a sledge track. Expect it was the one made by the Padre + his party. It leads us to a comfortable down trail on to the sea-ice.
>
> On inspection the ice was thin therefore treacherous. We decided to climb the hills. Proceeded to an easy slope. Before ascending same we thought it advisable to lunch, in case of accidents.
>
> After satisfying the inner man we packed + abandoned the sledge, carrying ice axes we assisted Wild up the gradual slope. His feet still very painful. Reached the summit of the hills which leads down to a plateau between Cape Armitage + Hut Point.
>
> I remarked, let us play chances? Slide down + see where we land. We let ourselves go, in 2 minutes we found ourselves at the bottom + about 10 yds from the edge of a drop of about 30 feet. Our breath exhausted.
>
> In ½ an hour we were at Hut Point.[8]

Hayward:

> 25 Mar: I suddenly heard voices apparently coming from the Hut, & of course knowing that we had left Cope, who is no better, by himself, could not make it out, but needless to say lost no time in making investigations. It turned out to be the Skipper, Joyce & Wild, who having left their sledge on the Barrier Edge, had made their way over the fresh sea-ice barely one inch thick & on foot to the Hut.

I cannot describe their ghastly appearance, the Skipper looked dazed, Wild had an ear completely frost bitten, his nose & one foot. Joyce had his hands & nose & feet gone, they looked awful.

Of course we were all pleased to see each other & Jack & I set to work to make our visitors as comfortable as we could. We sat yarning nearly all night & I will not say too much as to what it meant.[9]

Mackintosh:

25 Mar: Having our breakfast and have the luxury of sitting in front of the primus while it goes full. Here we are at last, our troubles of sledging and sleep at least over!

We found here even a blubber-fire, luxurious, but what a state of dirt and grease! However, warmth and food are at present our principal objects. As there are only three bags here,* we take it in turns to use them. Our party have the privilege.[10]

Joyce:

26 Mar: After dinner we had a medical examination. Wild is in the worst condition his feet are raw + his big toe will have to be amputated. His face is a picture and one ear is a big blister. Hands badly blistered. I do not think he could have travelled another day.

Mac seems to have got off the best. His feet slightly blistered hands slightly, face cheeks + nose blistered, hands slightly.

My feet and hands badly gone but not serious. Nose I am afraid of. It is a big black blister from cheek bones across. Anyway we are in a hut + we have a doc, so that is something. Cope started on his doctoring right away.[11]

Wild's big toe had to be amputated, a part of his ear came off, it was a couple of weeks before our faces straightened out again. It was painful to laugh but with the good management of Cope who was working under extreme difficulties, we were soon about again.[12]

---

*   There were only three sleeping bags because Mackintosh, Joyce and Wild had left their sledge with their sleeping bags on the hills around the Barrier in their rush to get to Hut Point.

Mackintosh:

26 Mar: This is indeed comfort – the trials & tribulations of the past (months) week can make us appreciate them.

Yet to see our habitation, this room (a space in the hut divisioned off) is full of smoke, we are sitting over a stove that has been made to use blubber – our clean faces which were so when we arrived are black with soot, this does not worry us, we are warm, we can turn in sleep, real sleep, no dreary shivers.[13]

27 Mar: The change in scene from a few days ago is remarkable. Here we are now leading a life of a primitive people, black now with grime and soot from the impoverished stove, all this so in contrast to the fresh air open life.

Although we have not been here yet long enough to wish to be back to sleepless nights and frozen fingers.

Today we have cleaned out some of the debris littered about, also the blubber which has overflowed from the stove laying all over the place, so that one is walking in it, we have now cleared this up and made an overflow ledge to receive the blubber and made a platform round the stove to walk over, the part we are living in has also been screened round, so we can retain more of the heat given out by the stove it has certainly made the place more habitable.[14]

Our clothes are rapidly becoming begrimed with blubber, as are our faces. We have not quite got used to the method of using the stove so perhaps this accounts for the smoke that issues from it. Washing is a thing we are unable to do, for one thing we have nothing to wash in, also the trouble of getting the water melted is all against us, as well as the room when we can do so.

Joyce's and Wild's frost bites are very bad, my principal damage is my nose and a couple of fingers – lanoline is our principal medicine.

28 Mar: The sea is freezing all round, but open water to the north, still.[15]

30 Mar: Now we have the shelter here and have been comforted I feel myself wishing to be back at Cape Evans (*Aurora*). I hate this idleness, besides the clothes we have are getting in a sad way. A bath would be just glorious. The ice all round is freezing fast tonight.

Joyce's nose is not a pretty sight being a resemblance of what one sees of Aly Soper.[*16]

Hayward:

30 Mar: Late last evening I watched Killer Whales in the Bay here, sporting about & breaking up the sea-ice which we are relying on to get to the ship as soon as possible. This was 8 inches thick & these whales simply made great lanes through it with the utmost ease, it is not nice however to see ones ground as it were, broken up under ones feet, & especially under ones very eyes.

We are endeavouring to thaw out a leg of mutton which we have discovered here, it was left in 1901, Scott's first Expedn so is nearly 15 years old, still fresh meat is always acceptable what!

Enjoyed mutton immensely.[17]

April 1915 – six men wait at Hut Point

Joyce describes their life inside *Discovery* hut. He was wondering why the ship has not come down to Hut Point and picked them up. He blamed Mackintosh for failing to direct Stenhouse, the acting captain of the *Aurora*. Joyce:

It is impossible to wash, there being no utensils, soap or towels.

The Blubber stove is a peach. Every time a piece of blubber is placed on it, it throws out black smoke + the fumes are very disagreeable.

The sun went North on 22 April until 22 Aug. The darkness gradually coming over the Antarctic until there is no daylight at all.

So one can hardly realise what it is to be in a hut that was built for 45 people two thirds full of snow one corner blocked off with provision cases, no windows, table, chairs or bunks.

3 men in sleeping bags, 3 men sitting around the blubber stove. 2 out of the 3

---

*   Ally Soper was a comic strip character from the early 1900s, who sported a large red nose.

bandaged up, no lighting except an improvised blubber lamp, which was an old tin full of blubber, a piece of canvas as a wick floating about which gives out plenty of fumes and very little light.

The food which is seal meat cooked in blubber oil, biscuits + now + again dried veges but in spite of all this everyone seems to have a good appetite.

The position here is there are only 3 sleeping bags so we will have to keep watch + wait until the others are brought from the bay. They will take about a week to dry as they are full of ice, the weight of a bag is 10 lbs + when brought in + weighed they were over 30 lbs. This shows the quantity of ice that accumulated through the heat of the body.

There is an assortment of stores. No clean clothing. One can exist here for some months. It is remarkable how one overcomes difficulties – what with the blubber + grease + our frostbites, which gave us a terrible time.[18]

(Twelve months on and Joyce, with others of the Mount Hope Party, would again be at *Discovery* hut, living in the same conditions.)

Joyce:

The nonappearance of the ship causes very heated arguments. Before the darkness came on there was open water as far as one could see from the hills. Even now there is open water as the sea is only frozen over to the South of Hut Pt.

I asked Mack one day what instructions had he given to Stenhouse regarding the returning sledging parties. He was very vague on the subject. Cape Evans is only 13 miles to the North + the ship could be here in 2 hours. Stenhouse knowing the conditions ought to have anchored here until the sledging parties were picked up. There being good anchorage in the bay, or landed coal, stove, lanterns, clothes + stores. In our arguments whoever is right or wrong only common sense ought to have been heard.

It does not take any thinking and until we found out otherwise Mack is in the wrong for not leaving instructions. Anyway we are going through the mill. Although we are heated in our arguments it is forgotten soon after.[19]

(It appears that Joyce may have been wrong to believe that Mackintosh did not leave instructions for Stenhouse. In his diary of 27 January, when at Hut Point, Mackintosh had written: 'I wrote instructions here for Stenhouse

to leave provisions here for our return in case we were not back in time to
be taken off by the ship'.[20] Stenhouse may not have seen the instructions
because if he had, he it is hard to imagine that he would not have left stores
at Hut Point when he picked up the party with Richards and Spencer-
Smith in early March.)

Mackintosh and Hayward anxiously wait for the sea-ice to freeze

However, the men managed, by reading and singing and in friendly arguments. Hayward mentioned a 'friendly' argument where it appears that
Hayward was arguing the case for a 'Canadian Cowboy' being able to go out
in tougher conditions than a sailor, who he called 'Broach Buster the Sailor'.

For Mackintosh, the conditions at Hut Point were now intolerable and
understandably, he longed to be home. He tells us he was reading a book
by a Richard Whiteing, written in 1899. No. 5 John Street was a hovel in
the heart of a slum in the West End of London where Whiteing had gone
to learn what it was like to live on half a crown a day, and to earn it. Mackintosh compared his predicament to that of Whiteing.

Mackintosh and Hayward had an overwhelming desire to be at Cape
Evans. (Twelve months later they would again be at Hut Point and repeat
their almost daily ritual of checking the sea-ice between the two locations.)
Hayward was regularly taking walks, usually with Mackintosh to check the
condition of the sea-ice.

On Thursday 22 April the sun did not rise and they noticed the diminishing light.

The men did not mention the First World War in their diaries and Richards tells us, in an interview, that the men placed little importance to the
war because most of them thought that the end of the war was a foregone
conclusion. He remembered that sometimes one of the men might say they
wondered if the war was still going on and the others would look at the
person who spoke as if they were mad. They did not imagine that the war
could still possibly be on.[21]

Hayward:

1 Apr : Weather so bad that it is impossible to venture outside the Hut. I have been wondering what you are doing more than usual, in view of the close proximity of the Easter Holiday. 8 pm: Weather cleared sufficiently to enable Skipper & I to get a little walk in, very acceptable too.[22]

5 Apr: Lovely day. Skipper & I walked to Gap.

To-night from 7 o/c until 10.30 I have been engaged in an argument against Skipper Joyce & Wild on the respective merits of the Western Canadian Cowboy & Broach Buster the Sailor, of course I was up against a strong majority & took on rather more than I bargained for, nevertheless the Skipper thanked me for the debate. Debates have been suggested for a daily or rather nightly part of our entertainment whilst here.[23]

15 Apr: Strong wind from South has unfortunately completely broken up ice & again a heavy sea takes its place, this of course destroys our hope of reaching the ship without much more delay as we began to expect.[24]

22 Apr: Lovely day. To-day we saw the last of the sun till Sept next.

23 Apr: The sun is leaving us rapidly & will disappear altogether within the next few days. Wind sprung up from the S & brought all the ice in packing tight with a very loud grinding & crunching. I should say that the ice now in the Sound is about 2" thick. 2 or 3 more days & we shall be able to clear I hope.

This evening we found a sort of Christmas Pudding in a linen bag, 14 years old & it was jolly good too. [25]

25 Apr: Blizzard set in last night & lasted all to-day. Hope it will let up to-morrow, strong wind doing its best to break up ice again.[26]

29 Apr: Less windy & brighter. Sea-ice promising.[27]

Mackintosh:

1 Apr: This place is really an appalling mess, much worse than I like to see but under the circumstances I don't like imposing tasks. I find myself getting more resigned to the grime and dirt, one minute I may be poking a lump of blubber on to the fire, one has to kneel down to get at the stove, your hands consequently get smothered in blubber lying all around.[28]

1 Apr : In the evenings songs are sung and everyone keeps more or less merry and bright. Yet we are grateful, I shall never forget the relief we found on getting back here safely. Arguments are rife. We have so much to settle and decide when we get back to the ship. I am sure if we should remember all that we have argued upon and not decided it will take us many days finding out.[29]

7 Apr: Great arguments go on. Hayward is a champion for Canada, having lived there for some time on a ranch. He and Joyce have been at it fist and tongs. Hayward stating that the blizzards in Canada are more severe than we get here and that cowboys are able to get out in any weather. This I should state goes rather against him, as I am sure no one could face some of the winds we have to. Hayward sticks to his guns however, so the point is still unsettled.[30]

8 Apr: Reading *No 5 John Street*, the inhabitants there were clean in respect to ourselves, but who on earth could be filthier? Our clothes are deplorable, Hayward is walking about on his 'uppers',* all of us have an odd assortment of clothing, odd shoes etc. A decent bed and wash are constant thoughts. Oh the joy of getting back to the other hut, or the ship![31]

11 Apr: Got all hands to clear out living space, it's been neglected I am afraid unless one keeps them up to mark they will soon get slack – discipline, the only thing down here, the filth we have cleared out is remarkable. We still remain more or less black with grime, but while here we have got quite immune to being without water; I am glad to say, all here are cheerful and bright.

---

*   Uppers are that part of a shoe that does not normally contact the ground.

The smoke though is terrific, we breathe it and our clothes are practically ooz-
ing with blubber.[32]

12 Apr: I try to get out as much as possible, breathing all the carbon we do can't be
good for one, so a little fresh air acts as an antidote. Have been making a wrapper to
tie around my head to keep my ears from frost bite. What a joy it will be to get back
to my cabin on the *Aurora* and have that wash and put on clean clothes once again![33]

13 Apr: I am thinking of this time next year – Home Sweet Home, all that life's
worth living & hoping for.[34]

15 Apr: Hayward and I went for a short stroll feeling lack after our lengthy period
of inaction. A grand sunset, the sun diffusing to the NW, the reflected rays cast a
shadow of gold in the Bay here, the heights were all bathed in gold, twinkling ice
crystals made the place appear like some fairy bower instead of being what we experience it. We can look round and see a perfect kaleidoscope of changing scenery,
wonderful. No one could write a description of what we see.

Do so hope the sea will freeze over and release us.[35]

Their day-to-day routine at *Discovery* hut revolved around killing seals.
Richards tells us the killing of seals was the main activity for the men at Hut
Point because they provided blubber for fuel and lighting, and meat for eating. If the weather was reasonable they would go out before breakfast and
walk by a crack in the ice looking for them. At that time of the year it was
dark and practically the only area they could find seals was near a break in
the sea-ice, near the edge of the shore. They would search for seals before
breakfast, then before lunch and again after their midday meal. Richards
recalled that each session might involve 5 or 6 miles of walking, so they
would do between 20 and 30 miles a day, on some days 'without finding a
single thing'. At times their supplies of blubber for fuel were very low but
they never managed to quite run out.

Richards remembered in specific detail how the seals were killed. The
seals were completely harmless and they would just put up their nose ready
to be hit. The men used an iron-shod pick handle to give them 'a smack on

the nose' which would stun them and then their throats were cut, resulting in 'two great gushes coming out from the arteries'. Straight away they would run a slit right up the body of the seal so they could put their hands inside to warm them otherwise the hand would 'go'; that is, freeze. They had to use their bare hands with a sealing knife because with mitts on it was too dangerous, the knife could slip and cut their hands badly. But they could only hold the seal knife in their hand for a minute or two before their hand would start to freeze. Richards says the knife was just 'like cold metal and your hand would stick to that'.

If they were just taking the blubber off the seals they would run long slits down the body and with a cargo hook pull up the blubber in a strip, right down the body, just easing it with the knife as they went. It would be a strip 6 feet long, or longer. They would lay the strip out on the ice and leave it there where it would freeze like a plank. They would usually come out the next day, load the frozen planks onto a sledge and back at the hut they would cut it up with an axe. When they wanted food from the seal they would take flesh from the middle section of the body, the waist.[36]

Mackintosh made extensive diary notes in April on the seal-killing. We learn of his dilemma; the immorality of killing seals versus his survival instincts, but he cannot finish his notes without yet another comment on the filthy conditions. Wild wrote the notes on seals, and tobacco, later in the year.

All the men smoked, usually pipes, but a major problem now arose – their tobacco supplies had ran out – so they tried to improvise and make their own. Wild's tobacco making ('Hut Point Mixture') did not impress Richards, who remembered it as 'a villainous concoction' which everyone tried but only Wild ended up smoking. He tells us that those who smoked it found they were forever spitting out saliva and phlegm and they could always trail Wild over the sea-ice by the 'black gobs' that marked his track.[37]

Mackintosh:

> 6 Apr: We are rather up against it as our store of blubber for the stove is nearly done, also our candles, for the latter we have rigged up kind of lamps out of empty corned-beef tins, but running out of blubber is rather serious, as seals to enable us to get a further supply have not yet shown up.

The worst job here is to get the fire going; sometimes while the blubber lasts, it flames fiercely, but more often it gets low, then down we get on our knees, a piece of blubber is placed in the opening, then a flame is applied and after gentle manipulation which requires much patience we can get it going, but every 10 minutes we have to keep it poked up or some more blubber is applied. This is one of the aids* we have to get an addition of dirt, soot and grime on to ourselves.[38]

15 Apr: To our joy we found seals lying on the ice which remains in the Bay along the edge of the Gap. We did not waste the opportunity, going out with the available knives to do our butchery.

It really is murder killing these innocent harmless brutes who roll their eyes and start with fright when they see you, the only sign of objection they show you is to open their mouths and perhaps a swish with the tail. They try to reach back to their ice holes which are close, but we think of it in rather an obscene way so as to make the crime more satisfactory to our consciences, for after all it's a case of survival of the fittest. If we don't keep warm we should probably freeze, hence we take a large club, bang the poor old seal on the tip of the nose, then while he is unconscious his throat is cut, so it's done as mercifully as possible.

At first I detested the job, especially when the seals looked beseechingly at me in their large eyes, but after starving in the tent I am afraid the tender instincts, if any, in us soon vanish. Now most of us can go out without turning a hair, kill and skin seals without any trouble or feelings of reluctance. Although this appears brutal, it means our only method of procuring fuel and food, but the butchery is by no means an easy task for the temperature is below zero and a 'nipping' breeze blowing, while we keep our hands while skinning well under the folds of the blubber, once we expose them to the cold air we would have frostbite.

While one of us skins the other holds the 'flinch' (as we call the hide) back. In this manner we accounted for 5 – what a mess we have left, the clear white snow bespattered with blood, a regular battlefield.

The trouble of this though is that we are unable to clean ourselves and the clothes are getting 'blubbier' and 'blubbier'. Of course our hands get washed in the seal's blood, so they can remain clean.[39]

---

* 'one of the aids' – meaning another helpful way to make his life more uncomfortable.

Here is Wild's take on seal-killing:

Gaze & Hayward were the seal hunters but when they found any Joyce & I used to go and help them. We were burning seal blubber all this time you know so it took quite a lot of seals to keep us going.

It was a weird sight to see us killing & skinning seals by candle light. It was no joke especially if there was a little breeze on. Sometimes with a Burberry helmet on, we would make a terrific blow at a seal's head and what with the light & the helmet would miss it and nearly fall on top of it. They look very savage too opening their mouths & showing their teeth.

We used to have rides on them sometimes; you have to look out they don't roll on top of you because they weigh anything from 700lbs to 20 cwt.

While skinning seals you have to keep dipping your hands into them to keep them from getting frozen.[40]

Joyce:

What an oasis in the wilderness if only a case of tobacco had been landed. A pipe of this soothing weed makes all the world akin. Various substitutes were tried with varying degrees of satisfaction to the consumer. We failed however to top the high water mark.

Tea was attempted, also coffee. I tried some dried mixed vegetables but was speedily requested to cease. Then the inventive genius of Wild asserted itself.[41]

Wild explains:

When we finished our tobacco at Hut Point we tried all sorts of things to smoke such as tea, coffee, sawdust, senna grass, different kinds of dirt scudding about, etc. We found a mixture of tea, coffee & sawdust to be the best substitute so we called it Hut Point mixture.[42]

April 1915 – the four men at Cape Evans

While Mackintosh, Joyce, Hayward and Richards (with Cope and Jack) waited at Hut Point for the sea-ice to freeze, Spencer-Smith and Richards remained at Cape Evans. The *Aurora* was anchored by the Cape Evans hut as the intention was to freeze the ship in over the winter months, most of the men lived on the ship. However, Spencer-Smith and Richards (and Stevens and Gaze) all worked and slept on shore, carrying out scientific work and killing seals for food and fuel. Very little in the way of stores or equipment was landed with these men and the view generally held then, both by the shore party and those on the ship, was that the ship was reasonably safe. The ship was tied up to the shore only 30–40 yards from the gravel beach by the hut and the sea-ice was usually firm so people would walk freely on it. Parties would come ashore from the ship and those on shore would go onto the ship over the sea-ice, just as a matter of routine.[43][44]

Spencer-Smith seemed to enjoy life at Cape Evans. He, Richards, Stevens and Gaze slept and worked at the hut and they ate some meals and enjoyed the entertainment on board the ship.

Spencer-Smith:

4 Mar: This stay in the Hut is becoming noteworthy for a series of pleasant dreams of home, Woodbridge, Cambridge, Edinburgh. I had the best sleep of the trip last night: thoroughly warm and comfy all night, the sleep being taken in two hour periods, with half-hours of lazy thought in between.[45]

6 Mar: More reading.

John of Gerisau (Oxenham)

City of Beautiful Nonesense [sic] (E.T.T.)

Cardinal's Snuffbox (Harland)

Hound of Heaven (Thompson)

The last fascinates me more every time that I read it – every stage in the flight is so real, and so true to my own experience. S.Luke 24.44 'All things … concerning me.'

Also 45 and 46 and the story of the two Emmaus id.13 et seqq.

It suddenly struck me tonight that I have always spoken and thought too lightly of O.T. history and prophecy. We know little of individual's hop[e]s & fears but the aims of the prophets in arousing the national consciousness of God's personal working in Israel's affairs is clear.

The instinct of man, especially in contact with supreme joy or sorrow, love and death, cries out 'It must be so!' And the meaning of the coming of the Blessed Lord is simply this – that it is God's answer (revelation) to man's cry: 'It is so'.[46]

23 Mar: It is very cold but nice to be on one's own and a good sleeping bag makes up for much else. Stevens and I have the corner formerly occupied by Evans and Wilson:[*] nice and private and next to the dark room: plenty of shelving too. Our books and beds make it look furnished and I have mother's photo too.[47]

12 Mar: A great singsong after dinner tonight, gramophone first, and then piano: all sorts of songs, solos and chorus – 'The Wearing of the Green', 'Auld Lang Syne', 'Three Fishers', 'Old Folks at Home', 'Little Grey Home', 'Where my caravan has rested', etc.[48]

1 May: Several visits & there was much tobacco & talk around the fire. I went on board about 5.30 to fetch a plum-duff presented by the cook, who seems rather better, and stayed to have yarn aft – all in good spirits.

By invitation went over again about 8 and played for a singing aft. Hymns first of all. 'Lead Kindly Night' – 'Nearer My God to Thee', 'Eternal Father', 'Adeste Fidelis', 'The Church's One Foundation', 'Old 100th', 'Rock of Ages' and many other old favourites, in which everyone joined.

Then we had some songs, mainly by Sten. and I did not come ashore until 10. Had a cup of cocoa with Irvine[†] and turned in at 11 for a short sleep, tired but happy.[49]

The loss of the Aurora

Then the most serious of calamities occurred – the *Aurora* was carried

---

[*] 'Evans' would be Lieutenant Evans and 'Wilson' was Dr Edward Wilson; both members of Scott's *Terra Nova* Expedition.

[†] 'Sten' would be Stenhouse and 'Irvine' would be Irvine Gaze.

out to sea. Richards tells us that she was tied up close to the shore, with her bows to the sea and with seven steel hawsers attached to bollards in the stern attached to two huge anchors which were iced into the shore. Holes had been dug for the anchors and water poured in, which became like concrete. From time to time ice formed around the ship but the wind blows and the tide took this ice out into the bay. Every now and again the men would equalise the tensions on the hawsers on the stern and they all thought the *Aurora* was quite safe for the winter.[50]

6 May 1915

Richards clearly remembered the night of 6 May 1915. In his book *The Ross Sea Shore Party* and in interviews he tells us that the breakaway of the ship came suddenly and unexpectedly. That afternoon the wind had begun to freshen, and by midnight a moderate blizzard was blowing. It was his turn to take midnight and 4 a.m. meteorological readings; however, Spencer-Smith offered to take the midnight ones and Richards tells us he gladly accepted the offer. Richards was up at three o'clock and he went outside to find nothing more than a moderate blizzard blowing, with snow drift about 20 to 30 feet high. The night was fairly clear – it was a moonlight night. He left the door of the hut and as he looked to his right down to the beach he knew he should have been able to see the tops of the masts of the ship above the snow drift. But there was nothing there. He walked the twenty or so yards down to the water's edge to find the anchor there in the sand but with the hawsers and the cables broken. The second anchor was further down the beach also with its cables snapped.

The *Aurora* was gone. The ice clamping the ship had been swept away from the base of McMurdo Sound by the blizzard, taking the *Aurora* with it. All Richards could see was open water. He woke his three companions who, like Richards, were naturally very concerned. They thought that, given a day or two of reasonable weather, they might expect to see the *Aurora* back again. Whatever hopes they had for the return of the ship were shattered when the worst blizzard they had experienced so far raged violently for the next three days. They now doubted whether the ship would return before January the following year.[51][52]

Richards, Spencer-Smith, Stevens and Gaze were stranded at Cape Evans. Richards recalled they immediately discussed what they had on hand and what they needed to survive, for they were certain that they were marooned until the following January or February. They were wearing their only clothing except for a few extra items in their bags. Apart from a few sledging rations, no stores of food had been landed from the *Aurora*, but fortunately Scott from his *Terra Nova* Expedition had left a stockpile of food on a hill to the east of the hut. They estimated they had general stores, flour and similar items to last ten men for two years. They had almost no fuel for the stove but they could rely on seals for fresh meat, and seal blubber for fuel. They had little or no soap for washing, matches were scarce and they had no luxuries in the way of tobacco or spirits.[53]

There were now four men at the Cape Evans hut, and six others living in quite primitive conditions at *Discovery* hut, who intended to walk to Cape Evans as soon as it was safe to make the crossing.

Chapter 7

'I THINK THE O.M. HAS A GOOD SOLUTION'

May 1915: The six men at Hut Point wait

MACKINTOSH, JOYCE AND Wild made few diary entries at Hut Point in May although Hayward continued to write, usually focused on their prospects of going to Cape Evans. Joyce made a note of the severe blizzard that took the *Aurora* away from Cape Evans. Hayward and Joyce mentioned that Wild fell into the sea and Wild made a comment on the relationship between the men in the hut, and on Mackintosh's behaviour. He was very critical of Mackintosh's ideas on how to make a dash to Cape Evans. His diary note for May is the only one, by any of the men, that mentioned any friction in the hut.

Hayward:

> 2 May: Another lovely morning. Sea-ice very promising indeed. 2 more days will see us on our way to C. Evans providing weather continues favourable. 5 May: Topping morning. Skipper & I had a walk towards C Evans ice seems pretty good & we expect to get away shortly. We afterwards killed a couple of seals & hauled in

the skins, Jack lent us a hand.[1]

Joyce:

9 May: A blizzard sprang up which lasted 4 days. The velocity at times 70 to 100. As a rule when the wind is Southerly the temperature rises, but in this case the temp dropped 20 to 20 below zero. The hut temp was well below zero even alongside the blubber stove the water was frozen. One had to keep in their sleeping bags for warmth.[2]

Hayward:

18 May: We are all more or less experts at draughts, having made a board & using pieces of sugar and biscuit for men. Time passes quickly this way. Went for a walk this afternoon, the Aurora Australis was really magnificent to-night.

19 May: Had our usual walk. Wild distinguished himself by falling through the ice into the 'ditch' (sea) luckily we were not far from the Hut.[3]

Joyce:

Late May: Towards the end of May Wild + I went north a couple of miles over the ice which had been frozen for 3 days. Found it bearable, on rounding the point on our return Wild fell through a seal hole which was snow covered. The temperature being almost 20 below, he was stiff as a board before I got him to the hut which was only 150 yards distant on.[4]

Wild:

24 May: Everybody has had a go at me (except the Captain) for making too much noise so I thought I might as well start the log again. We have been here two months & nobody knows the date so I am guessing it. The people who have been keeping their logs are all different. We have been keeping eight hour watches & I believe when they do another watch they sometimes fancy it is another day & that has put them ahead a bit.

I managed to fall in the pond the other day & went through the ice up to my waist.

Joyce was with me, we were about a mile away from the Hut & the temp was about 30° below, so you can bet I soon made tracks back as fast as possible.

Of course I've got no other clothes here so it wasn't much of a joke. Hayward lent me a pair of his pants and Jack supplied a sweater.

I knew the Skipper had a combination suit so asked him for a loan of it, till mine were dry. He wouldn't lend it to me said it was frozen. Joyce and I cleaned the sledges yesterday and the combination suit fell out of the Skipper's bag as dry as a bone.

He and I are sharing one bag in the hut and he didn't even ask me if I would turn in to keep warm while my clothes were drying, but calmly turned in himself and went to sleep.

He has got some daft ideas about getting back to the ship. One, he wants to start back himself or with one companion & try to walk back taking nothing with them. If it comes on a blizzard he says they will lie down & cover themselves with their Burberrys until it's over. I don't know what he means. He has got all sorts of impractical schemes.[5]

(Twelve months later Mackintosh would actually put these ideas into practice.)

I can't understand the people here at all; they've got no business down here at all. I don't know what they come for (with one or two exceptions) I mean the people on the ship as well; they've got no sense of humour at all.

I'll give just one instance. The other morning they were howling because they couldn't sleep, so in a jocular way I said, 'of course not, you get too much sleep'. Then Jack sat up with a most ferocious & eyes sticking out like hot pegs sort of look, 'who are YOU to say I've had too much sleep'. I had to laugh. I couldn't help it.

I suppose the light (or absence of it), food & dirt made us all bad-tempered.[6]

June 1915: The six men leave Hut Point for Cape Evans

By the end of May, the sea-ice was starting to become firm, and with a full moon to give them some visibility, Mackintosh, Joyce, Wild, Hayward, Jack and Cope planned to trek the thirteen miles to Cape Evans, on 2 June. Joyce noted some of their difficulties as they made the crossing, which may have been similar to those encountered by Mackintosh and Hayward some twelve months later, when these two men again attempted to walk from Hut Point to Cape Evans.

Hayward:

> Surface good & we passed Tent Island 5 miles from our destination about 8 o/c pm, having replenished ourselves with biscuits, & shouted at frequent intervals. About 3 miles from Cape Evans picked up a flag giving instructions as to course arrived at Hut 10.30 pm.[7]

Joyce:

> 1 Jun: Mack + I went North + found the ice bearable, so decided to trek tomorrow weather permitting. Cape Evans is 13½ miles to the North.

> 2 Jun : Under weigh for Cape Evans the moon shining brightly had not been trekking more than an hour when the moon became obscured and this was unfortunate. A large formation of ice 8 miles from Hut Point juts out from Mt Erebus to the West for 5 miles and is about 1 mile wide.

> Unfortunately through the darkness we trekked right into the churned up ice around the Glacier which placed us in an awkward predicament as we were liable to fall through the ice. Our sledge overturned several times. After a struggle we managed to get out to the West. A huge mass loomed up which was Inaccessible Island.

> It is very weird sledging in total darkness. Wild said: 'I think I can hear dogs barking' so we listened and sure it was – so when it is calm one can hear miles over the ice. When Wild heard the first bark we must have been 5 miles away. Eventually we made Cape Evans.

> The dogs gave us a great welcome although there were only 6 of them. They made enough noise for 20. Arriving at the Hut the inmates came out + wondering why the dogs were making such a noise. We found the Padre, Gaze, Richards + Jack.[8]

(The large formation of ice Joyce mentioned is Glacier Tongue. Inaccessible Island is a small 300-foot-high island approximately 1 mile to the south-west of Cape Evans. Joyce mentions six dogs but there were only five: Oscar, Con, Gunner, Towser and a female, Nell, who did not go out to Mount Hope.)

June 1915

There were now ten men at Cape Evans, where conditions were significantly better than at *Discovery* hut. They were fortunate to have made the crossing safely so early in June, in light of the changing state of the sea-ice that were still occurring. Richards and some of the others at Cape Evans thought that they took a considerable risk in making the crossing as a water stretch had been opening up consistently between the two huts during blizzards.[9]

The men were satisfied with the sledging efforts of their first season. Six of them, Mackintosh, Joyce, Wild, Spencer-Smith, Hayward and Richards, would form the Mount Hope Party of 1916. The other four, Stevens, Cope, Gaze and Jack, would assist with the early sledging but they would not participate in depot-laying after early January 1916.

The loss of the *Aurora* was the most significant news for the new arrivals. Hayward:

> 2 Jun: We found Smith, Gaze, Stevens & Richards in residence & heard from them that the ship after various incidents both hazardous & uncomfortable had been frozen in for a week (about) but on the 7 May a bad blizzard came up & the ship was blown out of the Sound carrying away in the process 6 wire hawsers & 1 heavy chain cable all made fast ashore & dragging her anchors.
>
> She has not been seen or heard of since & we can only hope for the best, that is that she has been blown clear of the ice-pack & made her way to Hobart in which case we shall not see her till next January when she will come down to our relief, we cannot feel very hopeful however as when she went out her engines were undergoing repairs & instruments & her wireless gear unshipped.
>
> At the best we are ten men who have to relieve Shackleton at the Beardmore Glacier 400 miles distant without any equipment to speak of but luckily Scott left sufficient stores in the Hut here to relieve us from any immediate anxiety in this

respect.[10]

Wild:

> 2 June: Cape Evans. We have got here at last, after a bit of a struggle. We ran out of tobacco at Hut Point so the first thing we wanted when we got here was a smoke & a drink.
>
> We got both I'm glad to say & then we had a great disappointment we found out that the ship had been blown away on the 11 May so we are only a little better off than we were at Hut Point. However I suppose we will get over it alright.[11]

Joyce:

> 2 Jun: On entering we could not see for quite a long time the acetylene light was too strong so we had to put on snow goggles. The hut looked like a Palace. A lovely coal fire was burning + the hut party looked very clean. Our party looked like scavengers.[12]
>
> When we arrived and found the ship gone, oh my! As it was the only clothes I had was a signet shirt, Drawers, 2 Pairs Socks, Pair finesscoe, 1 Cardigan. What a prospect to look forward to. I think the worst hit of the lot is no tobacco.[13]
>
> We had been out practically 129 days laid depot to 80° + travelled 288 miles. A good breaking in for the coming sledging season.[14]

The winter routine at Cape Evans

From his diary we can see that Mackintosh was clearly in charge, the expedition leader. He outlines their daily routine and tells us his concerns, including the need to be 'civilised'. We learn of a (poorly attended) religious service, and of the 'luxuries' at Cape Evans, compared to Hut Point.

Darkness had now set in for twenty-four hours but the winter was a busy period for all the men. As it was at Hut Point, the search for seals took up a great deal of their time and when they were visible on the ice, the men would make every effort to kill as many as possible and store the blubber and the meat. Water was obtained by digging out chunks of ice from a clean ice supply and sledging them to the hut where a large container was kept filled on the cooking range.[15]

Richards was left to do much of the scientific work over the winter months. He occupied himself with the construction of a dust counter for estimating the amount of dust in the air. He also started recording soundings and temperatures, observations on the rate of formation or dissolution of freshwater ice in the sea and the rate of removal of ice by evaporation.[16]

Mackintosh:

5 Jun: The day after my arrival here I gave an outline of our situation and explained the necessity for economy in the use of fuel, light, and stores, in view of the possibility that we may have to stay here for two years.

We are not going to commence work for the sledging operations until we know more definitely the fate of the '*Aurora*'. I dare not think any disaster has occurred.

Meanwhile we are making all preparations here for a prolonged stay. The shortage of clothing is our principal hardship. The members of the party from Hut Point have the clothes we wore when we left the ship on 25 January. We have been without a wash all that time, and I cannot imagine a dirtier set of people. We have been attempting to get a wash ever since we came back, but owing to the blow during the last two days no opportunity has offered.

I would like to state how indebted we feel to Capt Scott's British Antarctic Expedition for the supply of stores that have been left here and for which we are now reaping the benefits, in fact but for them we would be in a poor way.

Four of us, myself, Stevens, Richards, and Spencer-Smith, have breakfast at 7 a.m. The others are called at 9 a.m., and their breakfast is served. Then the table is cleared, the floor is swept, and the ordinary work of the day is commenced.

At 1 p.m. we have what we call 'a counter lunch,' that is, cold food and cocoa. We work from 2 p.m. till 5 p.m. After 5 p.m. people can do what they like. Dinner is at 7.

The men play games, read, write up diaries. We turn in early, since we have to economise fuel and light. Night-watches are kept by the scientific men, who have the privilege of turning in during the day.[17]

13 Jun: I took the opportunity, the first one I have had, as my clothes I have taken off – of having my first wash for 139 days. Stevens also cut my hair & whiskers, with the

result I felt much warmer – I wonder if anyone has had more dirt come off them. It really makes one feel much better. Stevens has given me a hair brush so now that I can brush that, which will be another luxury. I feel we are gradually getting civilised.

Smith held Holy Communion using the dark room as a chapel, where he had rigged up an altar. I suspect this is the first occasion in which Communion Services have been held on the shores of the Antarctic. Unfortunately I was the only member of the congregation.[18]

My thoughts of the fate of the ship are so constant that I find myself dispirited – which I strive to fight against. I miss the services of an officer, although these are a sterling lot of chaps, it requires an intermediary.[19]

Hayward: '2 Jun: Such a treat having a spring mattress on my bunk & slept like a log.'[20]

'5 Jun: An impromptu sing-along provides entertainment indoors during the day & bridge does the same for eve.'[21]

He tells his Ethel:

21 Jun: Of course one is never idle & it would be erroneous to think that I have done as little as my note might imply. There is always something to occupy ones attentions. Incidentally since my return from sledging amongst other things I have read the following books:

Edmond Thackeray

The Mill on the Floss Geo Elliot

It's never too late to mend Chas Reader

The Virginian Owen Wister

Robbery Under Arms

No 5 John St

Kipps H G Wells

The City of Beautiful Nonsense

The Wales of Gordon

White Fang Jack London

For the term of his natural life.[22]

22 June 1915

The 22nd June is 'Christmas Day in winter' in Antarctica and it was a day of celebration, which the men enjoyed immensely.

Hayward:

> Mid Winters Day Tuesday 22 June 15: Had a jolly good day. Fine dinner Christmas Pudding etc, etc, etc. Afterwards potato race (with tins of milk as potatoes), putting the tail on the donkey and many other dangerous & exciting parlour adventures. Thoroughly enjoyed it all.[23]

Spencer-Smith:

> We drank to the King and the Boss and then sat around singing shanties, particularly improvised. These included 'Ranzo', 'the Yankee Ship' (Blow boys blow), 'Farewell, Spanish maidens' (We'll rant and we'll roar), 'Grace Darling', 'Pull for the Shore', and other fragments.
>
> Cope told one or two stories and recited 'The German at the phone' … the last revellers went off to bed at about 3 leaving Cope & self on watch to clear up.
>
> If only the ship is safe somewhere – God keep them and bless them, as he has kept and blessed us too.[24]

Late July 1915

Mackintosh called a meeting for a discussion of future plans. Richards remembered that all the men agreed that the number one priority was to place food depots for the six men of Shackleton's party at least as far south as the Beardmore Glacier, and at every degree of latitude northward from there.[25] Their planned journey from Cape Evans (at 77° 38′ S) to the gap location at the foot of the Beardmore Glacier (at 83° 30′ S) and their return would be almost 800 miles. However, the total distance to be travelled would be closer to 1,500 miles as they planned to make a number of trips out and back to fully stock the depots that had been laid in February and March.

Mackintosh's diary note of 26 June gives us an idea of his leadership style – by consensus rather than strict or dogmatic instructions.

Mackintosh:

> I gave an outline of the position and invited discussion from the members.
>
> Several points were brought up. I had suggested that one of our party should remain behind for the purpose of keeping the meteorological records and laying in a supply of meat and blubber. This man would be able to hand my instructions to the ship and pilot a party to the Bluff. It had been arranged that Richards should do this. Several objected on the ground that the whole complement would be necessary, and, after the matter had been put to the vote, it was agreed that we should delay the decision until the parties had some practical work and we had seen how they fared.
>
> The shortage of clothing was discussed, and Joyce and Wild have agreed to do their best in this matter. October sledging (on the Barrier) was mentioned as being too early, but is to be given a trial. These were the most important points brought up, and it was mutually and unanimously agreed that we could do no more ... I know we are doing our best.[26]

Hayward tells us more of their plans:

> Discussed sledging arrangements for the relief of Shacks.
>
> Resulting as follows:
>
> Start 1 Oct.
>
> 4 Trips to bluff to be made & from there to 83.30 South.
>
> Getting back approx middle of March.
>
> A stupendous undertaking & as the Skipper says if accomplished will be almost a record of S. Polar travel. Of course we must all realise that we are up against a stiff proposition but can only wait see & do our damndest.[27]

Joyce:

> I do not suppose that any party of men have ever left to go on a sledging journey, under such circumstances.

The first part of the programme is to sledge the great bulk of the stores, about 4,000 lbs, to Safety Camp on the Barrier, about 23 miles, starting 1 September.

The second part of the programme is to trek all stores to the Bluff Depot about 100 miles south, after which parties will be arranged.

From the Bluff Depot stores will be laid at every degree to Mt. Hope, at 80°, 81°, 82°, 83°, 83° 40′.[28]

Spencer-Smith had every confidence in Mackintosh:

Spent most of the morning discussing the sledging problem … and it's a pretty big problem too, tho' I think the O.M. has a good solution already worked out … if his weights are correct, the job will D.V.* be done, tho' there'll be 10 very much played out men at the end of it. It's all in the game…

We shall have a very rough time for five months, especially at the beginning and at the end but D.V. shall get through all right.[29]

They had some sledging equipment that they had used in February and March of 1915 and this was supplemented by equipment that had been left behind by Scott's 1910–13 *Terra Nova* Expedition. They had one new tent from the *Aurora* but they would need to use at least two old ones that had been left at the Cape Evans hut. They were also forced to use two old primus stoves. They only had their original issue of clothing but they did find a certain amount of old underclothing in the hut. Footgear and windproof clothing were a problem, particularly fur boots. It was arranged that an old tent be cut up and made into windproof canvas shirts and trousers. The deficiency in footgear was met by making canvas boots and cutting up old sleeping bags and a horse rug for fur boots. They had adequate sledging food, left from Scott's previous expedition.

Over the winter months of June to August the ten men worked on various activities to enable them to be ready to depart south in September. Joyce and Wild made the lion's share of the canvas trousers and blouses. They also made about 500 calico bags, with strings attached around the mouth, which were used to hold sledging rations.

---

* D.V. – *Deo volente*: God willing.

The sledging food allowed for per day, per man was:

Pemmican	8 oz.
Oatmeal	1¾ oz.
Sugar	5⅓ oz.
Glaxo	⅔ oz.
Chocolate	1¼ oz.
Tea	¼ oz.
Biscuit	1 lb.[30]

The two navy men, Wild and Joyce, worked as a team.

Wild: 'Joyce & I were very busy making clothes, etc. First of all we cut up a canvas tent and made a pair of trousers for everybody. Then we started making things for sledging such as boots, etc instead of finneskoe. It kept us busy all the winter.'[31]

Tongue in cheek Joyce claimed the trouser cut was 'similar to that of Oxford bags'.[32]

Mackintosh:

All is working smoothly here, and everyone is taking the situation very philosophically.

Joyce is in charge of the equipment and has undertaken to improvise clothes out of what canvas can be found here.

Wild is working with Joyce. He is a cheerful, willing soul. Nothing ever worries or upsets him, and he is ever singing or making some joke or performing some amusing prank.

Richards has taken over the keeping of the meteorological log. He is a young Australian, a hard, conscientious worker, and I look forward to good results from his endeavours. Jack, another young Australian, is his assistant.

Hayward is the handy man, being responsible for the supply of blubber. Gaze, another Australian, is working in conjunction with Hayward.

Spencer-Smith, the padre, is in charge of photography, and, of course, assists in the general routine work. Cope is the medical officer.[33]

July 1915

The men appeared to work well together. Richards could not remember any animosities among the ten men, saying they got on exceptionally well, so far as he could judge. He remembers the occasional flare up but nothing serious; arguments were usually over trivial things. He related in one of his interviews that they had 'fierce arguments about everything under the sun' and they would refer to a copy of the *Encyclopaedia Britannica* at the hut. Stupid arguments, said Richards, like the number of miles around the Australian coastline for example, and the arguments would 'get quite heated', but he stressed that relationships were astonishingly good.[34]

Life, even in mid-winter, was pleasant and an undated Spencer-Smith diary entry gives us an idea of their daily activities. By late July they could see some light in the sky and Mackintosh writes of the beauty of Antarctica but he also notes how swiftly the weather could change – a feature of Antarctic weather which Mackintosh was acutely aware of at this time, but chose to ignore twelve months later.

Mackintosh:

1 Jul: My birthday. This evening we had our usual game of bridge, with a prize an ounce of tobacco. Joyce who at present is my partner and as myself had been constantly losing – I did not anticipate much hopes but as it turned out I was pleasantly surprised when we won the rubber – so I now have an ounce of tobacco.[35]

16 Jul: Richards is an excellent fellow, working hard & doing twice as much as ordinary people.[36]

30 Jul: Beautiful tints of purple over high cirrus clouds gave a grand tinge of colour to the surroundings. A day like this one can scarcely realise that this is not some earthly paradise of beauty.

All this was in the forenoon – in the afternoon a veil of clouds slowly swept over, partially obscuring everything & by 8pm the wind was blowing at 50mph, the drift obliterating everything – from Paradise to Hades in a few hours.

The dirt on us is remarkable – how we keep healthy is marvellous – although I don't expect we are dirtier than the Eskimos.[37]

Hayward:

6 Jul: Went out ski-ing with Gaze very enjoyable had some fine tobogganing afterwards. Weather glorious.

11 Jul: Went out with Gaze Ski-ing afterwards tobogganing, on the 3rd run hit a big rock going all out, stove in bows of sledge Gaze ricked his ankle & took off a piece of his nose on my back, I sprained my wrist, so we decided to pack up.[38]

Spencer-Smith:

Jul: Rather an idle day, finishing two packs of cards, after I've been out for a short exercise on ski with Stevens. The band of daylight to the NW seems extending. The dogs gather even for the shortest walk and are friendly, usually to one another, as well as to us. A little tea-party in my darkroom & plans for home! Richards & Jack are busy on stores weighing, Joyce & Wild on clothes: all in argument.[39]

August 1915

22 August was a welcome date, for on that day the sun reappeared and they were buoyed by its return.

Mackintosh:

26 Aug: We had hoped to get out and see the sun rise but the sky was too overcast so we shall not have that pleasure. Anyway it is good to feel the sun is about us now. I trust before he dips again for this long spell without him, that we have experienced, we shall be in the dear Homeland.[40]

Over Erebus the sun's rays peeped through ... and where the rays broke through gave us a most joyous scene of cloud effect. The light made us all blink, as well as to feel excitement of spirit.

Personally I felt like as if I had been released from being a prisoner – or imagined
what one would feel like, who had been one. I stood outside & looked at the lovely
wonderful scenery all around.[41]

Before starting sledging again they made an attempt at cleaning. Their
Jaeger clothing and Burberrys were run through with petrol, a task they
found to be very cold and painful. They also endeavoured to sponge themselves down as best they could. Owing to the shortage of soap it was the
first wash for eight months for Mackintosh, Joyce, Hayward and Wild, and
five months for Richards and Spencer-Smith.[42]

Mackintosh asked Cope, as the medical officer, to examine all the men
and he reported that Mackintosh was perfectly fit, Hayward and Wild quite
sound but Spencer-Smith, although perfectly sound in body and limb,
was found to have 'an intermittent heart'. Cope told Spencer-Smith he
was able to go sledging but if he felt any effects of his heart he was to turn
back at the earliest possible moment. Joyce and Richards did not want an
examination.[43]

At the end of August they were ready to start the sledging of stores from
Cape Evans, first to Hut Point, then on to the Barrier.

Chapter 8

'CAPTAIN ABOUT
1½ MILES AHEAD'

September 1915

T O STOCK DEPOTS out to Mount Hope required a huge volume and weight of stores, far more than the men could haul in one load, so a number of intermediary trips were planned, with three three-man teams taking out a portion of stores and then returning to base to take out more.

Mackintosh planned for the depots to be placed at each line of latitude, about 70 miles apart. The stores that would be left at each depot on the outward journey had to be sufficient for the returning men to reach their next depot. This was usually one week's worth of provisions, to cover the 70 miles. If men were delayed for any reason on their homeward journey, such as losing days because of a blizzard – and it took longer than a week to cover the distance between depots – they would be forced to go on reduced rations to make the food and fuel last until they made the next depot.

Mackintosh had worked out the total volume of stores needed, and it was a complex calculation. In the first season of sledging they had placed some stores at 80°S, at 79°S at Minna Bluff, at the three Cope depots, and at Safety Camp.

In the second season, stores had to be left at Mount Hope for Shackleton's anticipated team of six men; then stores all the way back to Hut Point for his use – at 83°S, 82°S, 81°S, 80°S, the Bluff depot at 79°S and at the Safety Camp depot on the edge of the Barrier. They were just the stores that Shackleton would need. In addition, stores had to be carried for their own use – in travelling out to Mount Hope and back. To move from one depot point to the next on their return journey they would pick up stores that had been deposited on the outward journey.

The first stage for the ten men at Cape Evans would be to take all stores from there to Hut Point. This was planned to be carried out in September, involving a multitude of trips between the huts.

The second stage, in October, November and December, would involve five trips taking stores from Hut Point to the Minna Bluff depot, a journey of approximately 70 miles each way, plus a trip to add stores to the 80°S depot, 140 miles from Hut Point. Their plan was to have the Bluff depot well stocked because it would be a base from which stores would be taken further out on the Barrier.

Once this work was completed, the third and final stage would begin. It was then planned for nine men to be at or near the Minna Bluff depot towards the end of December, and push on south from there. They would take from the Bluff depot all the stores they would need to lay the depots out to Mount Hope.

September and early October

The taking of all the required stores to Hut Point commenced on 1 September. The leading sledge party left Cape Evans with 600 lb of stores and it was quite an occasion. Richards wrote in his book that the others gave the leading team an enthusiastic send off as they set out tugging their load over the sea-ice. They pitched a tent halfway across to Hut Point and left this 'halfway house' for the use of subsequent parties on journeys between the huts.[1] The five dogs were used.

At this time, the dogs hauled sledges between the huts. The sea-ice

surface would have been hard and smooth and on that surface the men
would have skied, which meant they could have worked in harmony with
the dogs. Skiing speed was similar to the dog's normal rate of hauling;
faster than a man's normal walking pace.

The Joyce diary entry from 1 October below describes the usual routine
as stores were taken across the sea-ice to Hut Point. Mackintosh wrote only
a few notes in September, one on the cold affecting his right eye (his glass
eye), and his enjoyment in meeting inquisitive penguins.

By early October all the stores and equipment needed for the sledging
program were at Hut Point and the dogs were taken back to Cape Evans,
as the men planned to now haul the sledges themselves.

Mackintosh's diary entry, before leaving Cape Evans for the last time,
includes a list of the men in the sledging teams. He also mentions 'another
book' in which he would continue his diary notes but that 'book' has never
been found. There are no more diary entries from Mackintosh after 30
September. All that has survived from that date onwards are a number of
letters he left at various depots, which were usually instructions for Joyce,
and two long letters he wrote on 28 February 1916.

On 30 September Spencer-Smith wrote a poignant letter to his parents, mentioning they had had some 'misfortunes', presumably meaning
the loss of the *Aurora* and the death of most of the dogs. He appeared to
have doubts he would survive.

Hayward: 'Saturday 18 Sept 15 to Friday 8 Oct: During this time have
made trips between Cape Evans & Hut Point sledging stores I got very
useful work out of my dogs Con, Gunboat,* Towser, Oscar & a little bitch
Nell, they were good up to 600lb.'[2]

A typical Joyce daily entry:

1 Oct: Temp -7.

Weather very heavy clouds to N. Turned out 7 o'clock 'breakfast', got under
way 10.30.

3 sledges, load about 1700 lbs, surface very fair, doing about 1 mile p. hour, arrived

---

*   Hayward, like Spencer-Smith, used Gunboat as the dog's name, not Gunner.

at half way camp about 3.30. Left there one sledge we were pulling, about 300 lbs, as we found the load rather too much for us.

Proceeded to Cape Hut Pt. About 7 o'clock came on to drift + blow very hard from the SE decided to abandon sledge as we were still 3 miles from our destination, and to make things worse we had not eaten since breakfast, and most of us were getting rather bad frost bites through not having any food. Found it very hard to steer all land being obscured.

Eventually arrived at Hut about 10 o'clock. Soon had a fire going with plenty of Hoosh + forgot the tough journey. Fingers badly frostbitten. Turned in midnight. 13-240.[*3]

Mackintosh:

8 Sep: Temp -11 min to -15.5 max, my right eye and cheek are completely swollen up, my left cheek is a blister.[4]

21 Sep: Saw a large band of emperors (31) away west, hurrying up to inspect me – first in mass, then in line ahead, then in colonies of ½ companies, with a Captain and two Lieutenants ahead. One of the latter saluted me first and got pecked by the Captain for his pains.[5]

30 Sep: Everybody is up to his eyes in work. All gear is being overhauled, and personal clothing is having the last stitches. We have been improvising shoes to replace the finneskoe, of which we are badly short. Wild has made an excellent shoe out of an old horse-rug he found here, and this is being copied by other men. I have made myself a pair of mitts out of an old sleeping-bag.

Last night I had a bath, the second since being here. I have gradually been able to discard clothes, to wash them, so now I have a clean lot to start sledging. This too and having a bath.

I close this journal to-day (30 September) and am packing it with my papers here. To-morrow we start for Hut Point.

---

*   Joyce often wrote the distance travelled in the day, in this case 13 miles and 240 yards.

Nine of us are going on the sledge party for laying depots — namely, Stevens,*
Spencer-Smith, Joyce, Wild, Cope, Hayward, Jack, Richards, and myself.

Gaze, who is still suffering from bad feet, is remaining behind and will probably be relieved by Stevens after our first trip. With us we take three months'
provisions to leave at Hut Point. I continue this journal in another book, which
I keep with me.[6]

Spencer-Smith letter of 30 September 1915:

My dear Father & Mother,

Owing to various misfortunes of which you will hear in due course – for which
no one is blameworthy, we are setting out for the season's sledging under rather precarious conditions; equipment poor, time of year too early load heavy, etc. So there
seems to be an unusual element of risk, wherefore a short note to say 'au revoir' in
case I should not come back.

We've had a pretty stiff time, taking it all round, but I can't feel any regret about it
all, except that I should have liked to have been with you during the horror of the war.

Believe me that if anything does happen to me I will face it as cheerfully as I can
– with a hope that is really 'sure & certain' of seeing you all again with everything
unworthy in myself done away with. I have tried to be 'good' & to do good without
preaching – & even so I don't feel worthy of you two dear ones.

Goodbye for the moment.

I am your loving son
Arnold.
Please keep the communion vessels in the family.[7]

Sledging starts from Hut Point, to the south

In early October, stage two of the second season started, the sledging of
stores from Hut Point to replenish depots on the Barrier that had been

---

*   Gaze, not Stevens, ended up being a member of the sledging teams.

laid back in February and March. They were delayed by a blizzard until 9 October then a start was made with nine men pulling three sledges, one behind the other. Progress was very slow towards the start of the Barrier, owing to overladen sledges and a heavy surface, and camp was made that first evening by a very tired and dispirited party.[8]

10 October 1915

Joyce: 'Distance done during day about 4 miles. I don't think in all my experience down here I have had harder pulling – Temp -18. Turned in wet through.'[9]

11 October 1915

They tried nine men hauling three sledges at first and then three men pulling one sledge, but their progress was still slow. Joyce was very critical of Mackintosh and some (or all) of the Australians (Richards, Gaze and Jack) did not impress Wild.

Joyce:

Started away on our physical farce, found loads worse to pull than yesterday. Hauled up + took weights + found out there was about 2,000 lbs instead of 1566 proposed in the 1st place.

I think the man must be mad to think it is possible to pull such a load in the conditions on which we are placed. Only one thing he thinks of that is the men at the other end but he won't take good solid advice how to make good out of a bad thing.

There is not the physical status here to pull heavy loads. Hearts are willing but strength will not avail. Why won't he say take 180 lbs a man and get the journey done in a fortnight + make 5 trips out instead of 4 + try and save the men a bit instead of dragging here 220 odd pounds pr man.

I suppose he will learn to his regret that he has not taken good advice. Well after this hard struggle we hauled up in a snowstorm at half past three having struggled 4 miles. I think I shall have to tell the Skipper off.

Turned in 6 o'clock. Weary, worn + sad.[10]

Hayward: 'After loading up got under way for a couple of hours & did 3 miles. Going slow & heavy in fact I am quite sure that with such loads it will be imposs. to carry out the seasons programme.'[11]

Wild: 'We pulled the heaviest sledges & the others couldn't keep up. It's the foreigners that do it; they give everybody a bad heart.'[12]

12 October 1915

Mackintosh then decided that he, Spencer-Smith and Wild would travel as a separate unit, while the others (Joyce, Richards, Hayward, Cope, Gaze and Jack) would operate as a six-man party under Joyce's leadership. There is no indication from their diaries why Mackintosh decided to split up the party. All Richards could say later was that progress was almost impossible with the heavy loads so Mackintosh, Wild and Smith went on as an independent party while the rest under Joyce's command undertook four depot-laying journeys from Hut Point to the Bluff depot, some 70 miles south.[13]

Joyce:

Blizzarding. Spent half an hour in the Skippers tent regarding the load etc. The same old thing he is going on ahead with Smith + Wild with his load and to push on.

I to take over the other 5 + use discretion + to carry on from here to Bluff + visa-versa to get things out the best way I can. Now this proposition sounds alright on paper but if we sum up things it is impossible to carry on in these conditions. Why he is deserting this party which is supposed to be the weakest no one knows.[14]

Wild felt for (Ernest) Joyce: 'We've left the others behind with poor old Ern in charge, d____d glad.'[15]

Two teams: Mackintosh's team of three
and Joyce's team of six

From this date, 12 October 1915, until early January 1916, Mackintosh, Spencer-Smith and Wild travelled separately from the others. Possibly Mackintosh preferred working with only two men, leaving Joyce in charge of five others. Travelling away from Joyce meant he could leave him written instructions from time to time; which he did, placing notes for Joyce at various depot points.

Their first task for both teams was to restock the Bluff depot. Joyce's team immediately started relaying. Joyce was now maintaining a daily diary record and his 18 October diary entry is similar to many other days. He writes without any fanfare. The first trip to the Bluff depot for Mackintosh, Spencer-Smith and Wild was also uneventful, but now and again they commented on the conditions.

'Rouse out! Rouse out!' would be a common call to the men start a day. 'Right-oh', would come any replies. To pull down their tents they would first clear snow blocks from the skirting, lift it up from the windward side so it blew out and then shake off some of the more icy lumps, then fold it up. After packing they would look at each other's faces for frostbite. A dead-white nose tip or a white spot on a cheek were common signs and these would be nursed back to life with the warmth of their bare hands.[16]

Joyce:

> 12 Oct: The Skipper + party started off Noon. We started 12.30 found load too hard started relaying found it much easier work but 3 times the distance to do carried on until 5 o'clock. Skipper just in front. Camped. Temp -26.[17]

> 18 Oct: All hands had a good night's rest. Temp rather warmer + 0–12. Very fine sunny day blowing slightly from the SE. Under way usual time passed over several crevasses some as wide as streets. Came onto very hard sastrugi as white + hard as marble at about 10.30.
>
> Lunched noon. After lunch clouds obscured sun very bad for the eyes as everything is obscured + one cannot see the hummocks on the snow everyone falling

about, looking so much like classical dancers, done very good pace as the sledge comes over very easy. Distance done 9 to 10 miles record?[18]

Spencer-Smith:

17 Oct: A severe day: overcast and a strong and very cold wind from nearly dead ahead. Temp -10° F rising to +1° F in the evening.

The whole day was a long slip, stumble and fall: all glare surface and quite impossible to see where to place one's foot even when the drift ceased. The wind was so strong that it actually blew Wild and self backwards sliding on our feet at one halt.

We did 6 miles 1150 yds nevertheless and camped at 3 o'clock, quite fed up. If only the wind would stop, the surface is perfect for quick work.[19]

Wild:

20 Oct: Had to pack up at three o'clock on account of a strong head wind. I fell down or was blown down 5 times. Once the wind blew me 3 or 4 paces to the rear. I was just sliding. It would have been a lovely surface for travelling had there been no wind.[20]

More stores are laid at Minna Bluff

In late October Mackintosh and Joyce's parties added provisions to those already at the Minna Bluff depot and went back to Hut Point to pick up more supplies. With a southerly wind behind them and lighter loads (having deposited stores at the Bluff depot), the trek back was much quicker than coming out. Diary entries casually mention some of the hardships they endured.

In one diary entry by Joyce we learn of his party finding a note written in 1912, left by Apsley Cherry-Garrard, for Scott. Cherry-Garrard was the youngest member of Scott's *Terra Nova* Expedition. In early 1912, while Scott's party was struggling back from the South Pole, Cherry-Garrard made a supply run to a depot called 'One Ton Depot', about 140 miles from Hut Point – he had hoped he might meet Scott returning from the Pole.

Joyce:

23 Oct: Had another bad night. Cold + shivering warm when we turned in but got very cold in the night. Temp -30.

Under weigh usual time a cold S wind temp –20 –2. Just before we started Hayward + Jack opened sleeping bags + a very heavy drift struck us + before they could be closed were filled up. Hard luck.

Could not see anything to steer by so going by drift. Set sail found we had to run to keep up to sledge. Came on to an ivory surface. So had to take sail off. The wind was so strong that it still carried the sledge forward one man had to brake. We came some awful croppers on the hard Sastrugi. Going along between 2 + 3 miles an hour. Lunched usual time took all hand to spread out tent + then it took some 20 minutes. Under way usual in the afternoon drift eased but wind + surface the same as forenoon, going at a good rate. Slipped all about the place.

Camped @ 6 oclock. Distance done from 16 to 18 miles. I am bruised all over. Temp –20.[21]

Spencer-Smith: 'Spent the morning playing hunt the crevasse. Wild went down 2 little ones. We spotted 12 in all, including 4 or 5 large ones ranging from 7 to 30 feet width.'[22]

Joyce:

26 Oct: Sighted a sledge or part stuck up. NW. Made for it arrived at 4-10. Started digging out, then found it would be a long job decided to camp, made cocoa + carried on.

Came across a note from Cherry Garrard to Capt Scott, tied on a 12ft ice pick as follows:

19 March.

Dear Sir.

We leave here this morning with the dogs for Hut Point. We have laid no Depots on the way as being off course all the way. I have not been able to leave a note before.

Yours Sincerely

Cherry Garrard

Rather pathetic picking this note up + dated I think after Scotts death.

Finish digging about 8. Found 4 cases of Spratts Biscuits + some Wolseley Motor

Oil. Made a Depot, had dinner, turned in 9 o'clock. Temp -26.[23]

Late October 1915: All the men are back at Hut Point

The dogs at Cape Evans had not been used, except for taking stores to Hut Point in September. This was in spite of Joyce's experience with dogs – he first worked with them on Scott's 1901–04 *Discovery* Expedition and then again on Shackleton's 1907–09 *Nimrod* Expedition. Richards, in one of his interviews, tells us that they had decided not to use the dogs because they felt that men and dogs were not compatible. The pace of a man hauling a sledge with a heavy load behind him was just trudge, trudge, with one foot a few inches in front of another in the snow. Dogs liked to go at a reasonable trot when they were pulling sledges. They thought it would be quite impossible to marry the two.[24]

It is not clear why they then decided, in late October, to start using the dogs to help with the sledge-hauling. Joyce wrote there were five dogs used but only four were taken, Oscar, Gunner, Con and Towser.

Richards recalled that it was not Mackintosh's idea to take the dogs. He tells us that he (Richards) persuaded Joyce to try out the four dogs and that Joyce then had to 'sell' the notion to Mackintosh. The dogs were then brought from Cape Evans to Hut Point and they required some time to adapt themselves to the men's slower rate of progress, but to Richards the decision to take them was justified. He wrote later: 'None of us who made the southern journey will ever forget those faithful friends of the dog world – Con, Gunner, Oscar and Towser.'[25]

The men enjoyed travelling with the dogs, yelling instructions such as 'Ready' for the dogs to stand and be ready to start, 'Mush' for the dogs to go, 'Ha' to turn right, 'Gee' to turn left and 'Whoa' to stop.[26] Oscar was Richards's favourite. He described him as a powerful brute, a massive dog at about 110 lb, but not a lovely-looking dog. He had a broad leonine head and a low 'criminal type' forehead. Richards thought he was disliked by the other dogs on account of his homosexual activities. To Richards he was a lazy brute usually but 'when the chips were down he came through, when the other three chucked their hands in'.

Gunner (called Gunboat by some of the men) was as big as Oscar. Towser was the lightest and not much use for pulling in Richards view. Those three were Canadian huskies and Richards remembered them as lazy and quarrelsome, with no interest in hunting seals or anything else. Whereas Con was a samoyed dog and completely different in character. Richards described him as a 'good living dog', lively and keen on hunting seals. He believed that the other three dogs 'hated his guts' and they often tried to kill him.[27] But as far as he and the others were concerned, in the sledging, they all did 'yeoman's service'.[28]

Neither Joyce nor any of the others write on the sledging arrangement used at this time. From photographs we can see the dogs usually travelled in single file, not a fan formation, harnessed onto one rope back to the sledge. At the front of them was the leading man who the dogs followed. The other men were attached to the sledge separately, not in single file like the dogs.

Joyce:

> 28 Oct: Had a very good night's rest. Rather too warm with a roaring fire going all night. Temp +16 +30. Southerly blizzard was drying clothes + Bags.
>
> Had a yarn with the Skipper about things. So we have decided to take on the 5 dogs next trip + see what we can do.
>
> All our appetites are of the best so having a good stock of seal meat such as Liver Kidneys Steak etc. We found a seal with young so they are breeding now + we shall be getting up a great many. Had a bonzer dinner of seal. Turned in 9 o'clock.[29]

Hayward: '23–27 Oct 15. Arrived Hut Point after very favourable run back. Have decided to make use of dogs next trip.'[30]

Additional stores are taken out to the Bluff depot

From late October through to late December the two parties trekked out to the Barrier and to the Bluff depot, also loading up other depots on the way.

Mackintosh's party (he, Spencer-Smith and Wild) would now not return to Hut Point, preferring to pick up supplies from other depots on the Barrier, such as the one at Safety Camp, and go back south from there. Joyce's party, now with the dogs, would return to Hut Point on a number of occasions.

Some of the men maintained a daily log over these three months but most of their notes relate to day-to-day activities, or simple aspects of their existence. Wild seems to keep his peace with Mackintosh as there is no mention of any arguments, although he often included diary comments on Mackintosh, for dropping and losing things, and acting irrationally. Spencer-Smith often wrote of his thoughts and his dreams. Hayward's diary entries, so detailed when he first arrived in Antarctica and on his early sledging journeys of February and March 1915, had now become quite brief, and devoid of any reference to his fiancée, but he regularly made a note of the distance travelled each day.

Mackintosh gave Joyce instructions to place more stores at the Bluff depot:

28 October 1915

Dear Joyce,

The plans for you to carry out your next trip to the Bluff Depot will be as follows

- *Stores to be left at the Bluff by each unit (3 men) to be 159 lbs. To enable you to undertake this five of the dogs will be used each day to pull a weight equal to 70 lbs, their ration to be 1.5 lbs per diem. ***

- *To enable two efficient sledge parties, they should consist of yourself (in charge) Hayward and Gaze. For the other party, Richards, Cope & Jack with the dogs.*

- *The party under you then can pull the load according to the programme (560 lbs), while the other party with the dogs should easily manage that amount or I hope over without undue overloading.*

---

* Per day.

The above is what I require you to do, anything you can to better this or to accelerate the speed (3 weeks out and back) will be to your credit.[31]

Joyce:

5 Nov: ...broke our shovel a rather serious thing, as it will mean both parties to use one.[32]

6 Nov: Dogs doing their best. I suppose they find it strange pulling in harness with the men. Now + again we would get a heavy snow drop making a great noise + the dogs would get frightened and jump forward with gusto.[33]

Wild:

16 Oct: We saw one of Scott's bamboos with the remains of a flag on it this morning. We dug down about 8 feet but didn't come across any bacco. Still on Hut Point mixture.[34]

21 Oct: I found one of Skipper's finneskoes which had dropped off on the way out.[35]

1 Nov: Skipper lost his watch & I found it on the sledge.[36]

2 Nov: Another record, the Skipper didn't drop any mitts today.[37]

9 Nov: Started back at 10.15 & have come 9 miles that's without counting & meter & a few trifles. I took meter off when Skipper wasn't looking because I knew he would want it on if he saw me. Ha-ha.[38]

17 Nov: Skipper broke the compass and we had to mend it between us.[39]

19 Nov: Skipper acted wet just now & took his boots & socks off & ran around in the snow. He says he reckons it will be alright to go on the march with them off. I'd like to see him.[40]

9 Dec: Skipper's boot fell off. Smithy went back ¼ mile for it.[41]

Spencer-Smith:

5 Nov: Cam* has been trotting in and out of my mind all day. I Wonder why? A huge halo has encircled the sun all day; sun very warm, almost windless. Temp morn +13, evening +8°F.[42]

7 Nov: Graft! Graft! Graft! Even the sun deserted us at 10am and the sky became overcast, so that steering became very difficult: we must have passed within 150 yards of a cairn without seeing it.

Dreamt last night I had promised to preach today in London, but had not written the sermon, nor could remember where the church was. Joan† could not find the text about Absalom's complaint of David's niggardliness in forgiveness (a crib of Dr Macgregor's sermon in part).[43]

Hayward:

9 Nov: Under way punctually 8 o/c. Surface A1.‡ By lunch camp had done 4 m. After lunch fresh N. Easter sprang up, set sail, great assistance. Total for day 9M. Excellent. What!

11 Nov: Weather lovely. Going excellent. Dogs A1. Total mileage for day 9½ M

15 Nov: Richards & I took dog team & fetched back stores depôted by us last trip 2 m from our Camp these stores we left here, this being a more convenient point & also right on our course.

Got under way 10.30 heavy going weather bright & warm, so warm in afternoon

---

*   Cam would be Cambridge.

†   'Joan' – we do not know who Spencer-Smith is referring to, possibly a female acquaintance at a church in England.

‡   A1 – meaning excellent.

in fact that I indulged in a wash snow making quite a good substitute for water, soap & towel. Mileage 5½ m.[44]

Mid-November 1915

Mackintosh, Spencer-Smith and Wild seemed to enjoy each other's company. Spencer-Smith made diary notes on their debates, such as on 'Home Rule',[45] on the sledge-meter,[46] and with 'the Skipper about laymen taking scientific observations'.[47] There is no diary note of any conversations between Mackintosh and Wild; however, it is not hard to imagine that they would have discussed their shared Bedfordshire connection and their naval experiences. Mackintosh was at Bedford Modern School from 1891 to 1894.[48] Wild lived at Eversholt, a tiny village in Bedfordshire, from 1884 to 1894. Mackintosh served as an officer on a number of ships, working for the merchant shipping company P&O from 1900 to 1909, and Wild served with the Royal Navy on battleships, cruisers and gunboats, from 1895 to 1913.[49] [50] But, from a Mackintosh diary note from the year before, we have some insight into the conversation between these three men:

> After our sledging and while at our hoosh, all kinds of subjects are discussed from meals we'd like to be eating to quandaries as to what's happening at the Front; religion, seeing we have a parson; politics, in fact there's precious little that is not turned over in conversation.[51]

On 12 November Spencer-Smith fell into a deep crevasse, giving thanks when rescued. Wild gave us his version and there is no embellishment of the potential danger. He used the phrase 'in his warming pan', which no one explains, but presumably it meant down the front of the pants.

A 14 November diary note by Wild is highly relevant in light of Spencer-Smith and Mackintosh later succumbing to scurvy before the others. Spencer-Smith:

12 Nov: Turned west after lunch and after 200 yards found myself 10 ft down a

crevasse: caught O.M.'s rope as I went and nearly pulled him down too. Wild went in up to his waist.

It seemed a long time before I finished falling – only sensation one of wonders as to when I'd stop descending. Couldn't see the bottom and it seemed to stretch a long way along, about the same width all the way.

Able to brace myself with knees and back, with the O.M. pulling on my lashing hastily brought by Wild. Unpleasant experience and might have been serious as the sledge was in a dangerous position, lying along the line of the crevasse. Laus Deo!*[52]

Wild:

12 Nov: Passed over a lot of crevasses & went right down one, nearly sledge as well. At least Smithy went right down to length of harness. I got caught up just under the armpits & the Skipper was lying across it somehow, behind me. However we got out alright. I fell down after another, what they call Bergschmund† this morning, i.e. a big open crevasse. A carriage could easily have fallen down it.

The one Smithy fell down was so deep we couldn't see the bottom. I threw two or three big lumps of snow down but they only disappeared out of sight in the darkness. His hands were all gone when we got him out. He had to put them in his warming pan.[53]

Wild: '14 Nov: Arrived back at Safety Camp about three o'clock. Couldn't find any fresh meat but had jam & onions extra.'[54]

15 November 1915

In mid-November Joyce and Richards had worked out a plan: for Mackintosh's party to take stores from the Bluff depot to 80°S and then to 81°S, but Joyce's party (with the dogs) would take stores onto 82°S. The implication

---

* 'Laus Deo' – Praise to God.

† 'Bergschmund': the correct spelling is *bergschrund*. It is a German word for a crevasse that was formed when the ice of a moving glacier separated from stagnant ice.

with this plan was that he (Joyce) would be the one to go on and lay the final depot at Mount Hope, and not Mackintosh.

Joyce:

> Decided if dogs are fit on the 4th journey to take on South + sacrifice then as I think they will be the mainstay of the work on ac of the good work they done coming out.
>
> Richards + I quite agreed and worked out the plans that is the Skipper + party work from 80° to 81° our party carry all stores to 80° + then on to 82°. If not! well? I think we shall carry it out just the same.[55]

However, outside his diary notes Joyce was still respectful to Mackintosh. Here is a letter he left at a depot, on 15 November:

> *To: Captain Mackintosh, (Leader), Ross Sea Base*
>
> *Dear Sir,*
> *Can you let me know what there is to bring out after the next trip which I suppose to be the last to Safety Camp? I will try to bring out something after the same load as before, weather and surface permitting.*
>
> *I remain*
> *Yours sincerely*
> *Ernest E Joyce*
>
> *PS: Kind regards to Wild S. Spencer-Smith & Self hoping you are in the Pink.*[56]

25 November 1915

Mackintosh also left pleasant notes at depots for Joyce, but Joyce described this Mackintosh letter rather unkindly:

Mackintosh: '*I am leaving here … I sincerely trust you are all well and I am wrong in surmising that some accident has befallen you. Hoping to meet you soon and please push on for all you are with. Yours sincerely.*'[57]

Joyce: 'Arrived at Depot 5-20. Letters from Skipper usual whining tones etc. turned in at 10 o'clock.'[58]

Mackintosh and Joyce do not see eye to eye – 28 November 1915

On 28 November the nine men met up on the Barrier and Joyce spoke with Mackintosh of his plan, but Mackintosh had other ideas. It is not clear from any diary notes but the presumption is that Mackintosh wanted his party to go all the way out to Mount Hope, with Joyce's party returning, probably at the 82°S depot point.

Joyce was not impressed but Richards tells us that there was no outward antagonism between these two men, with Joyce always respecting Mackintosh, the commissioned officer. There was nothing in the least hostile in their relationship – Mackintosh was always 'sir' to Joyce, who had never lost the typical sailor's old time respect for authority. Joyce always took commands, and always loyally obeyed instructions.[59]

Joyce:

> Skipper came into our tent. Richards + I gave him a really good working plan to go on, but as usual he thinks he knows best, but will find out before long he is in the wrong + on one occasion he tried to ride the usual high horse but I wasn't having any then he practically accused our party for spoiling his plans but apologised.
>
> I told him straight, he would be getting into trouble one of these days through his foolishness.
>
> I never in my experience come across such an idiot to be in charge of men!![60]

Early December 1915

On 4 December Mackintosh left a letter for Joyce at the Minna Bluff depot congratulating him on his party's work in laying more provisions than he expected. He issued Joyce with further instructions – to continue laying provisions on to 80°S.

Mackintosh, Spencer-Smith and Wild then pushed on south, to lay more stores at 80°S. Then they would go back to the Bluff depot (70 miles to the north) and restock before turning south again for the final time, aiming for Mount Hope. From late November onwards Spencer-Smith had started to record his ailments and injuries.

Mackintosh:

Dear Joyce,

I was very pleased on my arrival here to find the two good loads your party has brought forward. I must admit they were beyond my expectations.

On your return trip which I expect will be in advance of us, I want you to carry forward to the 80 South Depot, another full load, equal to that which you have already depoted here – a 10 weeks full provisions.

If you will make an effort to manage this & I shall have no cause to feel any anxiety in forwarding the relief as far as possible, the course to the Depot will be N 29 E, but you will find it cairned, the distance is 68 miles.

We thank you for the books found here.

Yours faithfully
AE Mackintosh
Commander
Ross Sea Party

Please don't forget to bring full supply of this equal to 10 weeks not the others.[61]

Spencer-Smith:

18 Nov: Heavy pulling after our long rest: feel it very much in the ankles.

2 Dec: Tendons sore again.

3 Dec: Rather seedy this morning, with left tendon bad.

14 Dec: a very sore right foot.

16 Dec: My poor old neb* and lips are very sore. Very heavy pulling though the sledge is as light as we've had it: the surface is very woolly. Right foot feels better: I removed some dead flesh from big toe (side of nail) last night and that seems to have done the trick.[62]

Joyce's party leave Hut Point for the final time

Joyce, Richards, Hayward, Jack, Gaze and Cope had continued their depot-laying in October and November with a number of trips out to the Bluff depot and to the smaller depots closer to Hut Point. On 13 December, these six men then left Hut Point for the last time, having now stocked the Bluff depot with between 2,800 and 2,900 lb of provisions.[63]

13 December 1915

Joyce: 'We got under way at Noon. Had to leave Bitch behind in an interesting condition,† as our time is limited and I want to get out to the Bluff by the 19th.

'... Thank God this is the last load.'[64]
Hayward: 'Left Hut Pt all fit.'[65]

14 December 1915

Joyce was starting to become disillusioned with two of his party: 'Had

---

*   'neb' – his nose.

†   'interesting condition' – Nell, the bitch, was pregnant.

some words with Jack + Gaze. Gaze who was getting too big for his shoes had to be taken down a peg + Jack is like an old gossiping washerwoman. (Least said the soonest mended, needless to say more peace in the party.)'[66]

15 December 1915

Out on the Barrier, 140 miles from Hut Point, Mackintosh, Spencer-Smith and Wild laid more stores. These three men then turned around and headed back north to the Minna Bluff depot at 79°S to pick up their last load of stores. (At this time Joyce's party were approaching the Bluff depot from the north.)

Spencer-Smith: 'At 80° South. Took several photos and was taken – with flag – the depot as background. Wild suggested title "First Parson at 80° S".

'At lunch one of the tent-hoops cracked through so now we are spliced in 7 places & patched like B Esmond.'*[67]

Wild: 'The rib of the tent broke right off today at the bottom joint. I've lashed a bit of bamboo on. It doesn't look so bad now. I don't know whether it will stand a blizzard.'[68]

22 December 1915

Held up by a blizzard for a day, Spencer-Smith read, and he was hungry. Hunger craving was at its worst when they were inactive. And there was usually a pattern to their hunger pains, starting with a gnawing emptiness in their stomach so intense it would dominate all thoughts to the point of obsession, a feeling close to panic. Then they felt they could eat anything, even their boots. But they had learnt to recognise this feeling and that it would pass eventually, their mind and body accepting somehow they must go on without immediate nourishment.[69]

---

*   The meaning of his reference to 'B Esmond' may relate to Beatrix Esmond in the 1852 Thackeray novel *The History of Henry Esmond*.

Spencer-Smith: 'No travelling. It is now 9pm and we are about to have a little food for the first time since yesterday. It has been slow work, waiting, and every page in '*A Gentleman of London*' seems to mention eating!'[70]

24 December 1915

Mackintosh, Spencer-Smith and Wild slowly laboured their way back. Wild:

> 7½ miles after a struggle. It cleared up last night & after a light breakfast we got under way about 10 o'clock. Just as we got everything in for the night (day) the Skipper saw the Depot. It's about six miles away I should say.
>
> We hope to get there tomorrow Xmas Day, & then What O for a feed.[71]

25 December 1915

Mackintosh, Spencer-Smith and Wild came up to the Bluff depot after lunchtime on Christmas Day. Spencer-Smith's long diary entry extols their day, topped off with a surprise of cigars from Mackintosh:

> Christmas at the Bluff. Slept like a log and had a dream meal of very hot curry and stewed prunes. At lunch the O.M. sprang the surprise of the century on us – 4 cigars, saved from Cape Royds – awfully generous and incredibly acceptable.
>
> We arrived about 3am & settled down to a 'glut' … and we have eaten as much as we had each day for the 4 days past.
>
> Menu 3 S (supper ration) and 2 Bovril and onions. Thick chocolate cocoa. Biscuits. Streimer.* Raisons. Feel quite full. Previously my hands used to 'go' after half an hour after a meal.
>
> The others are not here yet; probably they have tried to run it too fine and the wind that helped us kept them back.

---

*   Streimer was a polar nut food made by a company called Streimer.

R. foot sore again. Our 4 day fast seems profitable now; and we are thankful to be so well out of it.

Nous devons beaucoup au Pere Tout puissant qui a entendu mes priere et qui nous a protégés pendant ces jours d'anxiete.*

Now that we are safely inside, there is quite a strong S.W. blowing, with drift. There is a delicious smell of tobacco: the Primus is still going to keep us warm, hunger is far away.

At lunch we sang 'While Shepherds watched' and 'Adeste Fideles' and Wild gave one verse of 'Christmas Awake!'. All conduces a little to Heimweh;[†] but only six months should put all right again.

W.P.[‡] we start south for the last time on the morning of the 26th: 279 miles to go then homeward bound, northwards all the time.

Evening. Slept like a log (or hog) and woke up at 4am to another meal. Then we went out – still drifting and blowing a bit, but not cold – and dug out all stores (they were pretty deeply in) and loaded our sledge, ready for tomorrow. We shall have a load of about 590 lbs or a bit more to start with. The others are not in sight yet.

Quite a library of new books found here. '*The Rogue's March*', '*Robinson Crusoe's Return*' (b. Pain), '*Intriguer's Way*', '*A Drama in Sunshine*'.

10.30pm. We are about to have supper – almost super-erogatory, before turning in. Foot feels better a bit. Temp. +21° F.[72]

Wild was missing a drink, but a surprise pipe of cigar tobacco made his day:

Smithy dreamt he had a good feed last night and actually ate it, so he didn't want as much as us other two.

The Skipper had saved up four cigars and has divided them between us. We are smoking them in our pipes. The best smoke for years & years. I still smoke Hut

---

*   His French quote means: 'We are indebted to the Father Almighty who has heard my prayer and has protected us during these days of anxiety.'

†   'Heimweh' – a longing to be home.

‡   'W.P.' – 'with pleasure'

Point mixture but can't say much for it. This is the second time I have been on short provisions & can't say much for that either. I hope it will be the last.

This is the driest Xmas ever I've had & I hope it will remain so. [73]

27 December 1915

The final phase then began for Mackintosh, Spencer-Smith and Wild – they left the Bluff depot heading for Mount Hope. That day an unusual event occurred.

Spencer-Smith: 'The Christmas Holidays are over and we are on the road again – Southward Ho! A heavy load – an indifferent surface – a cross wind – 6¾ hours work, distance 4 miles 1828 yards only – graft.' [74]

Wild:

A wonderful thing happened this morning. A skua gull* came flying over us and settled in the snow. The Skipper and I got a large bamboo pole each and went for it and most wonderful of all I caught it with a clout when it flew over my head. I fell over myself and knocked the gull over too.

We have plucked, trussed and washed it and going to try it for dinner tomorrow.[75]

Spencer-Smith gave a fuller description:

At about 11am the O.M suddenly shouted. We looked up and saw a skua gull close by us, about 7 feet in the air. It had probably dropped from the blue on seeing us black specks below and hoping for the best.

The Skipper outflanked him in the east armed with a flagpole: Wild in the west, with another bamboo. The bird rose. W struck; fell over but stunned the poor bird.

Soon dispatched, plucked and drawn by the O.M. It is now hanging (in bits in a bag) high up on the long bamboo. We hope to eat this tomorrow: anti-scorbs.†[76]

---

* The men call the bird a 'skua gull'. The correct description is simply 'skua'; a family of birds related to gulls.

† 'anti-scorbs' – the men knew that scurvy was caused by a shortage of ascorbic acid (which we know now as Vitamin C).

29 December 1915

Wild:

> As we couldn't travel we cooked our Xmas Turkey, ie: skua gull and it was A1. I boiled it for 3 hours and then fried it in pemmican fat and it was as tender as a chicken. We had a little dried onions with it, & six raison each for dessert.[77]

Spencer-Smith was not as complimentary:

> At 2.30 pm Wild started to cook the skua. It was stewed for 3 hours with a little pemmican (old) and onions and then fried in pemmican fat and served with thin hoosh. Very fat and bilious but none the less nice. Topped off with rich cocoa and a few raisons.[78]

30 December 1915

Wild:

> Last night we heard a row outside & on looking out we saw a skua walking about. The Skipper & I immediately gave chase, with a boot & flagpole each. However it was too artful & wouldn't let us get near enough to bang it & at last it flew away to the Bluff.[79]

Spencer-Smith: ' Another skua came pecking around the tent after we had turned in: it tried to carry off one of the Skipper's sandals. The other two sallied out to slay, but failed.

'The other party is in sight.'[80]

Christmas Day 1915 for Joyce's team

On their Christmas Day, Joyce, Hayward, Richards, Cope, Gaze and Jack were camped only a few miles short, that is, to the north, of Minna Bluff. In contrast to Mackintosh, Spencer-Smith and Wild's Christmas Day of cigars, a sing-along, and a 'glut' of food, Joyce's diary entry for Christmas Day mentioned no such luxuries, only the basic facts of a day's hard hauling.

Joyce:

> Glorious Xmas. Under way 7.45. SW wind + drift very heavy going sometimes sinking up to your knees. Wondering how are all friends. Very sorry cannot drink to their health.
>
> Would give anything for a smoke – when one is on the march no one speaking then you think of these things. Camped as usual.
>
> Dist 8¾ miles. About 5 miles off Depot.[81]

On 29 December Joyce's party could see a myriad of black objects spread over the white snow and they had no idea what they were, until they came up to them and found the area littered with feathers. They guessed that Mackintosh's party had killed a skua.[82]

Joyce: 'Dec 29: Captain about 1½ miles ahead.'[83]

The two parties meet, south of the Bluff depot – 31 December 1915

Meeting the others gave Joyce an opportunity to have a smoke (using tea leaves as tobacco) with 'Ern' (Ernest Wild) and to also come to an agreement with Mackintosh as to who should push on to Mount Hope. It is not clear from Joyce's diary but presumably the two men agreed at this time that some of Joyce's party would continue on to Mount Hope.

In his last diary entry of the year, Joyce atypically included a number of personal comments.

Wild: 'The others caught us up when we stopped about 10 o'clock. They have given us some more books, seal meat, butter and tinned paste so we will have a good New Years dinner tomorrow.'[84]

Spencer-Smith:

> The others came up when we stopped in the morning and friendly calls all round were the order of the day. Irvine and Jack brought us a splendid present of seal-meat,

potted meat butter and a parcel of books. We were able to give them a few books in return, including Browning's plays for Irvine. They are pulling a great load.

I had a long talk with Irvine and Jack in their tent in 'rebus divinus inter alia'.* They are camped some way to the left. Temp 20, Evg 23.

Finished 'Drama in Sunshine' during supper (of seal-meat) this evening and am now to begin 'The Old Dominion' and 'Evolution' (H. Univ. Lib.) now. This is the last entry for 1915.[85]

Joyce:

Had a pipe of tea with Ern + a long talk with the Boss. Made all arrangements for the final spurt which after a talk came to a mutual understanding (at last). It must I think it is clearly time he woke up.

We had a nice cup of tea together to drink the peace tomorrow being New Years Day. I thought it would be a fair thing to be at peace with all the world.

I wonder how many of the old pals are quaffing a merry cup + making all kinds of Good Resolve for the coming Year.

I often think of the brother, his wife + nephew + wondering how the world is treating them.

I suppose I am now starting on the biggest job of my life that is to get to this 83° S + if poss to relieve S. We are now 90 days out from C. Evans & all feel fit let us hope that Providence will look on us + give us fine weather.

Goodbye Old Year. Good Luck to the New. 'KiaOra'.†[86]

The nine men now had their sledges fully laden. They were south of the Minna Bluff depot and heading for Mount Hope. On the way they would stock new depots at each degree of latitude, which were about 70 miles apart, with enough provisions for Shackleton, and for their own return.

---

*   rebus divinus inter alia – 'among other things of God'.

†   'Kia Ora' is a Māori language greeting, meaning 'be well/healthy'. Joyce, like most British Antarctic explorers of his time, had fond memories of New Zealand. He had spent three weeks there in 1901 when the *Discovery* was being prepared for her departure to Antarctica, and the men returned to England via New Zealand in 1904. New Zealand was also the place of departure and return for Joyce on the *Nimrod* in Shackleton's 1907–09 expedition. After 1917 Joyce lived in New Zealand and married a Christchurch lady, Ms Beatrice Curtlett.

Chapter 9

'FEELING RATHER SEEDY. HEAD HOT; EYES ACHE'

The first week of January 1916

THE TWO PARTIES, one with Mackintosh, Spencer-Smith and Wild, the other of Joyce, Richards, Hayward, Cope, Jack, Gaze and the four dogs, continued on south. On 1 January they were well past the Bluff depot and coming up to the 80°S depot location. They were about 250 miles from Mount Hope.

The two parties continued to travel separately – Mackintosh's party travelled during the night-time hours and Joyce's party during daytime hours – but they now stayed reasonably close to each other. They travelled by the clock, not the sun's daylight hours, because at that time of the year the sun did not set, circling between 2° and 5° above the horizon. At this stage, Mackintosh, Spencer-Smith and Wild were man-hauling, each man attached directly to the sledge. Joyce's team were also man-hauling – heavier loads, but with the assistance of the four dogs. In his party Joyce was in the lead, followed by the dogs in a single file attached to Joyce's rope, which went back to the sledge. The other five men were attached to the sledge.

They had some clear days where the sun could be so hot that it scorched their skin and they had to wear a large sun hat. But the cold in the shade under the hat was such that their 'moustaches and whiskers became frosted and covered with ice, making their nostrils sting and tingle painfully'.[1]

Joyce's party of six men had two primus burners, one for each tent, but one started to play up. Joyce was undecided on whether to have his team stay together to help take stores to the 81°S depot point, or to send back three men at 80°S. They attempted to fix the primus by putting a wire ring made from a dog muzzle inside the primus burner to try to prolong its life. The primus then seemed to be working reasonably well, cooking their hoosh in nineteen minutes where the specified time was twenty minutes, so the heating capacity was not affected.[2] However, on 5 January Joyce made the decision to send back three of his party.

Mackintosh's intentions were that he, Spencer-Smith and Wild would be the only party to go all the way out to Mount Hope, with Joyce's party turning back at some stage. On the first day of the year he issued Joyce with more written instructions.

1 Jan 1916.

…On arrival at 81 South the party of which you are in charge will separate. Your-self, Messrs Richards and Hayward proceeding to 82 South or beyond. Messrs Cope, Gaze & Jack returning to Hut Point.

I would like it to remain, as regarding your proceeding beyond 81 South, I will leave it to your own discretion, provisions, etc permitting.

Cairns & any distinguishing marks you will put up as you proceed. Wishing you all the best,

Yours faithfully
signed
Commander
RSP[3]

Hayward summarised Mackintosh's plan: '1 Jan: After some discussion

1914 – Aeneas Mackintosh says goodbye to his daughter Pamela before leaving England.

8 November 1914 – In Sydney, Spencer-Smith writes a long letter to his parents.

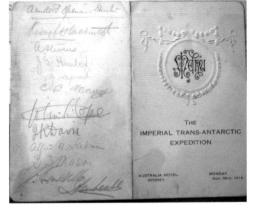

16 November 1914 – A special dinner menu made for the Imperial Trans-Antarctic Expedition from the Australia Hotel in Sydney, sent by Spencer-Smith to his parents. The menu was signed by Mackintosh, Spencer-Smith, Hayward and others.

December 1914 – The *Aurora* is about to leave Sydney. The photograph includes, in the top row, Hayward (third from left), Mackintosh in the light-coloured jacket, and Spencer-Smith to his left.

ABOVE 9 January 1915 – As the *Aurora* is approaching McMurdo Sound in the Ross Sea, the men can see the active volcano Mount Erebus, which Richards described as 'a magnificent sight rising steeply some 13,000 ft. from sea level'.

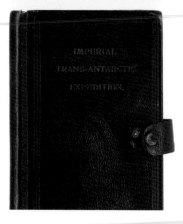

LEFT 24 January 1915 – On arrival in Antarctica, the men of the Mount Hope Party were issued with these diaries.

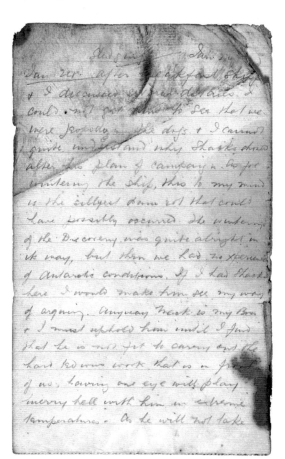

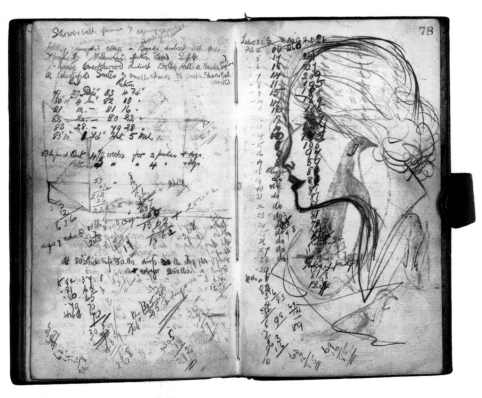

ABOVE 25 February 1915 – *Discovery* hut. On 25 March Wild tells us he and others first reached it after skiing over the sea ice from the ship. He adds that there was a blubber stove there which they lit and put some seal blubber on, but the smoke drove everybody out, except two men, who in Wild's words were 'Scotch so they could stick it'.

LEFT 11 March 1915 – The final stage of the journey back to *Discovery* hut was over sea ice between the Barrier and Hut Point. If the ice was not firm they would have to travel around the hills, rather than take a direct route to the hut.

RIGHT 6 May 1915 – Richards goes outside the hut at Cape Evans to take a meteorological reading and cannot see the *Aurora*, which was anchored close by the shore. All he finds are broken cables and anchors which were embedded in the frozen gravel to prevent the ship being blown away.

June to August 1915 – Inside the hut at Cape Evans. The men worked there over the winter months to prepare for the main season of sledging. The hut was very comfortable for the men to live in. It was insulated, with lighting, heating, bunks and a good supply of tinned food, jams, sugar, flour and biscuits, to supplement their main diet of seal meat. PHOTO BY DAVID BARNES

June to August 1915 – Each man was issued with two pairs of finnesko boots, made from reindeer skin with the fur on the outside.

June to August 1915 – After the loss of the *Aurora*, Wild wrote that he and Joyce were very busy making clothes. First of all they cut up a canvas tent and made a pair of trousers for everybody, which Joyce said looked like 'Oxford bags'.

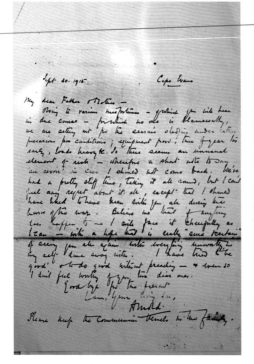

30 September 1915 – At Cape Evans, Spencer-Smith writes a letter to his parents. He tells his 'Dear Father and Mother' they are setting out for the second season's sledging and that this is a 'short note to say "au revoir" in case I should not come back'.

March to June 1916 – The *Discovery* hut's sole heating came from burning seal blubber chunks on this stove. Richards remembered that some of the blubber oil would run out of the back of the bricks and onto the floor and, every so often, when there was too much on the floor, they would shovel it up into a tin and use it again for fuel.

March to June 1916 – There was no lighting in the *Discovery* hut. The men were there over the winter months – the sun did not return until mid-August – so for lighting all they could do was make an improvised blubber lamp which was a bit of string or wick in some blubber oil, in an old tin, usually an empty corned-beef tin like this.

March to June 1916 – The axe the men used to chop up the frozen planks of seal blubber sits next to the blubber stove, in which seal chunks are still to be found.

11 March 1916 – Cans of McDoddies rhubarb. Joyce tells us that there were a few cans of these at *Discovery* hut when they arrived on 11 March, but they were soon eaten, and thereafter, at *Discovery* hut, the men ate only seal meat.

8 May 1916 – There is a hill by *Discovery* hut which has a cross on it, Vince's Cross, in memory of George Vince, who was a member of the *Discovery* Expedition. He died in 1902, the first man known to have lost his life in the McMurdo Sound region. Joyce, Wild and Richards stood at the top of this hill to watch Mackintosh and Hayward walk towards Cape Evans.

January 1917 – A wooden cross was erected on the hill behind Cape Evans in memory of the lost men from the Mount Hope Party. PHOTO BY DAVID BARNES

it was decided & written instruction given to Joyce that he, Richards & I were to go as far as possible taking into account quantity of stores available, whilst Jack, Cope & Gaze were to return at 81°S.'[4]

Wild: '1 Jan: The other party are about ½ mile ahead. We've just had a good feed of seal meat & pemmican & finished up with cocoa & raisons.'[5]

Joyce: '1 Jan: Skipper keeping up pretty fair. Dogs going well. Towser still short winded I have to stop every ¼ of an hour + give him 5 minutes spell. Work too hard for them.

'Distance during day 9-1200, a splendid performance on this surface.'[6]

Spencer-Smith: '2 Jan: The track of the others crossed ours at about one mile, almost at right angles. We can see them now far away to the right, probably they wandered in the mist.'[7]

Joyce:

3 Jan: Jack from the next tent called me over + reported his Primus was failing which makes things very awkward as their party have to leave us at 81°S. The thing is whether to send them back now or take them on to 81° + play chances with it ourselves. As no doubt we must get stores to 81° so after a lot of thinking I will do that if my 2 tent mates are agreeable.

There don't seem to be any happy medium 1st one thing or another but I think we shall win through at the finish with the aid of 'Provy'[8]

Hayward: 'Before reaching depot at 80° S primus in my tent went bang & Joyce with our approval decided that it would be best to bring into force the above mentioned arrangement on reaching the depot @ 80°.'[9]

Wild: '3 Jan: I'm just going to cut my whiskers & mous.'[10]

Spencer-Smith's thoughts were of home: '3 Jan: Spent the afternoon in a motor picnic to Stobo* with T&V and telling fairy tales to K&XXX.'[11]

Joyce:

4 Jan: Under way as usual. Overcast. Going about same as yesterday. Sun came out 11-30 First time we have seen it for some time. It has been very hot + we have been

---

* Stobo is near Peebles, south of Edinburgh.

travelling in singlet. I had my drawers turned up + got my legs badly burnt with the sun. The Distance done during day 10-200 a good days performance.

I had another look at Primus of the next tent + find it is worse than I thought as we arrive at 80° on Thursday with luck. I shall decide there.[12]

Joyce:

5 Jan: Told Cope, Gaze + Jack they would have to return when we arrived at 80° on account of Primus. I am very pleased to get rid of Gaze & Jack as they have not been playing the game very much but Cope has been rather good, always willing + doing his best.

But as the strongest have to go forward for the relief I had to send him back in charge of the others.[13]

6 January 1915

On 6 January Joyce's team reached and stocked the 80°S depot. Cope, Gaze and Jack then turned back to the north. Later that day, the party of Mackintosh, Spencer-Smith and Wild met the three men heading northwards. Irvine Gaze spoke to Spencer-Smith and told him that he believed Joyce wanted to go on to Mount Hope and meet Shackleton.[14]

Joyce:

Under way as usual. Sighted Bluff Depot. Weather very thick arrived at Depot 10-45. Told parties about returning. Gaze + Jack made usual silly suggestions but I told them they would have to go.

Loaded our sledge to 1200 lbs 12 Weeks + Dogs food. I thought + so did everyone we should have a bad time in starting but to our surprise, we ran ahead the dogs pulling for all they were worth. We then put on another case of Biscuits. Surface pretty fair. fair wind + sail set. Camped as usual Distance 5 miles-1400. A splendid performance. Load 1280 lbs.[15]

Hayward:

Without much opposition this was duly carried out & we (Joyce R & myself) got away from 80° @ 2 o/c pm on 6 Jan 16 (all fit) with 11½ wks of provisions fully prepared & able to lay depots for Shackleton's support at 81°, 82°, 83° & 83°.30´ Mt. Hope. This same afternoon we did 5 miles before camping.[16]

Spencer-Smith: 'At about 3.45 met Cope, Irvine and Jack sent back with a defective primus. They gave us news of Joyce's plans and also 1 lb of onions and of pair of finnesko. Joyce carrying 11 weeks has 4 hours start on us, we have 5 weeks. "TimeoDanaosetdonaferentes".'[17]

(His Latin quote translates to 'I fear the Greeks, even when bringing gifts', which may have meant beware of Joyce. However, none of the others wrote of Joyce's supposed intention to go on to Mount Hope and Richards made no mention of it in any of his later interviews.)

Wild: 'We met Cope, Jack & Gaze three miles off going back. Something the matter with their primus. The others have got 4 hours start on us. I hope we will catch them up in a couple of days.'[18]

Six men continue on: the Mount Hope Party

Now heading south with 210 miles to Mount Hope were six men, the 'Mount Hope Party'. They continued to travel as two teams: Mackintosh, Spencer-Smith and Wild in one, and Joyce, Hayward and Richards, with the four dogs, in the other.

7 January 1916

As they went south, they laid cairns, to help guide them on their return journey. Every quarter or half an hour they would stop and erect a cairn of snow about 4 or 5 feet high. They would back-steer using a cairn behind them if the visibility was poor, but primarily the cairns were set up as a guide for their way back – they would simply travel from one cairn to the other. At this time Richards started taking a bearing of the cairn that was behind using a prismatic compass and record this bearing in a note book. He did not really know why he started doing this; he recalled years later that he seemed to have an idea in his mind that it 'might become useful'.[19] As it turned out these bearings were crucial to their survival.

On 7 January, Mackintosh's party were some miles behind but they then made Herculean efforts to catch up – travelling over eleven hours to do so. It is not clear from any diaries why they wanted to travel with Joyce. Mackintosh may have seen his party falling too far behind. Joyce's team with the dogs may have looked to be travelling with less effort. He may have noticed Spencer-Smith weakening or he may have been concerned with his own physical state. But it seems more likely that Gaze's comment to Spencer-Smith, that Joyce was out to reach Mount Hope first, may have spurred Mackintosh on to catch up with Joyce.

That night Spencer-Smith made a long note in Latin, running the words all together in his diary and these words in Latin were Spencer-Smith's only mention of his discussions with his cousin Irvine Gaze. It appears that Spencer-Smith now believed that Joyce was out to win the 'prize' – that being to reach Mount Hope before Mackintosh. It seems likely that he would have discussed this with Mackintosh, resulting in them making every effort to catch up with Joyce, which they did, just before midnight.

Joyce:

> Under way as usual. Weather very foggy snow crystals falling heavily. Stopping every ¼ of an hour building cairns so there can be no mistake in following course + picking up our Depots. Fair wind + sail set surface very fair. Distance in the afternoon 4-1400.
>
> Under way as usual after lunch with fair wind, about 3 o'clock came onto very heavy surface sometimes taking 5 or 10 minutes in hauling out sledge – building cairns take up a fair amount of time but with all that etc we did 5-200 yds, making 9 miles 1600 for the day. A splendid performance.
>
> Dogs in splendid form we gave them a Hot Hoosh tonight. I will give them this twice a week. It is worth it + after all it is wonderful the amount of work they are doing. If we can keep them to 82° I can honestly say it is through their work we have got through.[20]

Hayward:

> After lunch about 4 o/c Richards picked up a party overhauling us.
>
> Camped as usual then & turned in, this party made our camp at 11 o/c pm this night & proved to be, Skipper Smith & Wild who had been working all hours to overtake us. Skipper said we would carry on in morning without alteration, we continuing to lay the course.[21]

Joyce:

> Last night about 11 o'clock dogs started barking. Turned out to see what was doing found to a surprise Skipper + party camping outside they had been travelling since 9 o'clock to pick us up + to carry on with us.[22]

Wild: 'Did 15½ miles & caught the others up. We had 2 lunches though & marched 11 hours. The first 10 miles were alright, fair wind & good surface, but after that the wind dropped & surface got very bumpy. Still we caught them.'[23]

Spencer-Smith: '*Quibusautemcognitis, ne fraudesummemlaudem aliiacciperent (!) noslongoitinereadeorumcastraprogressisumus Ad mediamnoctemdefessicastraposuimus post 11½ horas in via.*'[24]

(The quote translates to: Learning of this, however, to prevent others winning the first prize by trickery (!) we advanced by a long way towards their camp, to the middle of the night, worn out with the camp we have put after 11½ hours.)

8 January 1916

At the start of 8 January the six men were just over 200 miles from Mount Hope. In the morning Mackintosh talked with Joyce and it appears that Mackintosh did not want Joyce's team to go on to Mount Hope.

Joyce: 'Skipper had me in his tent + told me fresh plans. I think I shall have to disobey him again as I am sure if we are left to go as we are going we can easily lay this Depot. If it is not laid it will be to his bungling.'[25]

Hayward:

In the morning (8 Jan) a suggestion was made by Skippers party to tack on with us. We thought this arrangement would not be satisfactory & suggested carrying on for a bit & seeing how things panned out.

At lunch camp we compromised by relieving them of a tin of biscuits 50 lb & again got under way. Unfortunately this added weight (we having already 1200 lb up) made all the difference & pulled our pace down considerably & did not appear to help the others appreciably. Moreover the heavier load caused our sledge runners to break icily through frequent soft patches & made a satisfactory progress impossible.[26]

Joyce:

Anyhow I took 50 lbs. Sledges getting stuck in soft snow on account of heavy load off his sledge to ease their load which is 5 weeks about 570 lbs to make them come along faster.

We are now pulling something like 1350 lbs. Found he was still lingering. So stopped + asked him to join up with us, which he did without breaking up my routine.[27]

Mackintosh's team and Joyce's team are united

So they hooked the sledges together and pulled as one team of six men and four dogs. Richards tells us in his book that Joyce was in the lead at the end of a long rope. Behind him were Mackintosh, Spencer-Smith and Wild attached to this rope by harness, and then behind them were the four dogs, whose harness was also tied to the central rope. Behind the dogs he was tied to one side of the sledge with an 8-foot rope, and Hayward similarly tied to the other side. Richards says that 'tied' was hardly the correct word, as knots could not be loosened with the fingers in the cold conditions so all fastenings were made in such a way that they could be released by their hands encased in their fingerless mittens.[28]

They began to make excellent progress southward and Richards in *The Ross Sea Shore Party* tells us that the men now started to realise that the dogs would be an important factor in their attempt to lay the depot at Mount Hope and return. They were perhaps subconsciously aware that their own fate was linked to the dogs' well-being. From then on they began to take more and more care of them and whenever possible Richards tells us he heated up a hot 'hoosh' for them every night: dog pemmican and dog biscuits.[29]

Spencer-Smith often recorded the temperature, and those for that day, 8 January, were typical for January. The morning temperature was 9°F, that is twenty-three degrees below freezing, and the evening temperature was 18°F, fourteen below.

Hayward:

> Thinking that a trial of the arrangement suggested by Skippers party to tack on further might be tried, we did this – Skipper & Smith were obviously crooked & were not pulling an ounce.
>
> We of course had the benefit of an extra heave on the occasions when the sledges bogged & of course by so doing were not delayed so frequently as we had been previously.[30]

Wild: 'We went by ourselves this morning. In the afternoon we shackled the two sledges and pulled together. A much better day. We packed up early so as to have a good night's rest.'[31]

Spencer-Smith was also happy:

> We travelled behind the other party this morning and found the going very heavy, with too much pie-crust about. After lunch we transferred one case of biscuits to Joyce's sledge. They stuck twice and then we hooked the two sledges together and all found the world more pleasant after. Only about 7 hours work and the trek is 9m. 1050 yds. – and this after yesterday.
>
> So things looking rosy: the dogs pull well. Con has a touch of sun blindness – at the halts likes to have his head heaped over with powered snow: he lies still with head extended until the re-start.
>
> Morn 9. Evg 18.[32]

9 January 1916

On the morning of Sunday 9 January the six men were approximately 180 miles from Mount Hope. Richards remembered that Sundays were treated like any other day, even for Spencer-Smith. There were no prayers. Richards thought that even though Spencer-Smith was a clergyman he may have been a little hesitant asking people if they would like a religious service. It just didn't seem to occur to the men that a day was a Sunday.[33]

They mention 'pie-crust', which was a particular surface which would just take their weight for a second and then drop them down an inch or two. Richards remembered they found it a very tiring surface to march on.[34] Mackintosh described it as 'snow that gave in with every step taken on it',[35] and to Joyce it was the most difficult surface to travel over, 'you sink in to the ankles … so makes ones feet very sore indeed'.[36]

Spencer-Smith: 'Beautiful, though hot day, working rather longer hours we have done 10 m. 700 yds. Heavy going with a lot of pie-crust.

'Heb. 7.25. "To the uttermost".'[37]

Joyce:

> Skipper has had a sprained knee it is painful to watch go along. I don't think this surface will improve it much. Parties working harmonious together. It is a pity though they did not let us carry on as we were going.
>
> I am suffering very badly with snow-blindness hence this scribble. I have now been steering since Oct + I have not hardly been free since Nov.
>
> I have found a good easer + rub snow on them.[38]

He then added a note: 'Skipper asked me to take over the parties which I will do until the depots are laid.'[39]

(None of the others mention this claim by Joyce, to support it, or to discredit it, but there was no apparent reason why Joyce would write this note, if it were not true. In his field diary he simply recorded facts and events as they happened, or soon after and without any apparent embellishment. However, there were no comments by any of the other men that indicate Mackintosh had relinquished command to Joyce at this time. It is only when Mackintosh collapsed six weeks later that Joyce (with Richards) took over leading the party.)

10 January 1916

The previous evening it was clear and they could see Mount Markham, a 14,272-foot-high peak in the Trans-Antarctic Mountains, the mountains that stretch from the Ross Sea across the continent. But on the morning of the 10th they were forced to steer using the 'black cairn method'. A piece of black cloth was placed on a cairn before they left it and this back cairn could then be seen more easily – they would steer away from it, rather than steer towards a feature in the distance. They used the method in times of poor visibility. Richards recalled that the black cloth came from an old pair of his canvas trousers, ones that were covered with black blubber and soot. They cut them into squares of about 6 inches and placed that on the cairn they were leaving.

To steer when visibility was so poor they could not even see the cairn behind they used Joyce, who was in the lead, at the end of a 20–30-foot-long rope. Richards was tied on to the bows of the sledge and he would take a bearing with the prismatic compass on the correct route and put Joyce on that route. After a short while they would stop, Richards would take another bearing and readjust Joyce's line if he had wandered. If there was no blizzard it was easy enough to steer on a cloud or some feature in the distance, or back-steer from their own cairns.[40]

That day they trekked almost 10 miles but Spencer-Smith was now limping. Joyce inserted a callous note in his diary.

Spencer-Smith:

> Last night we had a glimpse of Mt. Markham, 13.5 miles away. This morning we
> could scarcely see 100 yds, but by the black cairn method we carried on. The sun
> came out at 10 and kept with us till between 3 and 4: and the days' hard pull shows
> 9 m. 1650 yds.[41]

Joyce:

> Snowing hard, I suppose the Skipper is wondering how we are going to steer.
>
> We are putting up cairns every 10 min with a little Black Bunting on, although we are halting so many times we are going along at a good pace doing 4 miles 1200 yds in the forenoon + 5 300 in the afternoon.
>
> To mark these cairns we have cut up a Richards pair of our trousers about a foot square to place on the sides so as to mark it more prominent.[42]
>
> Snowing all day, sometimes going in up to the knee which makes it rather hard for the dogs. They are doing excellent. We should not be able to get along without them.
>
> S + S* still not pulling.[43]

11 January 1916

The men were shocked at their appearance.

Wild:

> I borrowed a mirror from the others. I have just seen my face for the first time in four months. I fairly frightened me. I've had a trim up & wiped as much black off as possible, & now it will have to do till we get back.[44]

Spencer-Smith: 'A gruelling day – rather overcast. We borrowed Hayward's glass in evening & trimmed beards &c. We were all horrified at our faces. Lip very sore and looks nasty. Trek 10 m. 150 yds.'[45]

Joyce:

> Under way as usual, in very thick weather, going about same as yesterday.
>
> Skipper just jogging along. S still painful to watch.
>
> After lunch we came into a rotten surface sometimes sinking in up to the waist.
>
> Our little dog team is doing well. Gave dogs a hot meal of biscuits + pemmican + as much as they could eat. There is no mistake, they are a splendid team.[46]

---

*   'S + S' meant Spencer-Smith and Skipper, i.e. Mackintosh.

12 January 1916

On 12 January the six men reached 81°S (150 miles from Mount Hope) and left provisions for their return journey, and for Shackleton. Joyce was unable to steer because of snow blindness so Mackintosh took over. Their next depot was to be at 82°S, 70 miles to the south, and from there it would only be another 80 miles to Mount Hope.

Wild: 'Depot here 3 weeks provisions, 3 tins oil, & extra biscuits for dogs, nearly 200 lbs with the Skipper's boots.'[47]

Joyce:

> Under way as usual in a snowstorm. About 10 o'clock my eyes got so bad I had to ask the Skipper to steer, he made rather a decent job of it – better than I expected – he said one day was plenty enough for any man. It carried on thick all the day.
>
> I had several bad falls owing to the blindness. It seemed like a holiday pulling behind the Padre nothing to worry one, except pull & keep your feet.[48]

13 January 1916

On the first day out from the 81°S depot the weather was poor but they decided to march.

Joyce:

> Skipper asked me to look at weather as he did not think it fit to march, but as I am steering & Richards on the bearings on the cairns, after a little consultation with Richy, decided to get under way.
>
> Although it is thick + snowing a little patience with the cairns + direction, even if one has to put them up at 200 yds apart it knocks one forward. It seems that this weather will never break.
>
> The dogs doing splendid. I don't really know what we would do if it wasn't for them. Boys behind told me the Skipper had hardly been pulling the whole afternoon + he looked quite done up.[49]

14–17 January 1916

Over the next four days the six men edged their way towards the 82°S depot point, covering a similar mileage (around 10 miles) each day. Richards recalled in later years that that trudging along hour after hour, day after day, with a canvas harness over his shoulders and around his waist was a rather fantastic experience.[50] A northerly wind helped them at times where they could set a sail on the sledges and on these days, such as on 14 January, Joyce recorded that they 'went along at a good pace'.[51]

When the weather cleared they could see more of the Trans-Antarctic Mountains, including Mount Longstaff, a series of peaks 13,000 feet high which are to the east of Mount Markham. For Joyce, the mountains gave him direction to Mount Hope.

None of the men were recording lengthy diary entries, but it was particularly noticeable with Hayward, who had been such a prolific diary writer in 1915. Wild's diary over this period contained entries on basic necessities. At this stage of the journey one of the primus cookers had developed a fault – presumably it was an old primus that had been left at Cape Evans by Scott's earlier expeditions. The primus was absolutely crucial to their survival.

Hayward: '13 Jan 15 to 18 Jan 15. Pulled out from 81°S & made depot @ 82°S (3 weeks) on above dates respectively. Skipper & Smith very crocked.'[52]

Joyce:

> 14 Jan: In the afternoon land opened up ahead we think it is the Mt Longstaff place we are steering for at the base will be Mt Hope.[53]

> 15 Jan: Under way as usual. Strong SE wind. but clear surface improved though a cold snap in the night temp went down to zero.[*] The first zero temp since November it has been very cold all the forenoon. Distance in spite of wind which is right in our faces 5–1700.
>
> After lunch wind freshened + sky became overcast I could just see the land to steer by going pretty good. Skipper not going very strong. Distance in the afternoon

---

[*]   'Zero' was -32°F.

5–1400. Making Dist for day – 11 – 1072. Splendid going. My snow blindness is improving greatly.[54]

Spencer-Smith:

14 Jan: The land is very distant away to the west; great high mountains in a vast semicircle to the eastern horn of which we are approaching. Their names are still uncertain – the highest we can see is probably Mt Longstaff.[55]

15 Jan: Clear until late afternoon but cold headwind all day. Within Burberry helmet dreamt through the longest afternoon of the trip. Sermon – They shall mount up with wings, &c. (Last verse of II Isaiah, + poem 'Life and Death' cut out from '*The Lone Hand*'.) Our first zero last night.[56]

18 Jan: Very stiff in the legs (back & calf) still.[57]

Wild:

15 Jan: The temp went down to zero last night so we shall soon have some cold weather.[58]

16 Jan: Our primus refused duty and we had to borrow from the others to make supper. Richards has fixed ours up now. I hope it will be alright tomorrow.[59]

17 Jan: Primus not very grand. [60]

18 January 1916

The six men reached 82°S, just over 80 miles from Mount Hope, at lunchtime on 18 January. There they left provisions, for themselves and Shackleton's party, sufficient to make the journey back north to the 81°S depot.

Mackintosh's original plan was for him, Spencer-Smith and Wild to go on to Mount Hope and for Joyce, Richards and Hayward to return from the 82°S depot. However, there were two factors that arose to change this planned course of action: the faulty primus cooker and the slowly worsening condition of Mackintosh and Spencer-Smith. Richards, Joyce and Hayward by now had decided that they were not going to turn back. They had come to the conclusion that both Mackintosh and Spencer-Smith were sick men as they were both limping, especially Mackintosh. The end result was that Mackintosh agreed to them all going on.

Before continuing on south from the 82°S depot, Mackintosh made Richards sign an agreement – which Mackintosh dictated and Spencer-Smith wrote out on a page of foolscap. Richards thought that it may have occurred to Mackintosh, at 82°S: 'Well this bugger Richards, I suppose he may blow the gaff when he gets back, we had better seal him up.' Richards says that it was then signed by Macintosh and witnessed by Spencer-Smith. He thought that no other legal agreement had been made closer to the South Pole, or the North Pole.[61]

Richards's Agreement:

IMPERIAL TRANS-ANTARCTIC EXPEDITION

The Great Ice Barrier   18 January 1916

Lat 82°S

I R. W. Richards at present serving as a member of the above expedition under the command of Sir Ernest Shackleton CVO do in consideration of the salary by me of £* per annum, undertake to obey the lawful commands of the above named Sir Ernest Shackleton CVO or those appointed by him. I also undertake to hold secret all work in connection with the above Expedition – as regards publishing on return to civilisation – of news, diaries, photographs, or other material such as I now have, or shall have, as a member of the Expedition in my possession such property as above mentioned, to be considered as belonging to the above expedition. This is to hold good for a period of two years after the return of the Expedition to civilisation.

Aeneas A. L. Mackintosh   (signed) R. W. Richards

Commanding Ross Sea base[62]

---

*   Blank on the original document.

Richards had already signed such an agreement in Sydney, when he was interviewed by Mackintosh, so why he had him sign another is not clear. He and Mackintosh may have forgotten the original one. Certainly in his later years Richards made no mention of the original agreement, not in his book, in his letters or at any of his interviews. The Sydney original agreement resides at the SPRI in Cambridge, England, and the Antarctic agreement is at the Canterbury Museum, Christchurch, New Zealand.

Spencer-Smith starts to falter

The six men and four dogs pushed on southward from the 82°S depot and for the first three days, they averaged 13 miles a day. Joyce was preoccupied in determining which mountain in the range was Mount Hope.

Over these days Spencer-Smith's condition worsened, showing symptoms of scurvy, but he continued on. He made occasional diary notes on what went through his mind as he dragged himself along but there are no notes of wanting to stop, or give in. However, his thoughts may well have echoed those of Scott from December 1902. At that time Scott, Shackleton and Wilson were on the Great Ice Barrier, heading south towards the 82°S latitude line, where they would reach the farthest south at that time (82° 11′S). Then Scott wrote that while they could walk there was only one way they could go, that is south. He remarked that they could not stop, or go back, no matter how sickening the work was. There was no alternative.[63]

The lack of fitness of Mackintosh and Spencer-Smith was giving Joyce, Richards and Hayward increasing cause for concern. The two men both complained of lameness and showed unmistakable signs of exhaustion. Richards recalled that he and the others discussed this often in their tent, but there was little that could be done but to go on because, in their minds, the depot at Mount Hope just had to be placed. Richards tells us that Mackintosh was in charge of the party at this time and he was determined to see the final depot laid.[64]

Richards in later years wrote on how much he admired the effort

Spencer-Smith made in helping to pull the sledge. Spencer-Smith was on the rope in front of him and Richards could see him limping and obviously in pain.[65] Over the three days of 18–20 January they covered close to 40 miles and the trend of the mountains brought them closer. As they slowly drew near all the men were deeply impressed with their magnificent grandeur. Travelling slowly, as they were covering only 10 or 12 miles a day, Richards recalled they had abundant time to take in every spectacular feature. They had the mountain range to their west and the Barrier to their east, which Richards described as a 'featureless level expanse of the ice shelf [that] stretched away apparently endlessly'.

Richards's recollection was that the six men rarely talked as they trudged along. There was no conversation on the trail. One step forward was a little in advance of the last, and all their energies were needed for the job in hand. He remembered that the silence was acute, the soft crunch of their feet in the snow and the faint swish of the sledge runners merely serving to emphasise it. Profound silence, that is, unless a blizzard was raging, and then their tiny party was lost in what Richards called a 'howling shrieking wilderness of whirling snow'.

Richards also recalled that the hours of a day's march seemed endless. He did not know what went on in his companions' minds over those months while trudging along but in his case he used to perform long useless computations of one sort or another in his head. He did not think this was a deliberate act on his part but rather an automatic reaction to the monotony that was forced on him; 'an anodyne to the weariness of the body' he called it.[66]

He tells us he even spoke with Joyce and Wild, presumably when they were stopped for lunch or the evening, about coming back to the area the following year. Richards had become more and more intrigued with the region, especially that known as Shackleton Inlet, a re-entrant (a small valley) in the Trans-Antarctic Mountains, about 10 miles wide, which at this stage of their journey was quite close. He tells us that the three of them agreed to make a trip back to that area of the mountains in the 1917 summer season as they thought it might have some mining potential.[67]

Spencer-Smith:

17 Jan: Spent a nice afternoon at Cambridge & Edinburgh sledge ride.

19 Jan: Legs very stiff as before: quite painful walking.

20 Jan: Feeling rather seedy. Head hot; eyes ache.

21 Jan: Nearly fainted at 11 a.m. and had to tell at lunch how weak I am: much sympathy and an extra Bovril cube all to myself. Heart rather ricked, I fear, and knees bad – swollen and like a great bruise above and below knee, especially the right.[68]

Dreamt last night that the war was over – that all German rivers are now English rivers and Birmingham is ----------.[*69]

Joyce:

19 Jan: …Smith complained of his knees being bad. He has not been doing much pulling. I think the Skipper + him ought to have gone back with the other party. Now they are with us they will have to leg it out or camp until we come back. Time is too precious to waste.[70]

20 Jan: S complains of his legs. Mk + him walking along like old men. Shall now be glad when we have completed our work.[71]

21 Jan: S + S seems legs are worse I expect it will mean carting them on the sledge. I was steering for the clouds first of all when it cleared to the S. Very thick & black to the N. In spite of wind + surface we have done our usual 6–500 before lunch. After lunch clear all around & wind dropped.

I think Mt Hope is right ahead it looks as if it answers the description – about 30 odd miles off.[72]

Wild: '19 Jan: Primus working rotten. 20 Jan: Primus bit better. 21 Jan: Primus working all bands now.'[73]

The six men were now only 30 miles from Mount Hope. Mackintosh

---

*   There is no indication what Spencer-Smith meant by 'and Birmingham is ---------'.

and Spencer-Smith were having trouble walking but there had been no indication so far that they would not be able to continue. The weather had been excellent for most of the past two weeks.

Chapter 10

'WITH THE HELP OF 2 GOOD PALS WE CARRIED IT OUT'

22 January 1916

A T 11.30 ON the morning of 22 January, a few miles short of 83°S, Spencer-Smith suddenly sat himself down and told the others he could go no further. He said he had been just finding it too difficult to walk.[1]

Richards remembered in later years that the overriding thought on everyone's mind was that they must place the food depot for Shackleton at Mount Hope. They believed he would make the crossing and he and his men were dependent on that depot. So they made the decision to leave Spencer-Smith while they would go on the 30–40 miles to Mount Hope. There was no other choice – they couldn't go on with Spencer-Smith and there was no point in turning back at that stage.[2]

They pitched two tents, had a meal and put Spencer-Smith in his sleeping bag, fully expecting that when they came back that he would be able to get on his feet again. He was perfectly cheerful and he too was confident that after the rest he would be able to make the return journey. In Richards's memory Spencer-Smith happily agreed to stay; he said he would be quite alright. They left him with a supply of calico bags containing cocoa, oatmeal, cheese, sugar and pemmican, and a primus next to his bag.[3]

The others suggested to Mackintosh that he should remain with Spencer-Smith and rest; however, Mackintosh resisted that idea and decided to go on. Richards thought that Mackintosh, as the leader of the party, felt it was his duty to see that the depot was made. They could do nothing about it, short of restraining him.[4]

Spencer-Smith:

> After about 2½ hours struggle this morning, with the knees above and below getting heavier, hotter and more painful every step, I had to ask the Skipper to depot me here and carry on to Mt. Hope without me.
>
> Eheu! But it's no use howling.[5]

Joyce:

> 11-30 the Skipper asked me to camp as Smith could not proceed any further. We held a little consultation + decided to leave provisions and tent + sledge + Smith to stay until we returned as I expect we shall be back again under the week.
>
> I honestly think the S* ought to have stayed with him, as a good rest would do them both good + make them more fit for our long journey back.[6]

Hayward:

> Smith who had been visibly done up since they found us declared his inability to proceed & we were obliged to leave him camped.
>
> Rest of us went on, Skipper limping & hobbling & not pulling an ounce.[7]

Wild: 'We had to leave poor old Smithy behind; he has got a bad leg, so we are rather jammed up with five in a tent.'[8]

---

*   'S' – Joyce meant the Skipper (Mackintosh) should have stayed with Spencer-Smith.

Day One for Spencer-Smith alone

After the others departed, Spencer-Smith made his first diary entry. He was alone on the Barrier, 325 miles from Hut Point.

Spencer-Smith:

22 Jan: It is about 3 p.m. now and I reckon on getting 2½ – 3½ days complete rest before they return. They have gone off with one sledge and 5 weeks' food: and they rattled off at a tremendous pace with the dogs scrapping en route.

Skipper and Wild most sympathetic: the others kindly leave me a bottle of lime juice in case my complaint is some form of scurvy – which I doubt altogether. They have made the tent very comfortable for me so I should be all right. So I should be all right except for loneliness & disappointment (probably merited!)

A lazy afternoon and a good supper with a little vegetable in it; lime juice to drink – so ends the day – for me the trek was 4m 250 yds.

Not much inclined to sleep so finished the '*Sea Puritans*' – Childish stuff!.[9]

23 January 1916

Spurred on by their anxiety to get back to Spencer-Smith, the five men made good progress. They had a light load on because they only needed to carry provisions for the final depot for Shackleton and their own use. However, a blizzard caused them to lay up for a day and a half.

Joyce:

We found 5 of us in one tent pretty fair. Camping at 11.30. So camped + had lunch. Found it was still thicker in the afternoon so could not proceed. A rest will do us all good, dogs + us.

We can't afford the time still we will have half a day. We are now under 20 miles away from our destination. Hoping Prov. will look on us + give us a June day tomorrow.[10]

Hayward tells us: 'Skipper, Wild, Joyce and self played Bridge (auction) till turning in.'[11]

Wild: 'Had a game at "auction bridge"'* this afternoon. We lost. The Skipper was my partner.'[12]

Spencer-Smith's second day alone

Spencer-Smith read, dreamt and planned a comedy in his mind:

23 Jan: Heavily overcast all day, tho' the sun was shining through for a short time in the early morning. The knees feel no better so I had spent a day of almost total inaction. It is difficult to cook for one with these gadgets. Am well into the H.U.L. volume on Evolution[†] and seem to make sense of most of it.

Dreamt that we met Sir Ernest and Frank Wild with motor and one dog sledge – both clean and neat – FW wearing a very much Gold Laced Hat & Sir E clean shaven.[13]

Still heavily overcast and quite impossible to tell the time. I am about to have breakfast though I feel sure it is closer to lunchtime. Knees feel a little better but I haven't been out yet.

Colder but a little less overcast as the day goes on. Have mended my Burberry blouse and a blanket glove. Felt very poorly when I went outside for snow just now. It seems nearly midnight – but I can't see the sun himself. It was really 8 or 9 pm.

Half sleeping, half waking have planned a comedy 'Brown, Jones and Robinson' the dialogue rattles off beautifully until one begins to think of writing it down![14]

25 January 1916

The blizzard stopped after two days so the five men went on. They were now quite close to the mountain range along which they had been travelling since October, and were steering directly for a detached rounded mountain a few

---

* 'Auction bridge' is a variation on the normal game of bridge.

† 'H.U.L. volume on Evolution' presumably means the book *Evolution* from the Hull University Library.

thousand feet high which they were confident was Mount Hope. In the after-noon Joyce steered towards this mountain (which was indeed Mount Hope) but they came across crevasses and pressure ridges and were forced to camp.

In his book, Richards tells us that as they approached the mountains the surface had begun to change and they passed over huge gentle undulations, which would have been pressure ridges. Gradually these intensified until they reached what Richards described as 'a remarkably broken-up area' where they camped for the night. They had experienced a long tiring day during which they had made their record mileage (almost 18 miles), so they did not want to try to find a passage through the heavily crevassed area until they had rested.[15]

Richards says that Mackintosh had kept going gamely, but he was very lame at the end of the day. Behind his knee there was a considerable area of blue discoloration and the others were somewhat puzzled as to why this had not cleared up by now. It was not until they returned to pick up Spencer-Smith and found black patches on their own gums and behind their own knees that they realised it was scurvy. Mackintosh was able to gain some relief by massaging his knees with methylated spirits.[16] As their scurvy worsened they often rubbed their joints with methylated spirits, and this seemed to help. (Possibly the ethanol in the methylated spirits dried the skin and this eased the pain, temporarily.)

After weeks of scanty diary entries, Hayward returned to something like his earlier detailed notes.

Joyce:

> Turned out usual time. Weather very fine. Underway as usual going very good doing 8¾ miles before lunch. Altered course 2 pts after lunch steering for sup-posed gap of Mt Hope.
>
> 5.10 came into very heavy crevasse, carried on until 6 o'clock camped on the edge of the biggest ice pressure I have ever seen. Distance 9 M, making 17¾ for the day.[17]

Hayward:

> Going good. 8¼ M for run after lunch struck a very hard surface & travelled on some, when within 4 miles of destination Mt Hope 83.30 we dropped into a very

badly crevassed area. Made about 1½ miles through it & forced to camp 6.20 pm crevasses all round us. Will reconnoiter in the morning.[18]

Wild may have been missing life on the sea:

We haven't quite reached Mt Hope. There are crevasses all around us & we couldn't find a passage through. However better luck tomorrow. Just 12 months today since we left the ship. It is the longest time I have been off a ship for over 20 years.[19]

Another day alone for Spencer-Smith

25 January was Spencer-Smith's third day waiting for the others to return from Mount Hope. Not for the first time he mentions his heart, worrying that it may be 'ricked', and he was dispirited that his condition had not improved:

25 Jan: A year ago today we set off from the ship on our first journey – all clothes new and clean: a team of 9 dogs and high hopes. Only the last remain and even they should be accomplished now by the O.M. and Wild by now.

Sunny and warm again all day: I went out twice to try to enjoy it but my knees became painful at once and my toot ensemble is very weak: seems as if the heart is ricked after all: if so, it happened a day or two after we joined up.

More mending done. Finished my book 'Evolution'. Learnt 'So he died for his faith' and have no more literature.

The others should reappear tomorrow and I fear that they will have to find me, in spite of rest, cold bandages, &c – humiliating![20]

26 January 1916

On the morning of 26 January Mackintosh, Joyce and Richards set off to find a passage through the crevasses. The three men took great care as the surface became almost impossible to travel over. There were huge pressure ridges to haul the sledges over. Crevasses were everywhere but usually filled in except at the edges, where there was breadth enough for a man to drop in and hang up by his elbows and his harness.[21] They could see the crevasses quite clearly and in Richards's view they 'fatalistically believed' they would have no trouble with them; they simply had to find a place where they could get across.[22]

Eventually, they passed through the dangerous area and sixty years afterwards Richards still remembered the day, and the sights. He tells us it was a beautifully calm day and the sun was shining brightly as they climbed up a snow slope with Mount Hope on their left and the mountain range on their right. Below them was the Beardmore Glacier stretching away to the distance, 25 miles wide, and to Richards everything was on a 'gigantic scale'. He remembered that 'the scene was full of colour and simply magnificent'.[23]

The ice of the glacier was flanked by sheer steep rock faces splashed with vivid colours, and on the glacier itself below where the men were standing they could see a number of dark patches, which they thought was probably rock that had become dislodged from the steep sides.[24] Richards says he lay down with the glasses as he could see a blob of rock that looked the same shape as the tent they were using; like Shackleton used. He lay down for quite a long time looking at this 'tent' wondering if anyone would come out of it; if it was a tent. But they saw no sign of life.[25]

Hayward: 'We have reconnoitered in the morning at least Skipper, Joyce & Richards reconnoitered in the morning. Wild & I remained in camp & made tea several times.'[26]

Joyce:

> We decided to keep the camp up. Skipper Richards + myself roped ourselves together: I taking the lead to try + find course through this pressure. We came across very wide crevasses went down several, came on top of a very high ridge + such a scene. Can't imagine thousands of tons of ice churned up + the depth about 300 ft, we took a couple of photos then I carried on to the E.
>
> At last we found a passage through + carried on through smaller crevasses to

Mt Hope or we hoped it was the Mt by that name; the chart seems a bit off, so! Although we can see a great glacier ahead which we take for the Beardmore which this mountain is on, the position on the chart is wrong.

We had nearly arrived at the ice foot when Richards saw something to the right, which turned out to be 2 of Capt Scott's sledges. Then we knew for cert. this was the place we had struggled to get to.

So we climbed the glacier on the slope + went up about 1¼ mile + saw the great Beardmore Glacier stretch to the South. It is almost 25 miles wide, a most wonderful sight.[27]

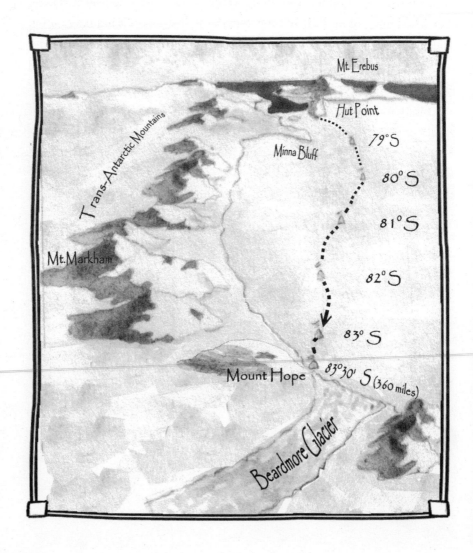

The final depot is laid at Mount Hope

Joyce, Mackintosh and Richards rejoined Hayward and Wild at their camp, arriving back at three in the afternoon, and then they moved camp closer to where the depot was to be laid. Richards had thoughts that the Mount Hope region could even be gold-bearing. In an interview many years afterwards he tells us he went to the land at the side of the glacier and picked up some quartz, and he noticed it was very much like the quartz found near his home town of Bendigo, a mining town in Victoria. He remembered saying to the others at the time: 'Well look, we've been wandering over this Barrier which has got nothing to offer. Next year, if the ship is not back, what about coming out to these mountains and having a look at what's there?'[28]

The final task was to lay the depot, which Wild, Hayward and Joyce duly completed later that day. They were very tired when they retired for the night and their sleep was disturbed by 'heavy cracks like pistol shots' in the ice beneath them; in Richards's mind no doubt due to the intense stresses to which all the ice in the area was subjected. However, he recalled that they all experienced a sense of peace knowing that they had placed all the depots for Shackleton, in spite of considerable difficulty.[29]

Wild:

> Have made the Mt Hope depot at last, 7 miles from where we were last night. 2 weeks provisions & 2 full tins of oil so they ought to be alright. We found two sledges here that had been left by Scott's party. The depot is 2 miles from here. Joyce, Hayward & myself laid it & came back here for supper. The ice pressure around here is tremendous. The B Glacier looks very rough from the Gap.[30]

Hayward: 'Immediately after pitching tent Joyce, Wild & self dropped off ½ one of aforesaid sledges & put on 2 weeks provisions for depoting which we three laid 2 miles up glacier running between Mt Hope & the mainland. Took photo.'[31]

Joyce:

> Wild, Hayward + myself then took the depot up the Glacier a fortnights provisions.

We left it lashed to a broken sledge + put a large flag up. I took 2 photos of it. We did not arrive back until 10-30. It was rather a heavy pull up.

I was very pleased to see our work completed at last. We had dinner when we arrived back the Skipper telling us how good it was of us to bring him along.

This is his first acknowledgement of the work we done. Still I don't want his praise. All I wanted to see was the work carried out what men are depending on. As I said when we started sledging I would do this + so with the help of 2 good pals* we carried it out.

Turned in 12 o'clock. Dist we done during day 22 Miles.[32]

Hayward was thinking of Spencer-Smith and Mackintosh: 'Smith will in all probability have to be put in the sledge. The Skipper is quite lame & I contend has hindered far more than he has advanced our main objective of laying these depots to 83.30 for Shacks support.'[33]

Spencer-Smith waits at 83°S

Spencer-Smith wrote of a person, 'T', possibly to write down the comedy skit he mentioned in his diary two days ago:

26 Jan: By the sun it is nearly 6 a.m. – I didn't have lunch until nearly 2, expecting the others any minute. I suppose Sunday and Monday delayed them by making it imposs to choose the spot for the depot. Knees no better. Sleeping bag, 2 mats and floor-cloth sopping wet under me.

Mind very active – if only I had T. here as secretary. Northerly wind all day: land partly obscured; sun shining brightly. Had a bit of a 'dish-up' effort and washed.[34]

27 January 1916

It was now late January and a blizzard on the first morning for the men

---

*   Why Joyce mentioned only '2 good pals' is not clear. He possibly meant Richards and Hayward, who he usually shared his tent with, although he laid the final depot with Wild and Hayward.

returning from Mount Hope was an indicator of what was to come. In such circumstances they felt it was dangerous to attempt their way back through the maze of crevasses and ice pressure, but during the day conditions eased somewhat so they began the long haul back to Hut Point.[35]

Richards tells us they were all anxious because they had left Spencer-Smith, obviously a sick man, with no one closer than 300 miles away to the north, and only their party to the south. They were naturally 'chaffing at any circumstances' that caused a delay. They thought Spencer-Smith would be alright and that he would be able to resume his journey, but Richards remembered that he was worried because they had to find him, which might be difficult if the weather was poor. They had to locate a little conical-shaped tent in a wilderness of ice and snow that was completely featureless; and there was nothing to guide them.[36]

Joyce was now suffering severely from snow blindness. He had to go off the lead position and bind his eyes with a piece of cloth, which meant he often fell and stumbled because of the uneven surface. Richards recalled Joyce saying he was falling down like a 'jumping jenny'.[37] Slivers of cocaine were used to help with snow blindness and if they could get any water they would dissolve them and put them in their eyes, but if they couldn't they would stick the cocaine in raw just to relieve the pain. Richards describes the pain when snow blind as being like coal dust in your eye from a steam train: 'very unpleasant'.[38]

Joyce:

> Found it snowing – good job we laid the Depot last night. Had breakfast at noon, cleared up 3-30, so got underway got through all the crevasses by about 6 o'clock then I turned the steering over to the Skipper as I had a very nasty attack of S. Blindness. Camp 7 o'clock. Dist 4¾ miles.
>
> We are now Homeward Bound. 360 miles to go. I think with the help of Good Old Provi we ought to be in by the 27th of Feb.[39]

Wild:

> I thank God – on the back trail. They say 'enough is as good as a feast' well I have had my feast of sledging this season. Now for a good run back to the Bluff where

I hope to find some bacco. Joyce is stone blind with snow blindness. He has been
hanging onto the Skipper's trace. I used it as a guide rope.[40]

Spencer-Smith looks for the five men returning

27 January 1916 was day five for Spencer-Smith, tent bound and alone. He
was completely isolated, 300 miles out on the Great Ice Barrier of Antarctica.
He was living in complete silence apart from the noise of the wind and occasional sounds from movements of the snow and ice refreezing and splitting
due to changes in temperature, but he makes no mention of this solitude in
his diary. He does not write copious diary notes of what went through his
mind hour after hour, day by day. He does not give us any reflections on his
relationships with any of the other men. He, like many others in Antarctica
at those times, seems to simply accept the situation as it was. Douglas Mawson on his 1911–14 Antarctic expedition was alone for over thirty days after
losing his two comrades when exploring the coastline to the north-west of
McMurdo Sound. To while away the time he thought of topics such as how
to fix his cooker and trusting in Providence to pull him through.[41] From his
diary notes Spencer-Smith was much the same; mending his clothes and
reading – but (surprisingly) making no reference in his diary on his religious beliefs to guide the others back safely. He pens no long diary entries
which might be expected from a man with his background and education.

27 Jan: Strong southerly and drift kept me at home, apart from other things – but
later in the day the weather became calm and bright. Spent part of the time in (1)
delivering a lecture, (2) a sermon, both in execrable French.
No sign of the others. Two meals.[42]

28 January 1916

On the 28th Joyce, Richards, Hayward, Mackintosh and Wild made over
16 miles for the day, so they were then only 11 miles from Spencer-Smith

and expected to be at his camp the following day. The dogs were pulling strongly as they only had a few days' food and fuel on the sledge.

Joyce:

> Under way as usual. I am now absolutely blind, hanging on to harness for guidance, but still pulling my whack which is little as the dogs are going well + we have only a couple of days provisions on.
>
> Lunched as usual. Skipper still weak on the pins. Distance during day 16½ miles.[43]

Hayward:

> Picked up our outward trail after travelling an hour and a half, after which going good tracks being easily followed. Total distance for the day 16½ miles, this puts us 20 odd miles on the homeward trail. We shall pick Smith up at lunch as he is approx. 11m on.[44]

Spencer-Smith starts to worry

On 28 January Spencer-Smith made calculations on the distances from his tent back to the 82°S and 81°S depots, to determine the distance the men had to travel to Mount Hope, surmising that their absence could be accounted for:

> 28 Jan: Felt very rotten this morning: fine with a gentle northerly, and mountains half-covered in mist.
>
> The mileage since the "80° Depot is as follow:
> 81° Depot 64m 972 yds.
> 82° Depot 68m 666 yds.
> (this spot): 44m 319 yds.
> Total: 176 m 1957 yds.
>
> If these figures are roughly correct and the 80° Depot is truly laid, then this spot is still 35 m. 71 yds from Mt. Hope. But if, as I have always supposed, the so-called 80° Depot is 8 miles north of true 80°, then this spot is 43 miles from Mt. Hope. In

either case the long absence of the party is fairly accounted for. But if we are 10 m. ahead of dead reckoning, then there's a problem! Perhaps however they laid up all the 23rd and 24th.

The mountains to the west are tremendous this evening. No sign of the others at p.m.[45]

Chapter 11

'HOPE TO REACH BLUFF DEPOT TOMORROW'

29 January 1916

JOYCE, RICHARDS, HAYWARD, Mackintosh and Wild came up to Spencer-Smith's tent in the early afternoon of 29 January. They had sighted his tent at midday but it was 3.15 before they arrived.[1] They found that he was still in his sleeping bag so they realised then that there was only one thing to do – they had to put him on the sledge.[2] His condition had deteriorated and it was obvious he could not walk. But Spencer-Smith was cheerful, and very glad to see them back as he had experienced a very trying time.[3]

Richards felt for the man, writing later that he had been left alone, 'a small speck on the vast ice shelf', and when their party had disappeared to the south a week before and 'the great silence of the Barrier had settled down' he must have been very lonely indeed.[4]

Spencer-Smith complained of pains in the back of his knee, and he put it down to tears in his windproof clothing. If they had a hole or a tear in their clothing they would get a sore not unlike frostbite – the flesh would become quite red because of the wind that came in. This is what Spencer-Smith thought had happened. Joyce was not sure if Spencer-Smith had scurvy; however, Richards recalled in an interview that when he saw the state of Spencer-Smith he realised that he did.[5]

They placed Spencer-Smith on a sledge, wasting no time, and by four o'clock were moving north again. They made him as comfortable as possible in his sleeping bag and arranged the load on the second sledge so as to give him the best ride possible. (From this day Spencer-Smith was never on his feet again.)[6]

The six men were back together, with Joyce, Richards and Hayward again sharing one tent and Mackintosh, Spencer-Smith and Wild the other. The layout of the party still had Joyce in the lead on a long rope, but now followed by the dog Con and then Gunner, these two dogs in single file behind Joyce. Then followed Towser with Wild one side of him and Mackintosh the other, and then Oscar the last dog closest to the sledges, flanked by Richards and Hayward. Spencer-Smith was on the sledge.[7]

It now dawned on the five men that they were going to be rather up against it because they had Spencer-Smith on a sledge and they had to pull him through 325 miles.[8] They were all worried how they would now travel.

'Praise to God!' Spencer-Smith wrote: 'Laus Deo! The others arrived at about 3.30, just as I was thinking of having lunch. It is strange but cheery to hear men and dogs again.'[9]

Joyce: 'Came on Smith's camp 3 o'clock. Found him in his sleeping bag unable to walk + black limbs swelled up. It may be scurvy but I do not think so as his gums + eyes do not shew it.'[10]

Wild was philosophical: 'Picked up Smithy this afternoon. He is still crook and we had to put him on the sledge. I'm afraid that will make us rather longer getting back. Still it can't be helped.'[11]

Hayward:

> Picked up Smith, one hour after moving on, found him very crook indeed & we had to put him on the sledge in his bag, needless to say this extra weight has pulled down our speed considerably & we did 3 miles before camping.

I think it will be too optimistic to imagine that we shall be able to do more than 12 miles a day under these circs unfortunate but que routes runs.[*12]

Joyce:

The Skipper is in his usual panic. As I said after we left 80° that we should have the both of them on the sledge as they have been both useless from that date. If it had not been for their primus I should have sent them back.

Now you see we have about 300 miles to go, provisions rather short & a sick man & one that is nearly as bad. Now comes one of the trials of the Antarctic. Well one cannot do more than their best.

The dogs are still keeping fit if they will only last to 80° we shall then have enough food to take them in. I guarantee they will live in comfort the remainder of their days.[13]

Spencer-Smith jotted down a summary of the others' depot-laying at Mount Hope:

They laid up on the 23rd and 24th and reached Mt. Hope on Wed. 26th. – it is the biggish rounded mountain in the distance. They found terrible crevasses, open some of them, and huge pressure. A party had to rope up to find a way to place the depot and found a narrow passage – about ¼ mile wide – and two of Scott's sledges.

They left 2 weeks grub there and have pelted back, their outward distance being about 33 miles.[14]

He added: 'The Skipper gave my knees a fierce massaging tonight which was very painful but I hope beneficial. I do hope to be all right before we get back. Again – Laus Deo!'[15]

30 January 1916

A blizzard stopped them on their first day after picking up Spencer-Smith

---

*   His term 'que routes runs' means 'what runs, runs', or what will be, will be.

– they were approximately 320 miles from Hut Point. Wild called the blizzard day a 'nothing day',[16] and to Hayward it was: 'Rotten luck. Blizzard laid up.'[17] We can visualise the scene inside their tent from Mackintosh's words, when tent bound in similar circumstances a year before.

Mackintosh:

> Still blowing, the door of the tent is covered high with drift so to get out we have to shovel the snow away, so our only place is the bag.
>
> What a weird scene this is inside the tent on such an occasion, here lie 3 forms stretched out with a hand and perhaps a book and a portion of the face appearing out of the bag, around our feet lie the cooker, various bags, finneskoe, all this enclosed in a small green tent.
>
> What queer places and positions man will place himself. The drift outside has heaped to about 4 feet in height and there is a regular lane through which we can walk out from the door being banked up on either side.[18]

Joyce: 'To our utter disgust found it snowing hard & blizzarding. So are obliged to wait until it subsides. Told the Skipper we would only have to have 2 meals a day, the 1st at noon + 2nd about 8 o'clock. That will save a little food.'[19]

Spencer-Smith: 'Snowfall all night and a heavyish southerly blizzard from breakfast-time onwards. So we have not moved – and had no meal till noon. Left knee feels a little better: right knee unchanged. Another meal at 6. Weather very slightly improved. Feel rather rotten.'[20]

31 January 1916

Joyce may now have taken over as leader; or at least Mackintosh was now looking to him for more advice. The weather cleared but they were slow to get under way with Spencer-Smith being carried to the sledge (and from it when they camped). They covered only 8 miles for the day but Joyce was not unhappy.

Joyce:

Skipper came in our tent and asked if we would travel by night. I told him no. Carry out the usual routine as we have over 300 miles to go + if once you break your routine it is hard to pick it up again.

He seems properly scared. I also told him that he ought to have known about the condition of Smith. He made the usual silly excuses.

Put Smith on the rear sledge & covered him up with a floor-cloth made him pretty comfy. It is very warm and the drift is covering everything with water + melting into water. All our gear very wet. After sailing all the time we have done 8 miles. Turned in very wet but cheerful.

As the dogs are the factor I am going to study them above everything as I am almost certain we shall have the Skipper on the sledge.[21]

Spencer-Smith: 'The blizzard went on all night, but it was sufficiently calm (!) for us to start off for a half day at noon. I was carried in my bag to the sledge and spent a mis. 4¼ hours – quite warm but feeling very weak, with crampy knees.'[22]

Hayward: 'Blowing like hell. Got under way however (11.30). It took us an hour & a half to dig out sledges before starting. Poor old Smith seems very sick indeed, & we had to carry his body in order to get him on to sledge.'[23]

Here's Mackintosh, a note from a year before:

Getting away in the mornings is our bitterest time. The putting on of the finneskoe is a nightmare, for they are always frozen stiff, and we have a great struggle to force our feet into them. The iced sennegrass round one's fingers is another punishment that causes much pain.[24]

We had to get our boots on – this is not such a simple operation as it sounds. We call it our 'hour of discontent' for getting into these frozen boards takes anything for ¼ to ½ hour's hard struggle and pain, especially if one happens to have a chapped heel, which I have.[25]

Wild: 'Didn't start till after 12 o'clock & stopped at 8 o'clock. We had a fair wind with drift & I'm wet through. Can't shift clothes, haven't got any. End of fifth month sledging. I hope another month will finish it.'[26]

1 February 1916

They managed 13 miles for the day.

Joyce:

> Starting a new month with a fair wind. Under way 9 o'clock as I overslept myself. 2nd time since Oct, not a bad record.
>
> Set sail going very soft snow in spite of our patient on the sledge we have done 6–900 miles in the forenoon. I went on until 6 o'clock to make up a little lost time. Dist for the day 13 Miles. Very good going.
>
> I told the Skipper he would have to do away with the 2nd sledge he is making a lot of excuses about it but I shall travel tomorrow with only the 1 sledge. We must make our 13 or 14 miles a day.
>
> Smith is no better he is quite useless & we have to lift him + carry him about we ought to be in by the end of the month. Skipper is still not pulling a damn.[27]
>
> Skipper black like Smith & his gums are badly swollen. It is a miracle to me how he gets along; his ankles are twice the size. There is one thing he has plenty of pluck.
>
> Hayward's gums are black and protruding, and he is slightly black at the back of the knees.
>
> Wild, Richy & Self gums turning black.
>
> I think the scurvy has got us & only one thing for it – fresh meat.
>
> Smith's bag is wet through & there is no way of drying it. Poor chap but he is a Briton – no complaint from him.[28]

Spencer-Smith:

> A beautiful day with quite a pleasant southerly breeze to help. The mountains are very distinct. – the cocoa-coloured bit is abaft to the beam now and we are opening up Shackleton Inlet. I spent the afternoon rather more comfortably than the morning – enthroned and encushioned on the front sledge.
>
> So tomorrow we will go on with only one sledge and with good weather shall not be long.[29]

Wild did not elaborate on something Mackintosh said: 'I have just been out and put the primus and oil boxes on the other sledge & the canvas tank. We want to keep the speed up if poss. The Skipper is evil minded: about Oscar and the pemmican.'[30]

2 February 1916

Joyce's plan was adopted – they went on with only one sledge. Joyce described the day's effort as 'a really good performance'.[31] They had travelled over 13 miles by his reckoning (15 by Spencer-Smith's diary) and were now within 280 miles of Hut Point. The next day they would reach the 82°S depot, replenish their food supplies and push on.

Joyce: 'Under way as usual but a little late owing to doing away with a sledge. Found it rather difficult to stow but managed very well. Stowed Smith very well on top. I am afraid his heart is very badly affected his lips very bloodless.'[32]

Spencer-Smith: 'A warm day – almost too warm this afternoon even for me on the sledge. A full day's work was done and the result is 15 m. 800 yds – great work. Everyone is very kind to wretched me. "O that this, too solid flesh would melt!"'[33]

Hayward: 'We depoted a sledge this morning & carried on with everything including Smith stowed on one only, good scheme, going good 15½ M for day. Camped 6 o/c. Skipper could hardly put his foot to the ground.'[34]

2–7 February: The trek from 82°S to 81°S

They managed to cover 17 and 18 miles a day to reach the 81°S depot because they travelled long hours.[35] Richards remembered that at the time he felt they were 'rather fantastic distances' to do in a day considering the loads and everything else that was against them. Their progress would depend on the weather and the surface. If a blizzard was blowing with a strong south-easterly, which was the prevailing direction of the wind, they would 'hoist a sail' and the wind would give them some assistance.[36]

The time taken to pack up after a stop was now becoming a major issue.

The men also found the morning, that is the forenoon march, always more tiring than the afternoon one, and the last hour before lunch particularly so. But lunch seemed to work a miracle of revival and they stepped out afterwards with more energy, which they attributed to the sugar they put in their tea.[37]

The well-being of the dogs was now paramount and wherever they could they gave them a hot 'hoosh' meal a day of about a pound in weight. Richards remembered that they watched them with a zealous care because just one bite on a foot might have meant a significant loss to the whole party. They could not afford to lose a quarter of the pulling power of the dogs, even though they weren't pulling as much as a man.[38]

3 February 1916

Joyce:

Under way 8-20. It takes rather a little longer to get ready on ac of our invalid so shall have to get up earlier 4-45. Had a fair wind so makes all the difference in pulling as the Skipper is not all that is required. Wind keeping up all day, so I carried on until 6-15 I am going to work overtime every night until we get in.

I forgot to add picked up 82° Depot 2-45 + left 2 weeks for the Boss. Distance done during day 17–900. S not very well but he will have to stick it.[39]

4 February 1916

Spencer-Smith:

Feeling very rocky myself until the afternoon: can't stand up even for a few seconds now and have to be carried always to and from the sledge – horrible but necessary. Nice and warm during afternoon and feeling rather better, thanks to some strong Bovril (emergency) at lunch. Repeat dose for some days, I think.

Tremendous excitement about an hour after lunch – black objects ahead: not the least bit like a cairn: but it was, with lumps of paper on it.[40]

Hayward wrote: 'Poor old S* rotten.'[41]

Joyce:

> Hayward Wild + Richy splendid condition. S – rotten.
>
> Dogs doing splendid. Shall give them a little extra feed now as we are doing so well.
>
> Smith had a little fainting fit this morning. We shall have to put our right foot forward. I am rather afraid we shall not get him in on time – still, no one being could do any more than we are.[42]

5 February 1916

It was a 'warm' day, only six degrees below freezing.

Spencer-Smith:

> Anniv. 3. 'Ne obliviscar.' Another fine day and a big march of 17 m. 1275 yds. We dipped Shackleton Inlet this morning. The land is rather misty and the sun blazing hot in the afternoon. The temperature at lunch was +26° F.
>
> Very bumpy progress and rather uncomfortable for me but one can't howl so long as we are making such fine progress. The dogs are doing splendidly – always keen. Passed halfway flag just before lunch.[43]

At this stage Joyce was still optimistic: 'Dogs are still in splendid condition + going as well as ever. They are little Marvels. At this rate we shall soon polish off the remainder.'[44]

6 February 1916

In one of his interviews Richards tells us how Spencer-Smith spent his days on the sledge. He would be down inside his sleeping bag and the other men could not see him. He would have the sleeping bag flap right over his face

---

*   S may refer to Spencer-Smith, or possibly Skipper, that is Mackintosh.

and part of the time he was unconscious. Richards was close to him on the bows of the sledge and at times he would hear him uttering 'wandering' thoughts and at other times he would 'hear him reciting a prayer in Latin'.[45]

Spencer-Smith: 'Been all over London and Althorne with dear old T&U – a dream surely to be realised in July or August of this year, if only the ship is safe: please God she is.'[46]

Hayward: 'Good going 10½ m by lunch. Breeze petered out after noon & surface bloody awful could only do 8¼ (18¾) before camping. We are in sight of depot at 81° S, 4½ m distant.'[47]

Wild: 'Skipper still as selfish as ever. Letting Smithy lay on a boot while he has got two big bed-fur mitts for pillows. The tent blew inside out like an umbrella the other day. I've just been mending the ribs again.'[48]

Joyce's watch stopped, much to the annoyance of Mackintosh: 'After we had done 2 miles and I looked at the watch and found it had stopped. But decided, to S---- disgust, to place it on the wrong side, the consequence was done over 10½ in the forenoon.'[49]

On Monday 7 February they reached the 81°S depot (209 miles from Hut Point – by Hayward's diary entry) and picked up a week's provisions again, to travel the 70 miles onto the next depot, at 80°S.

7–11 February: The trek from 81°S to 80°S

Spencer-Smith often recorded what his thoughts were during the day but the other five men rarely let on in their diaries what was on their mind as they trudged along, hour after hour, day after day. In an interview sixty years later Richards gave an insight into his thoughts. He tells us he could not talk to the other fellows as they were too far away so he had a world of his own to think about. Sometimes he would look at the peaks of the western mountains and guess the bearing when they were starting the day. Then he would guess the bearing when they had finished. He did it by eye, without the compass, and just for purely something to do, trying to work out in his own mind, the angle between the first two from the known distance they had travelled.

He tells us he did this sort of thing to keep his mind occupied because there was such intense monotony as they trudged along 'one step a little in front of the other' on the snowy surface. He believed that the others must have had something that occupied their mind because there was not much to see. The Barrier was a featureless surface although when they were close to the Trans-Antarctic Mountains they could look and admire them when it was clear, but there were parts of the journey where they were out of sight.[50]

At these times he simply pondered on the simple things that made up his day's existence. He remembered that he seldom thought of the outside world as he had heard nothing from it since December 1914; he had left all that behind. The only reality was what he and the other men saw. However, the pleasures of their day were just as satisfying as for someone in civilisation. There was the shelter of the tent at the end of the day, the easing of a blizzard, a smooth-running snow surface, the sighting of a food depot and ample food after being on short rations. These to Richards were the peaks above the drudgery of their day-to-day existence and he wrote in his book it 'produced a feeling of profound well-being'.[51]

Hayward's diary notes over the five days they took to travel the 70 miles between the 81°S and 80°S depots were very brief but he was now keeping a simple table of the date, distance travelled and miles left to reach Hut Point. The entries over the days from 81°S to 80°S were:

7	14	209
8	11	195
9	15	184
10	14	169
11	16	155[52]

(The first line means on 7 February they had travelled 14 miles and had 209 miles to Hut Point. The last line means that on 11 February they had travelled 16 miles and had 155 miles to Hut Point.)

Hayward: '8 Feb: Snow which fell during night made going very difficult, however with some effort we managed to put in for the day 11 miles not too bad. Old man very bad.

11 Feb: Made depot (80° S) at 14 miles. Time 5 o/c. Camped 1½ miles N. Total 15½ M.'[53]

Spencer-Smith:

7 Feb: I have spent most of the day with my Edinburgh pals (J. and C.).[54]

8 Feb: Spent the afternoon imagining 'tired man's' jobs for myself. Gums sore for two days – on lime juice.[55]

9 Feb: Pleasant afternoon in South Square, Gray's Inn. Gums are better.[56]

10 Feb: Feel very weak … Dreamt of the Stevens twins. I going to call on Mrs S. see twins in front garden and say 'Hello twins, you don't know who I am.' The reply in duet sans hesitation was 'Oh no, but you look like the devil!'[57]

11 Feb: A rather more comfortable day – mostly hovering around Gray's Inn, furnishing, &c, &c. If only the dream cd come true.[58]

Wild: '8 Feb: Short day & rotten surface. 9 Feb: Fair wind and rotten surface.'[59]

Joyce maintained a daily log, such as:

8 Feb: Blowing + Snowing all night Turned out 5-30 found it still snowing + too thick to get under way called hands 7-20 underway 9-50 very thick + bad light for steering but managed to pick up some of the Cairns.

Lunch 1 o'clock. After lunch it cleared up with a good blue sky very strange in this lat as we call this the gloomy stretch, as no party has experienced good weather in this Lat. Camped 6-40 surface got so bad that we were sometimes up to our knees. I think it is the hardest afternoon we have experienced. Dist during day 11¼ miles.[60]

On 11 February they reached the 80°S depot, 155 miles from Hut Point, where they again replenished their supplies and carried on.

12–17 February: They close in on the Minna Bluff depot

Richards recalled that from the 12th onwards their progress became slower because none of the men were in good shape and Mackintosh was usually hanging on to the sledge. As their weakness increased, they gradually jettisoned everything they could to lighten their load. They had already left the second sledge behind and then the sledge-meter, shovels, ice picks and other items were tossed aside.[61]

Over these days, lying on the sledge, Spencer-Smith dreamt or thought of England almost every day. He does not gripe or grumble, but simply puts down a brief statement of his ailments now and again. In his book *The Ross Sea Shore Party* Richards tells us that at every camp and at every midday halt Spencer-Smith was lifted from sledge to tent in his bag. Mackintosh, his tent-mate, was also an invalid so practically the entire care of Spencer-Smith fell on Wild's shoulders, he being the only other occupant of that tent. Wild tended to him for forty days with a devotion that in Richards's view could not be surpassed, and for upwards of 300 miles in increasingly difficult circumstances. Spencer-Smith never once complained although his thoughts wandered and at other times he lost consciousness. He was, however, often ready with a cheery word and he did his best to make their task as easy as possible.[62]

All their diary entries were meagre over these seven days although they wrote about seeing familiar landmarks. Joyce, who was leading the party out front, may have been becoming despondent at this time, and he was clearly annoyed with Mackintosh. Hayward's table of distances covered for the seven days from 12 February to 18 February shows their slow progress after the 80°S depot to reach a position of 81 miles from Hut Point. On the last three days they only travelled 8 miles a day.

Joyce:

12 Feb: There are about 4 lines of Cairns about. Another of the Skips silly whims & it is hard to keep on a straight course.

Sighted Bluff in the forenoon, miraged up & also Mt. Discovery in the afternoon.[63]

14 Feb: Surface pretty fair in the forenoon. In the afternoon came across the most rotten surface we have experienced since we have been out. I would not mind if we were all pulling our weight in but I am afraid not.[64]

17 Feb: Surface very rotten sinking in up to the knees. S----- pulling about the same 1 rat power.[65]

Hayward's table of distances:

12	12	139
13	12	127
14	10	115
15	8	105
16	8	97
17	8	89
18	Blizzard	81[66]

His other diary notes were scarce:

12 Feb. Very hard going. Mileage 12½ for day.

13 Feb. Dull steering difficult. 12 M

14 Feb. Going execrable, still dull. 10 M for day

15 Feb. Rottener & rottener could only do 8 m today.

16 Feb. The surface on this stretch is like ploughing ones way through treacle on stilts & we could only do 8 M

17 Feb. Surface similar to that before mentioned. 8 M again. Skipper very lame.[67]

Spencer-Smith:

12 Feb. Hardly any breeze and therefore very hard work all day. Spent the morning as above and the afternoon at Ardingley!*

'Gunboat' got adrift while they were putting up the tent and came to visit me. Day's march about 12 miles. The sledge upsets occasionally but without damage to me or it.

13 Feb. A dull, grey day – lit. and metaphor. Days march about 12. Gums rather sore again and feel cranky generally.

14 Feb. A dull day but cleared up beautifully in the evening. It is getting much colder now: the minimum showed -9° F last night.

I had a fierce argument with Wild at lunch 'de lege talionis'† in Belgium, S Africa, &c.: and spent the afternoon trying to see why he and I hold such opposite views. The simplicity of the solution made me kick myself – of course one's views of right and wrong here and elsewhere depend on belief in the Absolute Good = God – and this he has not realised yet: hence the strange contrast between his really fine character and his wild opinions.

Dreamt of Christmas day at All Saints last night – Procession of the Blessed Sacrament, hundreds of candles, incense, &c., the organ crashing out the first few bars of 'Adeste Fideles'.

The wretched Oscar loose outside woke me up – nor could I re-capture the vision.[68]

Wild:

12 Feb: 12½ m roughly. The meter has busted so we have to estimate it how we can. Sighted Old Discovery and the Bluff so we are getting among familiar places again.

13 Feb: Cold day & hard going.

14 Feb: 8½ miles. Hard pulling. Rotten soft surface. Hardest day & shortest distance since we joined up with the others.

---

*   Ardingley is possibly Ardingly, a village in West Sussex.

†   'de lege talionis' is an analysis of the Laws of Moses. Spencer-Smith and Wild seemed to have different views on the laws as they apply to social living.

15 Feb: 8m ditto. It's snowing like anything now.

16 Feb: 9m. Good fair wind or else we would have done about two.

17 Feb: 8½ Fair wind, hard going. Smithy still keeps pretty cheerful. He doesn't howl much, like I should. He is still very weak.[69]

17 February 1916

On the evening of 17 February, they camped, worn out but with less than 10 miles to reach the Bluff depot. Richards tells us in an interview that during the day their progress was particularly slow, and towards evening, with a low drift blowing, that they had lost their line of cairns (those laid on the way out to Mount Hope).[70] They had lost them because they had what Richards called 'carpet sweepers'; that is, snow drift, up to perhaps 4 or 5 feet. That day they had been going on a bearing which Richards recalled as being 'pretty right' but they were not on the line of cairns when they camped that night. They were not anxious as they thought they would pick up the line again in the morning.[71]

The men knew they still had a difficult job ahead of them but Richards does not remember feeling worried at that particular stage.[72] From their diaries of 17 February the others also appear unconcerned and their thoughts were on reaching the Minna Bluff depot, with its ample supply of provisions. However, their serious problems were about to begin, or as Richards remembered, from that time on things began to get 'distinctly sticky'.[73]

Wild: 'Hope to reach Bluff Depot tomorrow.'[74]

Joyce: 'If fine tomorrow, very doubtful heavy clouds flying around, we ought to reach the Depot.'[75]

Spencer-Smith prayed, 'Oh God hear O Lord': 'Given light we should be at the Bluff tomorrow afternoon. "Domine Deus exaudi".'[76]

It was 17 February and the six men, one being the incapacitated Spencer-Smith on a sledge, were only 80 miles from the complete safety of Hut Point. Autumn was now closing in.

Chapter 12

'OR ELSE WE SHALL BE SHARING THE FATE OF SCOTT & HIS PARTY'

Hayward's diary table summarises the six days from 18 February:

18	Blizzard	81
19	do	81
20	do	81
21	do	81
22	do	81
23	do	81[1]

'Do' means ditto. They remained 81 miles from Hut Point. They did not move.

18 February 1916

On the first morning of the blizzard, they found conditions were too thick for travelling. It had been blowing a blizzard all night so they decided to wait and see if it would clear. With the dogs curled up in the snow outside their tents, the men lay in their sleeping bags and waited for the blizzard to stop. They were not perturbed and even thought the enforced rest might even be of some benefit. Spencer-Smith was the only one to portray any unease in his diary that day.

Wild:

> Blizzard. Nothing doing.[2]
>
> Strong wind from S.S.W. accompanied by much drift & heavy snowfall, making it impossible to get under way, at this time, & we had 3 days provisions in our bag & perhaps a gallon of kerosene for the 2 parties of course ample in an ordinary way on which to make the Bluff depot.
>
> Following our customary practice during lay ups we had to-day 2 meals only.[3]

Joyce:

> Turned out 5-30 found it too thick to carry on before. 8 o'clock it came on to blow very hard with drift. 1 Days lay-up although against our grain will not harm us especially the Skipper, he is keeping up pretty fair, better than we expected.[4]

Spencer-Smith: 'A real fierce blizzard all night and all day so we are still in situ quo. The wind – still howling – seems about the strongest I remember and almost carries a note of personal animus. This tent stands it magnificently.'[5]

19 February 1916

Richards wrote later that they were not really worried at this stage. They went onto half rations but the depot was only 10 miles ahead, and they expected the weather would soon lift and enable them to travel again.[6]

Joyce: 'Still Blizzarding. Put ourselves on 2 meals a day for case of emergency let us hope for a June day tomorrow.'[7]

Hayward: 'No apparent change in weather conditions, & we further decreased our rations, having all day 2 pots of hoosh between the 3 of us.'[8]

Spencer-Smith: 'Wind eased a bit between 9 and 10 but still very thick. No chance of travelling: last Primus full of oil began for supper tonight. Unutterably boring. Dogs ate biscuits. 80 left.'[9]

20 February 1916

For the six men, Joyce, Richards, Hayward in one tent, and Mackintosh, Spencer-Smith and Wild in the other, this was their third day of blizzard. During the blizzard they could not get out of the tent, so they had to stay in the tent to have what Richards termed their 'natural motions'. He tells us that the man needing to go to the toilet would say 'heads under' and the other two would put their heads under their sleeping bags. That man would get up and with a knife dig a square out of the snow and lift it out. In Richards's words he would 'have a bog there' and put it back again. Richards tells us it 'was perfectly odourless and quite all right'.[10] Spencer-Smith had to be helped by Wild.

They were starting to realise that their position was becoming serious. Their food was running out and the sick men were not improving. The dogs were weakening and they now had no more fuel for the primus cooker, but Wild seems to retain his sense of humour. The men wrote about their food supplies dwindling and running out of fuel but they rarely wrote about the abhorrent conditions inside their tents. Hayward, twelve months before, had described what it was like trying to sleep in a wet sleeping bag, describing his 'bag coated with frost inches thick, inside also frosty'. The bag became 'positively wet, as it became warmed' and he 'did not sleep a wink & felt like an old man of 290' when he got up, 'stiff & sore all over. It was hell.'[11]

Joyce :

Still blizzarding. Things are serious what with our patient + provisions running short. Let us hope for the best. Dog provisions nearly out. Have to half their rations. We are now on 1 cup of 'hoosh' amongst the 3 of us & 1 biscuit, 6 lumps of sugar.

No tea or cocoa. The most serious of calamities our oil is running out. We have

plenty of tea but no ammunition to cook it with.[12]

Wild: 'We are on one meal a day again, about the same place too.'[13]

Spencer-Smith noted it was the ninth Sunday before Easter: 'Septuagesima. Somewhat calmer in the morning, but as wild as ever in the afternoon. We are now on one hot meal per diem: any further desire to be satisfied with hard biscuit and chocolate.'[14]

21 February 1916

With no sign of a break in the weather their position had now become critical, although Wild continued to look at their situation in a light-hearted manner. They had reduced their daily rations to a quarter of a pint of pemmican and one biscuit. Their oil was exhausted, and the only way to get something warm was to pour some methylated spirit into a mug and ignite it, which Richards recalled as being a very slow process.[15]

Joyce :

Still blizzarding. We are living in pools of water made by our bodies through lying in the same place for such a long time. I don't know what we shall do if this does not ease. It has been blowing continuously without a lull.

We made one cup of pemmican amongst the 3 of us + 1 Biscuit each & 2 cups of tea divided.

Richards improvised a spirit lamp out of an enamel tray although it takes half an hour to melt 1 mug it. It is the means of keeping up our strength as we are getting very weak.[16]

Wild: 'Still reducing rations. I shall have to make more holes in my belt.'[17]

Spencer-Smith: '*Même jeu!*[*] And the barometer going down again, after a

---

[*]   '*Même jeu*' – the same game.

short rise – Cheer O! N.B. though not particularly hungry I keep on thinking of new milk, creamy butter, cheese, salad, new brown bread, and jam:
sometimes new laid eggs and pickles intrude – all at Althorne.'[18]

Hayward was still optimistic: 'Proceeded again as yesterday confident
that we should wear it down by the morning.'[19]

22 February 1916

The blizzard surpassed in length and fury anything Richards had experienced. He wrote later that it was impossible to see or communicate with
the other tent because of the howling of the wind. The snow was now
almost covering their tent, and exiting might be difficult. The drift had
banked up against the frail walls and gradually restricted the space inside.
Their three sleeping bags were crowded together side by side, and 'hour
after monotonous hour' was spent in them as the days went by. By this
time there was plenty of ice adhering to the hairs inside the bags and they
found real rest impossible.[20]

Their position on the Great Ice Barrier was ominously close to where
Captain Scott perished. On 19 March 1912, Scott, Wilson and Bowers
were camped just 11 miles from their next food depot, the One Ton Depot,
which was at latitude 79° 30´S. The six men of the Mount Hope Party
were camped 10 miles from their next food depot, the Minna Bluff depot,
which was close to latitude 79° S. Richards recalled some years later that
they knew scurvy had taken hold on them and one of the effects of scurvy
was to lose one's will-power.[21] He also related in one of his interviews that
he was thinking at this stage that 'it was very easy to die'. He added that
he had no thought of dying; only that it occurred to him that it was quite
easy to do so.[22]

On this day the food for the dogs ran out. For themselves they had only
one meal, to have just before they started again. Richards, Joyce and Hayward then decided they would just have to make the effort to reach the
Bluff depot, or they would suffer the same fate as Scott, who in Richards's
opinion lost his resolve to travel and died in his tent. They were aware

that they were held up just a few miles north of where Scott died, and that they were a similar distance away from their depot as Scott was from his One Ton Depot.[23]

Hayward: 'Still no let up of the blizzard, in fact it seems to have increased in fury and with more drift and we naturally began to realise the serious-ness of our situation and still further curtailed our ration.'[24]

Joyce:

> Same old thing. No easing of this Blizzard. I think it has come to stay. Hardly any food left except tea & sugar.
>
> Richards, Hayward + I after a long talk decided if possible to get under weigh tomorrow in any case or else we shall be sharing the fate of Scott + his party.
>
> The other tent seems to be very quiet now + again we have a burst of song from Ernie so they are in the land of the living.[25]
>
> We gave the dogs the last of their food tonight so we shall have to push on as a great deal depends on them.[26] We are keeping 1 feed of pemmican to get under way with.[27]

Wild's only note for the day: 'Have had two biscuits and a chunk of snow.'[28]

Spencer-Smith: 'Sleeping bag sopping wet. Slight rise of Bar. No hot meal. The lee-side of the tent is drifted up as high as the roof: it will be a great struggle to get out tomorrow – or the next day. But Wild did it!'[29]

23 February 1916 – a momentous day

At the end of six days with no progress, and the blizzard continuing, Joyce, Richards and Hayward talked the matter over again and they felt the six of them had to make the effort and get under way.[30] They knew they just had to march, no matter what risk of disaster might be involved, even though the wind and drift were still as violent as ever. Richards recalled that under normal circumstances they would not have contemplated travelling.[31]

Richards recalled that they had difficulty in making Mackintosh start as he believed they could not march in the conditions prevailing. To Richards that was correct but only for Mackintosh and Spencer-Smith. He and the three fitter men knew they could march and they just had to make a start that day.[32]

There was an incident with Mackintosh on the *Nimrod* Expedition in 1909 that bears a correlation to the situation he was now in. He and a colleague had become lost in the hills around Mount Erebus and were attempting to reach their hut, but found their way blocked by impassable crevasses. Mackintosh later wrote that it was his companion, a sailor, who took control of the situation, over him, the officer. Mackintosh admitted to being morose and dejected: 'I became despondent and did not care what happened,' he wrote in his diary. Mackintosh said the other man was in better spirits.[33] This aspect of Mackintosh's character, becoming despondent when under pressure, not caring what happens when in a tight situation and allowing a non-commissioned officer to lead, appears to have now resurfaced. Sixty years later Richards could remember the situation of 23 February 1916 and in his opinion Mackintosh had lost all initiative and was quite content to remain. He was not particularly anxious to move as he did not feel well; however, he agreed to make the effort.[34]

Fortunately the weather eased slightly mid-morning.

Hayward: 'About 10 o/c we made out the sun dimly shining through our tent & immediately started preparations for getting under way, although the wind had abated nothing & still very heavy low drift.'[35]

Joyce:

About 11 o'clock saw a break in the clouds + the sun showing decided to have the meal we kept for getting under way for.

Sung out to the Skippers party that we should shift as soon as we had a meal.

Skipper asked if we had any Pemmican to spare. I told him we were on our last bit. I asked Wild + found they had a bag of oatmeal some Bovril cubes + 1 bag of choc + 18 biscuits so they are much better than us.[36]

Spencer-Smith heard Joyce's call:

Still blowing – but at about 12 came a shout from the other tent 'She's breaking!' – and so we are having some hot Bovril and we are going to try to start.

Poor dogs! There's no food for them. They get snowed clean over and only occasionally emerge to howl a protest.[37]

Joyce:

After we had our meal we started to dig out our sledge which we found right under. It took us 2 hours one would hardly credit how weak we were two digs of the shovel + you were out of breath, this was caused through our laying up and practically no food.[38]

Hayward:

It took us (Joyce Richards & myself) over 2 hours to dig out sledge, during which process we discovered that we were very weak indeed, & had great difficulty in getting our breath. I must say that I have never experienced such weakness in my life before & we all attributed it to short rations & the ill effects consequent upon our inactivity.[39]

About 2 o/c we got everything stowed, with Smith wrapped up in the best manner possible, the drift & wind being more violent than at any other time during this blizzard, altho the Sun appears at times fitfully.

Before getting under way the Skipper complained at being unable to walk & we told him to tie on alongside the sledge, easing his weight by it.

The surface we found to be very soft & deep, & at frequent intervals the sledge bogged badly & in our weak state it was as much as we could do to restart her, the 4 dogs we have altho having been on short rations for some days, worked splendidly and were as ever of the greatest help.[40]

Richards:

Just set under way at 2 p.m. this day after totally unexpected lay up of 6 days. Commencing this period with little food we are now reduced very low indeed. Dog food has been totally exhausted tonight despite the fact that we have for a few days been to a certain extent denying ourselves that they may have a better chance.[41]

The afternoon of 23 February

It was after 2pm on 23 February before the six men and the four dogs had started towards the Minna Bluff depot, about 10 miles away. Richards wrote in *The Ross Sea Shore Party* that it was incredible weather and they 'couldn't see anything, and it was howling wind, difficult to stay on your feet'. They were 'lurching along' due to the force of the wind and from being so weak, having had little food for the past six days. The wind was buffeting everything, a whirling snow, 'a sort of milky whiteness that was over everything', and they found it difficult to even move the sledge.[42] Richards felt that they must have presented a pathetic sight as they staggered along in their traces. Spencer-Smith was lashed to the sledge in his sleeping bag and protected as far as they could manage from the whirling snow, while Mackintosh teetered along holding on to the sledge at its rear.[43]

Joyce tells us that within an hour Mackintosh collapsed and called out:

'Stop Joyce I cannot go any further– Just wrap me up in a deck cloth let me lie there in the snow'.

He told me he was not feeling fit as his legs were swollen black. I had a look at his gums they were also black. I think he has got scurvy.[44]

In Hayward's words: 'After covering perhaps ¾ m in what must have been somewhat over an hour, the Skipper declared himself done up & unable to proceed.'[45]

Richards:

> …the Skipper gave in and could not possibly go any further. He wished us to wrap him in a sheet and leave him. He has for weeks been suffering from a strained knee and bleeding from the bowels… The Skipper has completely gone. I had to hold him up to prevent him falling.[46]

Years later Richards remembered his conversation with Mackintosh:

> Mackintosh said, 'I can't go any further, I've got to stop'.
> We said, 'Don't be a bloody fool'.
> He said, 'Oh my hands, my hands'.[47]

Mackintosh, Spencer-Smith and Wild are left behind

Joyce now appears to take command of the party. He, Richards and Hayward discussed the situation and quickly decided that Mackintosh would have to stay while some of the others would push on to Minna Bluff. Richards remembered that all the fitter men made the decision, not simply Joyce. The conversation with Mackintosh was brief – they told him they would put the tent up and he would stay with Spencer-Smith and Wild. In Richards's recollection of events Mackintosh 'wasn't all there, mentally'. He recalled that they said to Wild: 'You've got to stay with him because you've been looking after them and we'll go on and see what we can do to get food.' They told Wild he had to stay because Richards, Joyce and Hayward were a compact party and were the obvious ones to go on.[48]

Richards wrote in his book that, given the conditions prevailing, there was no time for discussion and arguments and 'Wild accepted this decision

without comment'. It was essential that a fit man be left to look after the
sick men and as Wild had been looking after Spencer-Smith it appeared
at the time the obvious course to follow. Richards thought that, in hind-
sight, it might have been better to have taken Wild, leaving Hayward to
look after the two sick men, but they felt that Wild was the better man for
maintaining their morale.[49] They left practically all the food with Mackintosh, Spencer-Smith and Wild, which Joyce noted as '20 biscuits, no oil,
4 cubes of Bovril a little tea'.[50]

Joyce: 'I held a consultation amongst Wild + party decided to pitch
their tent leaving Wild to look after them + make the best way to the depot
which was anything up to 12 miles away.'[51]

Hayward: 'It was decided by all hands that the only thing for it, was to
leave the Skippers party (himself Smith & Wild in camp) whilst we carried on in an endeavour to make the Bluff Depot.'[52]

Richards:

> We had been immobilised for 6 days with blizzard. At the end of this period our
> tent party took the initative in deciding as the lesser of two evils to strike camp and
> endeavour to reach the Bluff Depot.
>
> Had gone no more than a few hundred yards when Mackintosh collapsed.
> We made a quick decision in impossible conditions to leave the two sick men
> with Wild who was well. I do not think he liked the idea but he was in their
> tent we told him he had to do it. I would have felt the same as Wild in the con-
> ditions prevailing.
>
> When their tent disappeared in a few moments after starting I rather thought we
> would never see them again.[53]

Joyce:

> I told Wild I should leave as much as possible and get back 26th or 27th – weather
> permitting.
>
> So we made them comfortable & left them about 3-40, but just as we left them
> it came on to snow pretty hard.[54]

The evening of 23 February for Joyce,
Richards and Hayward

The blizzard picked up again after the men separated but Joyce, Richards and Hayward struggled on and covered about 3 miles to the north. Under those conditions the heel of the leading foot was never placed beyond the toe of the other and the gain with each pace, two or three inches at most, was often lost by back-slipping as the weight was brought forward. When they came to a particularly soft spot, they could do little more than mark time.[55]

Richards was clearly bothered that they had left the three men behind, so much so he now started to keep a more detailed diary, starting this day, 23 February 1916. The reason, as he explained some years later, was that he was becoming concerned. First of all, when they left the others he had no idea whether they would ever see them again. He did not know whether they would even find the Minna Bluff depot. Secondly, his diary record would be his account of what had gone on, in addition to Joyce's diary. Richards remembered that he saw Joyce keeping a meticulous diary, writing it up every night, but in Richards's words: 'Joyce was just a little bit unreliable, inclined to draw the long bow and to embroider a bit at times'.[56]

On this day, 23 February, Hayward wrote over 300 words on the day's events, his first detailed diary entry for some weeks. He gave no reason for suddenly reverting back to his earlier ways of keeping a complete record of the day. Possibly he was now thinking like Richards and was worried about their chances of surviving, or the day may have been so momentous (leaving Mackintosh, Spencer-Smith and Wild behind) that he was inspired to start writing again. He continued this expansive diary-taking until he was back at Hut Point, but all his notes from now on were on the events of the day. There was only one more mention of his fiancée, on 7 March.

They were now losing the sun for four hours a day. That evening Joyce, Richards and Hayward had a tiny meal. Hayward could not understand why they couldn't sleep.

Joyce:

Sun going in & we found even with the 4 dogs we could not make more than ½ to ¾ miles per hour. The surface is that hard that sometimes you go in up to your waist still in spite of all this we carried on until 6-35.

Camped in a very howling blizzard. I found my left foot badly frostbitten. After this march, we have gone into our banquet – 1 cup of tea + half a biscuit. Sleeping bags wet through, but still cheerful living in hopes for it to clear up. Turned in 9 o'clock.

Situation does not look very cheerful + this is really the worst day's surface I have ever come across in all of my journeys here.[57]

Richards:

…We have left Smith, Wild and Mackintosh camped roughly 9½ mile from Bluff Depot. Our idea is to push on and try and pick up the Bluff Depot in time to save the lives of the dogs – our own too for that matter as we are out of food all round.

He added later:

Note: The reason for emphasizing that we are primarily concerned with saving the dogs was a selfish one; we knew we could not get back if they gave up.

The weather is still full blizzard and our travelling conditions do not favour rapid work nor good steering. This afternoon we did roughly three miles.

Haywood Joyce and self are weak and feel the effect of the lay up. Our gums are swollen and slightly black – mine seem to be shredding.[58]

Hayward:

Since the 21st we have had no kerosene & have been unable to use our Primus – Between us we have formulated a scheme whereby we heat our grub, what there is of it, (a cup of tea each & half biscuit) with methylated spirit, the process taking something like 2 hours & a half.

However we eventually turned in but found it impossible for some cause or causes unknown to sleep a wink.[59]

The evening of 23 February for Mackintosh, Spencer-Smith and Wild

Mackintosh, Spencer-Smith and Wild were in their tent, their first night of waiting, and hoping, for the return of the others from the Minna Bluff depot. Spencer-Smith compared Wild's gesture, to stay and look after he and Mackintosh, to a Charles Dickens character, Emma, in the book *David Copperfield*. (She is the long-suffering wife of Mr Micawber, whom she swears she will never leave despite his financial difficulties.)

Wild summed up their day:

> Made a start about 3 o'clock, then the Skipper went crook so we had to stop again.
> After a bit of a palaver the other three went on. I stopped behind with the invalids.
> They are going to the depot and are going to bring food and oil back to us.
>
> I'm afraid they will have to pack up though as it is blizzarding worse than ever.
> However I hope to see them in 3 or 4 days time. I wonder if I'm right.[60]

Spencer-Smith:

> After less than a mile – deep snow, terrible graft they say – poor Mac collapsed. Symptoms very much the same as mine: aggravated, of course, by the long enforced rest.
>
> It was decided almost at once that Joyce, party and dogs shall dash on as lightly loaded as possible and bring back grub and oil as soon as possible. We wanted Wild to go too but he stoutly refused to desert Mr Micawber. So here we three are with a few biscuits, a few sticks of chocolate, 2 'meals' of oil, a ¼ tin of methylated and a few oddments, vegetables, Bovril and lime juice tablets. The weather did not improve as the afternoon went on, so the others have probably not gone far yet.
>
> We had a great and glorious cup of tea (Te Sol!) to warm us up and sat up talking pretty late, the wind still howling.[61]

The six men were now in two parties. Joyce, Richards and Hayward with the dogs had travelled 3 miles north since leaving the others. Mackintosh, Spencer-Smith and Wild were tent bound, completely dependent on these three men returning from the Bluff depot.

Chapter 13

'WE ARE ABOUT ALL IN'

24 February 1916

JOYCE, RICHARDS AND Hayward had travelled 3 miles the evening before, and were now 6 or 7 miles from the Minna Bluff depot. In the morning they found the weather much the same with a heavy wind, estimated by Joyce to be about 60 miles an hour.[1]

Without paraffin for their primus the only way they could melt snow was in a mug over a dish burning methylated spirits. They still had some spirits which were used to start the primus. At an interview, many years after, Richards tells us: 'You know what methylated spirits is like, when you put a match to it, it goes up like that, well down there in the cold it's rather hard to light. You just sort of get a match on it and coax it to light.' When the water was warm they would put a few tea leaves into it. They could not boil the water using the methylated spirits. In Richards's words: 'it just wouldn't boil'.[2]

They were now at a critical moment in their journey – they just had to find the Minna Bluff depot, but they did not know how because in the blizzard they could not see anything. Richards remembered that the conditions were simply impossible and they had difficulty in even maintaining their footing during the worst of the savage gusts of a hurricane force wind.[3]

He also wrote later on the lack of visibility. They could only see a few yards and the sky was no different in appearance to anywhere else. There appeared to be no up or down and with zero visibility they had extreme difficulty in steering. They were attempting to find and follow the course along the line of cairns that had been placed when they went out to Mount Hope but they did not know where their line of cairns lay – they had lost them the day before the blizzard started.

Richards knew the bearings of the line of cairns, they were in his diary, having been taken on the way out to Mount Hope, but they did not know if they were to the right or the left of them. However, they knew that if they stayed parallel to the line of cairns, by steering on the known bearings, they would be close to the right course.[4]

Richards and Joyce worked together, as they had before when trying to steer in a blizzard. Joyce was on the end of a long rope and Richards would take a bearing and set him on the right line. Richards wrote in his book *The Ross Sea Shore Party* that bearings were not easy to take because he had to get his hands out of his mitts to hold the aluminium compass. 'It was a really painful business', in the cold, with bare fingers, and he could only manage to hold the metal of the compass for a few moments before it had to be put away so he could return his hands to his mitts.[5] After giving Joyce the direction with the rope they would judge the wind, which was coming from the south-east over their right shoulder, and try to maintain that same course, based on nothing but the direction of the wind. They would only go on for a short time, about a quarter or half an hour, halt, and Richards would take another reading.[6] Richards tells us there was nothing ahead but 'a white featureless void', and nothing to guide Joyce to keep a straight course. The best they could do was to see the way the rope lay in reference to the wind and try to maintain that angle.[7]

To make matters even worse, they no longer had their sledge-meter, which meant they did not know how far they had travelled each day. They had discarded it days before to lighten their load. This meant they did not know exactly where they were when stopped by the blizzard or how far they had travelled since they had left the others. He wrote later that in their weakened state they finally decided that they would allow about a quarter of a mile per hour for their progress, and in Richards's words, 'this turned out to be a surprisingly correct figure'.[8]

They were very weak and had difficulty in hauling the sledge in the deep snow, even though they now had very little load on; the tent, sleeping bags and some equipment. Although the three men and four dogs were only pulling a light sledge, Joyce tells us they struggled to even move it at times. (Two months earlier, in January, the same team pulled 1380 lbs, 10 miles a day).[9]

Joyce: 'Up at 4:30; had one cup of tea, half biscuit; under way after 7.'[10]

Richards: '3pm. Blizzard continued throughout the night. Rose at 4-45 and took 3 hours to get underway on account of the spirit having to serve as fuel.'[11]

Joyce:

> Richards, laying the cairns had great trouble in getting the compass within 10 degrees on account of wind.
>
> During the forenoon had to stop every quarter of an hour on account of our breath. Every time the sledge struck a drift she stuck in (although only 200 lb.) + in spite of three men + four dogs we could only shift her with the 1 – 2 – 3 haul.[12]

Richards:

> Marched till noon – saw one cairn …We did perhaps three miles this morning – going very heavy and we and dogs are weak. Blinding snowstorm continued this morning.[13]

24 February: 'lunch'

They had camped for lunch after five hours of hauling and it was as meagre as their breakfast. They planned to march on but the wind increased so they could not move. As they lay in their sleeping bags the three men, Joyce, Richards and Hayward, made a number of diary notes. They were now completely out of food, resorting to eating scraps of unused dog food in their dog-tank. Joyce later described it as the worst-tasting meal he had ever eaten, but 'it had to go down'.[14] The dog-tank was a canvas tank in which they used to keep the dog pemmican. Richards recalled later they were scraping that 'for crumbs and stuff like that' and putting it into hot water to get some sort of nutrient. In his mind they were 'just about starving, there's no question of that and very weak'.[15]

An easing in the conditions did come, but they were still unable to move.

Joyce: 'Camped in an exhausted condition about 12.10. Lunch. Half cup of weak tea + ¼ biscuit, which took over half an hour to make. With scrapings from dog-tank it is a very scanty meal.'[16]

Richards: 'With difficulty pitched camp owing to the extremely heavy wind and snow. Our tent is torn and threatens to run at any time.'[17]

Hayward:

> Ready to resume at 2.30, but before we were able to stow our gear away the wind came up from the SW with such violence accompanied by such violent drift we were driven back into our tent which fortunately we had not struck.
>
> During the short respite we were able to get our bags into the tent, everything being chock-a-block with snow and after some difficulty managed to get them spread and ourselves in.[18]

Joyce: 'Richards and Hayward went out of the tent to prepare for getting under way, but the force of wind and snow drove them back. The force of wind is about 70 to 80. We decided to get the sleeping-bags in, which took some considerable time.'[19]

Richards: 'We all feel cold this afternoon. After lunch cannot risk taking tent down as wind is so strong and drift so thick. We have taken bags inside and are awaiting a lull in conditions, and urgent as the need is we cannot face the weather.'

He added a note to his diary later: 'The urgency was to march to the Bluff depot and return with food to the three men left behind.'[20]

Joyce:

> The wind carried on with un-abating fury until 7 o'clock, and then came a lull. We at once turned out, but found it snowing so thickly that it was impossible to proceed on account of our weakness.

The worst of camping is the poor dogs and our weak condition, which means we have to get out of our wet sleeping-bags + have another ½ cup of tea without working for it.

This is the 2nd day the dogs have been without food, and if we cannot save the dogs it will be almost impossible to drag our two invalids back the 100 miles which we have to go.

No chance must we miss. Turned in again. Wind sprang up again with heavy drift 8.30.

In spite of everything my tent-mates are very cheerful and look on the bright side of everything. After a talk we decided to wait and turned in. It is really wonderful what dreams we have, especially of food. Trusting in Providence for fine weather to-morrow.[21]

Richards:

5pm.

Wind has now dropped but it has started to snow heavily. Had a meal of ¼ biscuit and cup of tea. Can see nothing in any direction and it would be folly to proceed as no course could be steered.

Later. Decided to remain camped till 3a.m. It is hard to know what course to pursue at times when a wrong decision means wasting the working efficiency from our meagre food. A false start means a meal wasted to a certain extent. It is very cold.[22]

Hayward was now becoming fearful:

We are in a very bad case indeed being practically without food and means for heating. We have no means of telling how far we are from the depot; in fact it seems to me that taking everything into consideration that it is going to be a very close call indeed.

The dogs have had nothing to eat for 2 days and if they crack up it will be very serious.[23]

24 February evening

Many years afterwards Richards could not remember if they even thought of Mackintosh, Spencer-Smith and Wild, or if they would even reach the Bluff depot. He thought that possibly the 'trials of the moment' were all that they could take in, and they did not look past those. They were weak and to all intents and purposes out of food and fuel; and the dogs seemed to have lost their spirit.[24]

On this evening he wrote in his diary a long summary of the events that had brought them to this predicament. He was unsure of his dates at times:

> 29 December 1915. Joyce, Haywood and Self, Gaze, Jack and Cope set out from Bluff Depot southward.
>
> Met Skipper and party two days out. In conversation Skipper and Wild admitted they had little hope of reaching 83-30 S. (Where the final depot for Shackleton on the Transcontinental journey was to be placed.) In written instructions to Joyce, Skipper directed that all hands should proceed to 81S, and from there Joyce, Haywood and Self were to continue to 82S, and beyond if possible.
>
> We arrived at 80S on 6 January 1916. The primus belonging to Gaze, Jack and Hayward had commenced to burn away at the top and Joyce decided instead of carrying on with the full party to 81, to send back Gaze Jack and Cope.[25]

Richards later added a note:

> The tents and primuses and a lot of other gear was what Scott had left behind and had been in service previously. When our ship was blown away in April 1915 it took all our sledging equipment with it. The second hand gear we were forced to use plagued us continually as in the case of the primuses and the unsafe condition of the tent.[26]

(In fact, not all their sledging equipment was on the *Aurora*. When the ship was taken away in May 1915 the men at Hut Point still had their gear.) Richards's field diary continues:

> Consequently we left 80S on 6 January with 12 weeks' provisions on sledge and enough dog food to bring us back to this position. First afternoon we did 5 miles, 1800 yds. Second day saw 10 miles recorded. That evening saw Skipper and party caught up to us at 11p.m. by means of a forced march… Skipper has a bad leg. We joined parties.
>
> The intention of the Skipper was I believe to take us with him to 82 S and then send us back – he to take the dogs on. Long before this position was reached it was

evident to our party that Skipper and Smith were done men and we had determined not to allow Wild to go on with Smith and Skipper. I understand that Smith and Wild brought pressure to bear on Mackintosh to the same end. However there was no question of separation of the parties, but if there had been we were determined not to allow the other party to go on as it would have meant suicide. The primus in the other tent gave out and prevented any separation whatever of the two parties. I give as my opinion that even had the primus been working satisfactorily the safest and best arrangement would have been for Skipper and party to have returned from 81S and we could lay the depot at 83 30.[27]

Richards added later: 'Note – the primus was the vital factor. Without it we would be without liquid and unable to cook.'[28]

24 February for Mackintosh, Spencer-Smith and Wild

This was day two for Mackintosh, Spencer-Smith and Wild, waiting for the return of Joyce, Richards and Hayward. The weather was uppermost on their minds.

Spencer-Smith:

Worse than ever outside. Wild went out for snow at midday, after clearing the door, and came back full of it and half blinded!

The sun has been shining all the morning too! Quite calm in the afternoon – the horizon faintly visible – so the other party may have reached the depot.

I think a good deal of foods of various kinds – ice-cream yesterday at the A. & N. C.S.L. with Mother and then again with Margaret.

Wild has contrived a 'methylated cooker' and we are having 'bijou' meals twice daily.[29]

Typically, Wild was matter of fact:

Wind has dropped & it's snowing like h __ l now. Can't see two yards.

Made a tiddly feed tonight using methylated spirits for a fire. Boiled up some

Julian* & used a Bovril cube with it & it was lovely. We have a proper tiddly stove now.

It's astonishing how weak you get in a week. My back & legs were aching like anything last night after that little bit of exercise. [30]

Joyce, Richards and Hayward –
25 February 1916

The blizzard continued and Joyce again compared their predicament to that of Scott, and his struggles with Wilson and Bowers to reach their One Ton Depot in 1912. Joyce knew they had to keep moving.

They covered about 3 miles in the morning and Richards had fond memories of the dogs at this time, especially Oscar. He wrote in an unpublished document titled 'Four Dogs' that although they now had little on the sledge, the dogs had lost their spirit. Three were losing heart, but in the crisis the massive Oscar just lowered his head and pulled as he never did when things were going well. He even at times got a bit of a run on the sledge and tried to bite the heels of the dog ahead to make him work. To Richards the dogs were just as individual as humans, and by this time they had become very close to them and recognised their every mood. They, like the men, had been very short on food for days. It seemed to Richards that Oscar was aware that they were looking for something that would give him a full meal once more. When things were going well he was inclined to be lazy, but in Richards's opinion it was 'no exaggeration to say that Oscar alone gave them that little extra strength' to keep going.[31]

Hayward:

Spent a hideous night, lack of food allowing cold to do its worst upon us. We all feel we are about all in and I am sure that unless the weather changes for the better immediately and allows us to take our bearings there will be very little hope of us getting in as we are rapidly getting weaker.

However, we get underway! And to add to our troubles our tent has developed

---

*   'Julian' – Julienne is the correct spelling – thinly sliced dried vegetables they carried.

a rent 3 ft long during the night, needless to say neither of us has sufficient energy to attempt to repair it.[32]

Joyce's actual diary for the day is barely legible:

> Turned out 4.45. Richards prepared our usual Banquet ½ cup of tea ¼ biscuit which we relished.
>
> Under way at 7 – carried on halting every 10 min or ¼ of an hour. Weather Snowing + blowing – same as yesterday.
>
> We are in a very weak state but we cannot give in. We often talk about poor 'Capt Scott' + the Blizzard that finished him + party. If we had stayed in our tent another day I don't think we should have got under way at all + shared the same fate. Anyone would go to Hell for pasture after this.
>
> But if the worst comes we have made up our minds to carry on, on the trek + die in harness.
>
> If anyone were to see us on trek they would be surprised – 3 men staggering on with 4 dogs very weak; practically empty sledge with fair wind + just crawling along. Our clothes are all worn out & finescoes + sleeping bags torn. Tent is our worst point, all torn in front + we are afraid to carry on a/c of it + it is too cold to mend it [33]

Hayward: 'Joyce leading sets a good pace, the dogs especially Gunner, Oscar and Towzer are struggling on gamely, they seem to realise as much as we do ourselves.'[34]

Richards: '4a.m. Turned out and had ½ biscuit and tea. Wind has sprung up and nothing can be seen.'[35]

'Lunch' – 25 February 1916

At their lunch stop, they had no idea where they were and no idea where the Minna Bluff depot was. Richards did not want to travel on any further. He tells us he said to the others: 'Look, there's no use going on, we may overshoot the depot. We might as well wait here and see what happens.' He does not know whether they would have lasted much longer, saying in an interview decades later that if they had to go another day he did not know whether they would have been able to see it out.[36]

They did discuss eating the dogs, for their own survival, but realised such an action would not have saved their lives. Richards remembered it was the only time they thought of eating the dogs but without them they would not have been able to reach the Bluff depot, so they discarded that idea. They realised that if even they ate only one dog they would be signing their own death warrant – they could not make progress without the help of four dogs.[37]

25 February had been a day with no food, except a piece of biscuit and half a cup of warm tea for breakfast, another small piece of biscuit and some warm tea for lunch. They had travelled about 3 miles on the 23rd, 3 on the 24th and possibly 3 the morning of the 25th. They thought they must be close to the Minna Bluff depot.

Hayward outlined their morning progress:

12 o/c noon. Have done perhaps 2½ to 3 miles, there is nothing to see on which to steer & it has been snowing more heavily than ever, & we still have no idea as to where the depot lies.

At 2.30 pm at which time we had managed to obtain a warm cup of tea & hoped to proceed, the snow was thicker than ever accompanied by very strong wind, & we could not move. I hope we can make the depot before we are forced to pitch again. Our pace is approx. ¾m per an hour, quite knocking us out.

There is nothing to see on which to turn and it has been snowing more heavily than ever and we still have no idea where the depot was. [38]

Richards:

Later noon. Sun through murk … at times in the morning. Heavy wind and heavy snowfall and we do not know how we stand in regard to the depot or whether in thick weather we have strayed from the course. We are very weak.

The Canadian huskies are working pluckily but obviously weak and they have had no food for 2 nights. Con very groggy.

The weather is now thickening again and the wind very strong. The method of cooking entails … a loss of a good deal of time. A meal … takes a lot of preparation and at the end the warmth of the tea does not stay with one for very long.

Later. This afternoon we had perhaps the heaviest snowfall in this blizzard accompanied by heavy wind. Impossible to travel in this so have decided to camp till storm abates.[39]

We sat down in the tent to wait, as though our rough reckoning of distance had led us to believe that to go further might put us beyond the depot.[40]

Joyce:

We camped after our grand lunch at noon after 5 hours struggling I think we done about 3 miles. After lunch sat in our tents talking over the situation decided to get under way again as soon as soon as there is any clearance. Snowing + blowing force about 50 or 60. I do not think we will be able to pitch camp again.

Richards sang us his old Australian college song.[*41]

Three other men continue to wait

Mackintosh, Spencer-Smith and Wild could do nothing but stay in their tent. They were 81 miles from Hut Point, but only 10 miles south of the Bluff depot, from where they hoped Joyce, Richards and Hayward would soon return, to save their lives.

All Spencer-Smith could write was: 'Blizzard again!'[42]

But Wild was optimistic: 'Blowing worse than ever and snowing all the time. I hope the others reached the depot yesterday. Then they will be able to feed up. This ought to be the final blow now before it clears.'[43]

---

* There was no other reference to the 'college song'. It may have been The Melbourne Teachers College song at Melbourne University, where Richards studied.

Joyce, Richards and Hayward – 26 February 1916

On the morning of the 26th, four days after leaving their three colleagues, Joyce, Richards and Hayward were in a critical situation. They were now completely without food and they knew this day might have been their last if they had not reached the depot. [44]

However that morning (at 1 a.m. it was light enough to see) the weather cleared early and they could see the depot. On reaching the Bluff depot they knew, to quote Richards from an interview, 'we were in clover'. They could eat as much food as they liked because the depot was well stocked with plenty of food for Shackleton and themselves. [45] They made the decision to rest up and recover before heading back to pick up Mackintosh, Spencer-Smith and Wild. In addition, their tent was one of Scott's old tents and a few small rips had appeared. The steam from the cooking used to freeze on the tent and they had been desperately frightened one of the rips would tear completely. They fixed the rips using a canvas food bag with Joyce sewing from the inside and one of the others outside. [46] The tears in their tent had to be fixed before they could start back.

Richards remembered that it was at the Bluff depot where he first saw that Hayward could not straighten his legs. They were blue and black at the back so Richards started rubbing methylated spirits on them. [47] He wrote in his book that Hayward's condition was worse than that of either Joyce or himself, although he and Joyce had some stiffness and discoloration behind the knees and on the gums. Richards recalled that by then Hayward was more or less ineffective as a unit of the party; he had broken down. [48]

At the Bluff they had expected to find some news of the *Aurora*. It had been arranged with Stevens to leave a message at the Minna Bluff depot but there was no news. Richards tells us he felt 'somewhat gloomy' as he had hoped the ship might have returned to Cape Evans and sent a party out to the Bluff. They did not speculate a lot about what might have happened to the *Aurora*. They simply guessed she hadn't come back and thought they might be in Antarctica for another winter. But uppermost on Richards's mind was their own predicament, in that they still had to reach the safety of Hut Point. When interviewed many years afterwards he could not remember even saying 'well now we've got food we're alright' because they knew they had another 90 miles to go – 10 to go back and pick up the other three men and then 80 to Hut Point. He knew that would be a very hard 90 miles.[49]

Joyce:

Saturday 26th AM: Richards went out 1-10 and found it clearing a bit, so we got under way as soon as possible. At 2.25 Richards sighted the depot which looked like a mountain right on top us.

I suppose we camped no more than ¾ of a mile from it. The dogs sighted it which seemed to electrify them they had new life + started to run but we were that weak that we could not go more than 200 yds then spell.

I think another day would have seen us off.[50]

Hayward:

Unspeakable night. At about midnight weather cleared somewhat & we decided to get under way & we each knew that it would be the last time, in the event of our not making the depot.

Imagine our feelings when we found on a break occurring that we had been camped within a short distance of the depot which we made in somewhere under an hour, all absolutely played out, but thankful indeed for our deliverance.[51]

They struggled to cover the short distance to the depot.

Richards:

Under way at 2.am. Fairly heavy drift and thick weather. Shortly after start saw the depot practically ahead. We had been camped within ¾ mile of it and could not have seen it through thick weather.

We could not even travel more than a few yards without halting so short was our wind. Dogs bucked up at sight of depot but are weak.[52]

Years later, he modestly said: 'I laid the course and to this day I don't know how we did it, I really don't know.'[53]

Joyce:

> Arrived at Depot 5-25 found it in a dilapidated condition. Cases all about the place. I
> don't suppose there has ever been a weaker party arrive at any Depot either N. or S.
>
> After a hard struggle got our tent up + made camp then gave the dogs a good
> feed of Pemmican.
>
> If ever dogs saved the lives of anyone they have saved ours let us hope they will
> continue in good health so that we can get out to our comrades.[54]

Richards: 'Decided to halt here till dogs have had a couple of meals as it
would be fatal to them to turn … too soon and we depend on them for the
lives of Mackintosh and Smith.'[55]

Joyce:

> I started on our cooking. Not one of us had any appetite although we were in
> the land of plenty, as we call this Depot, plenty of Biscuit etc we could not eat.
> We decided to have Oatena* + milk for a start which went down very well + then
> a cup of tea.
>
> How cheery the Primus sounds, it seems like coming out of a thick London fog
> into a drawing room. After a consultation we decided to have a meal of pemmican
> in 4 hours + so on until our weakness was gone.[56]

Hayward found it surprising they were not hungry:

> We camped immediately, afterwards preparing a meal which strange to relate we
> could not go being quite past hunger. The dogs apparently did not suffer similarly
> as they easily disposed of the heavy feed given them.
>
> We turned in for 3 or 4 hours then had another go with rather more success & a
> still further attempt about 10 o/c showing marked improvement.[57]

Joyce adds: 'Mended our torn tent with food bags – this took 4 hours.
Feeding the dogs every 4 hours + Richards + Hayward built up a Depot.

---

*   'Oatena' is rolled oats.

It is really surprising to find it takes 2 men to lift a 50 lb case. It only shows our weakness.'[58]

Richards:

> We occupied the day in a rest and several meals very light in amount but at fairly
> short intervals … Joyce spent afternoon mending tent. This was most pressing job
> as if we needed to pitch camp again in a blow tent would rip to pieces before we
> could get it up.[59]

They packed the sledge, planning to head back south early the next morning.

Richards: 'Hayward and Self arranged depot stores and stores to take back to the other party. The depot was in an untidy condition and took considerable digging out. Weather is dull and heavy wind and drift continues. We intend to start at 5am tomorrow on a forced march back.'[60]

Hayward:

> Weather shows very little improvement but we hope to be in a fit condition enough
> providing the weather is at all reasonable to start back to the relief of the Skippers
> party at 5 o/c AM tomorrow.

> We are still very much troubled by weakness & shortness of breath but hope this
> will pass in due course, with full rations.[61]

Richards noted the deterioration in Hayward's condition: 'Hayward complains of stiff legs under knees. This was where the others (Smith and Skipper) first felt symptoms of their disorder. I hope for all our sakes that he has nothing of this sort. We must go carefully.'[62]

Joyce knew Hayward had scurvy: 'Poor Hayward collapsed. He had been getting weaker & tried to be cheerful but one could see he would not have lasted much longer. Hayward's legs are black & I am afraid he has Scurvy. Richy massaged him, rubbing in methylated spirit, which seemed to ease him.'[63]

A forlorn postscript ended Hayward's diary entry for the day: 'PS: There is no news here of the *Aurora* which needless to say is not exactly cheering.'[64]

Richards: 'No sign of a party here from the ship. I fear she has gone down probably with all hands.'[65]

Joyce recorded two entries on the weather during the night: 'Later – still the same weather. We shall get under way a make a forced march back as soon as possible I think we shall get stronger travelling + feeding well. Later – weather will not permit us to travel yet. Weather still the same force of wind at times about 70 to 90 really surprising how this can keep up for so long.'[66]

Mackintosh, Spencer-Smith and Wild wait, optimistically

Ten miles away to the south, Wild was heartened by the weather clearing:

Cleared up a bit today. Saw the Bluff in the afternoon & can see it now. (7pm).

Went out and built a cairn and put some black bunting on it as our tent only shows about a foot above the snow. The others will reach the Depot easily today and I should think I shall expect them the day after tomorrow, although they might do it tomorrow.[67]

And Spencer-Smith was confident:

Calm this morning. Wild built a cairn and cleared the tent front. Horizon in view all day and even the Bluff at times. Blowing a bit and drifting, but Bluff still in sight, so the other party should be in safety now, if not two days ago.

Great argument yesterday with Wild who stated that every word in the English language bar one had its rhyme. I took him up quite literally and had a good fight. Smoked two pipes of tea to-day: O.M. 2 cigarettes.[68]

Their food worries now resolved, Joyce, Richards and Hayward were recovering at the Minna Bluff depot before heading back south, although Hayward was starting to weaken. Mackintosh, Spencer-Smith and Wild could do nothing but wait, and hope.

Chapter 14

'WE HAVE HAD THE
CLOSEST OF CLOSE CALLS'

27 February 1916

I T WAS STILL a blizzard on the morning of 27 February and Joyce, Richards and Hayward were unable to get away from the Bluff depot. They could nothing but lie in their sleeping bags and wait. Hayward wrote diary notes but there was no reference to his fiancée.

Richards:

> Wind hurricane force and heavy drift. Impossible to see anything. We are now all sitting on our bags waiting. Dogs and men could not face this even if a course could be steered. This is awful – held up here knowing that the three men are starving and worse deathly cold 10 or 12 miles back. This is the 10th day of the blizzard.
>
> Our gums are swollen this morning, especially Haywood's.[*] His knee he says is a bit better but he can hardly walk …[1]

---

[*] Richards often wrote 'Haywood' in his diary instead of 'Hayward'.

Hayward:

After a short lift in the weather which occurred about 6 o/c pm yesterday eve – giving us cause to hope that we could carry out our intention of moving this morning as planned, – the wind again came very strong from the S.W. with drift starting approx at 10.30 pm.

We are very much disturbed to find that so far (10 o/c AM) it is a matter of physical impossibility to attempt to get under way the wind having abated nothing, if only we had to travel N we would have a cut at it but our return course would take us right into the teeth of it, & one can imagine what it would mean to travel into a cold wind of terrific force, with drift so thick as to prevent one seeing anything outside a radius of a few yds, even the dogs could not face it.

At the same time it is very distressing to have to remain here inactive realizing the serious condition of the party awaiting our return.[2]

Joyce:

Weather continued with fury the whole night, expecting every minute to have the tent blown off us. Up 5 o'clock found it so thick one could not get out of the tent.

We are still very weak but think we can do the 12 miles to our comrades in one long march. If only it would clear up for just one day we would not mind.

This is the longest blizzard I have ever been in that is to continue. We have not had a travelling day for 11 days + the amount of snow that has fallen is astonishing.[3]

Found the door of the tent blocked with snow. Had a hard job to get out. Could not see the dogs or sledges as they were completely buried under. Could only tell where the dogs lay by the round holes where they were breathing. After digging them out, made breakfast.

We are eating much better & one can feel themselves getting stronger. Turned in our bags again which is the only comfort we have, and they are wet through.[4]

27 February 1916

The dogs were crucial to their efforts to return and save the three other men, but they did not want to go back south. Richards thought that the dogs seemed to know instinctively they were going the wrong way and so they had to drive them north and slowly work them around to the south.[5] They worked until late that night, then believing they were over halfway to the others.

Joyce:

Later had a meal 10-30 decided to get under way in spite of the wind + snow.

Under way 12 o'clock. We have three weeks' food on sledge, about 160 lb., and one week's dog-food, 50 lb. The whole weight, all told, about 600 lb., and also taking an extra sledge to bring back Mac.

To our surprise we could not shift the sledges. After half an hour we got about ten yards. We turned the sledge up and scraped runners; it went a little better after. I am afraid our weakness is much more than we think.

The dogs have lost all heart in pulling; they seem to think that going south again is no good to them; they seem to just jog along, and one cannot do more.[6]

Richards:

After heavy snow and wind this morning signs of a break appeared at 10am. Had a meal and commenced to get underway at noon or thereabout. Took a good deal of time in starting sledge. Heavy wind blowing and drift. Dogs have no heart. Sledge took half an hour to start, though very light. Cleaned runners and made it a bit easier. Dogs unsettled and two fights occurred before starting. We got them apart in time...[7]

Hayward:

To add to our troubles the dogs seem to have lost heart in their work and all the whipping possible making no impression on them. They do not like the idea of turning again when they imagined they were on the trail for home & food. For some reason or other they engaged in a pitched battle shortly after starting & we all three were absolutely exhausted when at last we were able to part them.

About 9 o/c pm clouds at Zenith rolled away, & moon showed itself & we were expecting weather to clear permanently but within a very short period it shut down again & commenced snowing terribly.

We were very pleased to be able to seize an opportunity of getting under way presented by weather lifting slightly at noon, the wind was still strong & colder.

We were badly disappointed to find that altho we had a light load comparatively it was as much as we could do to shift it & our progress was irritatingly slow; there is no disguising the fact that we are still very weak.[8]

Joyce: 'I don't suppose our pace is more than ½ or ¾ of a mile per hour. The surface is rotten, snow up to one's knees + what with wind and drift a very bad outlook. Lunched about 4.30.'[9]

At the day's end Hayward was at the end of his tether:

We continued till 11 pm when it was quite impossible to steer through it & we were forced to camp & for my part I felt I could not have gone much further a feeling shared by my tent mates.

During the time we were travelling I should say we covered about 5½ miles.

Midnight. Wind has dropped & we intend to resume at 6 o/c AM.[10]

Richards:

The weather was again too thick to enable us to pick up our cairns and we had to steer in the same hit or miss fashion as on the trip to the depot.[11]

Worked until 11pm. One of the hardest days I have put in. Dogs have no heart for South journey now. When we camped too dark to steer. Weather dull but wind dropped.[12]

Joyce:

Hayward is in rather a bad way about his knees, which are giving him trouble and are very painful; we will give him a good massage when we camp. It was very dark making our dinner, but soon got through the process.

Then Richards spent an hour or so in rubbing Hayward with methylated spirits, which did him a world of good. If he were to break up now I should not know what to do. Turned in about 1.30. It is now calm, but overcast with light falling snow.[13]

Day Five for Mackintosh, Spencer-Smith and Wild

Mackintosh, Spencer-Smith and Wild now had very little food left and had nothing to write about as they lay in damp and sticky clothes inside their wet sleeping bags. Their sleeping bags froze if they were not lying inside them. During the day they spent most of their time toggled up inside their bags, with half-frozen fingers, listening to the ice crackling. Then drops of thawing ice would fall on their faces. At night it was dark and cold in the tent and as the night wore on the temperature would drop and they would start to shiver. A puddle of water would form underneath their body and it would be ice cold on top. They dozed off now and again but only for an hour or two at a time.[14]

Wild kept his sense of humour: 'Little difference, it clears up a bit now & then.

We have just got a dishy feed left for tomorrow & then we shall have to take after that Yankee fasting man if the others don't appear. My belly is singing "Rule Britannia" now.'[15]

Spencer-Smith:

> Very fierce blizzard during night – eased a great deal during the day. Wild burrowed out thro' great mass of drift at door.
>
> Sexagesima. D.V. the others will be back some time tomorrow, as we are on our last bijou rations or thereabouts. Very cold and wet and weak but not dead yet by any means, thank God.[16]

28 February 1916

Joyce's footwear was causing problems and Richards noticed that he now had symptoms of scurvy, but they travelled for three hours in the morning before the blizzard came on again. Richards then reckoned, by the number of hours they had marched, that they would be somewhere in the vicinity of the other camp, and that it would have been folly to proceed further. He remembered that they even shouted 'in the remote hope that they could be nearby'. They stayed in their tent and looked out at intervals to see if anything could be seen.[17] They knew the others must be nearby, but they could not see far.

Richards:

> Under way at 9am. Rose at 6am. Three hours taken to get under way because of bad gear. I suspect we were pretty slow too, owing to our condition.
>
> Joyce has finnesco with more hole than boot and yesterday suffered with snow filling up the finnesco. It was impossible to mend last night on account of lack of light.
>
> I spent ¼ hour this morning and ½ hour last night rubbing Haywood down with meth. spirits. He says, and it seems too by his walking, that the rubbing did him a lot of good.
>
> I am sorry to find that I have the dreaded black appearance on the back of my leg although up to the present it has given little trouble. I don't know whether it's scurvy or not but remembering that Smith, Skipper and Haywood each was affected there first it makes for unrest.[18]

Hayward adds: 'Start unavoidably delayed by necessity of repairing our gear which is in a terrible condition. Joyce suffering a frost bitten foot yesterday on account of his finneskoe being full of holes.'[19]

And Joyce: 'The reason of delay – had to mend finneskoe, which are in a very dilapidated condition. I got my feet badly frost-bitten yesterday.'[20]

Richards: 'We worked from 9 until a little after noon. For a start it was dull but clear on horizon. At about 10.30am the outlook was thick everywhere and steering became difficult. We camped at about noon in midst of heavy snowstorm and moderate wind.'[21]

Hayward:

> Worked three hours which should put us in the vicinity of Skippers tent.
>
> It has been blowing hard & snowing heavily all the morning & camped in weather so thick as to preclude all idea of picking up any object further than a few yards away, we are therefore obliged to wait, keeping a look out for a break which might allow us to locate the party, who must be within a mile of us.[22]

Joyce: 'I think the party must be within a very short distance, but we cannot go on as we might pass them, and as we have not got any position to go on except compass. Later: Kept on blizzarding all afternoon and night.'[23]

Richards was now apprehensive: 'It is distressing to arrive here within reach and be prevented rendering aid on account of the thick weather. We can only sit still looking out at intervals of 10 minutes or so.

'I fear what we may find on arriving.'[24]

As was Hayward:

It is impossible to describe ones feelings in this matter, here we are waiting to help these men & unable to do so, as the result of our good fortune of making the Bluff Depot, although under distressing conditions & yet unable to say in which direction they are camped from us even if the weather permitted us to travel, yet we are sure that it would take us no more than an hour or so to relieve them under conditions the slightest bit favourable.[25]

Richards:

7pm. Afternoon passed with no break in weather. Heavy snow and moderate wind. Can see nothing. Have shouted but no response.

We are standing by ready to start on the instant. I am watching the weather while Joyce and Hayward are trying to get a little sleep but with not much success.

I know I cannot sleep with the thought of these men starving and cold within perhaps a very short distance of help.

One keeps wondering how it will all end.[26]

The evening of 28 February 1916

In a long diary entry Richards recounted what had happened over the past few weeks. He was particularly struck by the break-down of Mackintosh but he lays the blame for their troubles with his Skipper.

Richards:

The pity of it is that Mackintosh did not realise the folly in passing 81S with Smith. I can see the two of them in my mind's eye neither able to pull much and both walking as I have seen Hayward and as I fear I will be shortly do myself…

… Then the long march back towing Smith on the sledge. The obvious agony of the skipper during some of the long marches, the slackening of pace before 80. The hard gruelling from 80 onwards reducing us to 7 miles a day, and then the great blizzard. Until then I believe most of our party were unaware of the full extent to which our heavy season had affected us. But that lay up searched out our weaknesses – shortened wind – knocked Hayward and broke the Skipper up completely.

I have never been so profoundly impressed with a change in a man's condition as that of the skipper after we struck camp on 23 Feb. His face was changed and he could scarcely walk and in a broken voice he said he would have to tie on to the sledge behind instead of pulling in the trace. We all had a struggle that afternoon – blinding drift and deep soft snow and we were weaker than ever. Then the Skipper's collapse … He kept saying 'Oh my hands are gone' and then 'I'm done' 'I'm done' over and over again and 'I don't care what happens'. I tried to comfort him a little. Poor Wild I was sorry for. I don't think he wanted to stay, but it was necessary to have one whole man to look after the two sick men. And so he stayed. And then our nightmare in making the depot – starved and through it all the blizzard never or practically never easing. And now we are here waiting for this nightmare to cease.

And this stems from the end of Mackintosh's folly in going South when done himself and in the company of other done men.[27]

Richards concludes with an explanation as to why he made the notes: 'I have written this down more to keep my mind occupied than anything else, putting on paper the thoughts passing through my mind. And now it's too cold on the fingers so I'll stop.'[28]

Mackintosh writes a 'Farewell Letter'

28 February was the sixth day of waiting for Mackintosh, Spencer-Smith and Wild. They had little food left.

Spencer-Smith:

At the most two very scratch meals to come.

A flat calm at 8 p.m. last night continued until about midday today and then to our great disappointment everything became obscured and so no help arrived. But the Bar. is rising and we are not downhearted yet. God's in His Heaven!'[29]

Wild: 'Another day gone & also all the scraps. The weather was clear this morning but blizzarding again a bit now and beaten Scott's record.* We have had an eleven day blizzard and are only nine miles from depot.'[30]

We have some insight to Mackintosh's thoughts at this time. On this day, 28 February 1916, he wrote a long note, possibly fearing that he might soon die. He explained their plight, and that he was not 100 per cent confident that help would come. He attempts to exonerate himself from any blame, writing in positive terms on their efforts and in particular Wild's behaviour. He acknowledges that he and Spencer-Smith succumbed to scurvy before the others, because of a lack of fresh food.

His words have an eerie similarity to some of Scott's last letters, and in particular to a short note Scott wrote titled 'Message to the Public'. As he lay dying in his tent in March 1912, Scott wrote up his journal, plus a number of letters; to his mother, his wife, Wilson's wife, Bowers's mother, Admiral Sir L. Beaumont, and Sir J. M. Barrie amongst others. In 'Message to the Public' he wrote that it was misfortune, not any fault on his part, that caused his expedition to fail. Scott stated that his logistical planning had 'worked out to perfection' but the loss of pony transport which resulted in a late start, the poor weather and the soft snow were events that they could not overcome.[31]

This is Mackintosh's long note:

I have this record in the event of anything happening to this party. Today we have finished the last of our food. A blizzard has been blowing 11 days. With the exception of 1 day when the wind fell light where horizon could be discerned as well as land around the Bluff.

---

* It is not clear exactly what Wild meant with this 'Scott's record' reference, possibly the number of days of the blizzard. However, Scott's journal of 1912 states the blizzard that halted him, Wilson and Bowers also went on for more than eleven days.

We were left here 4 days previously in order that Messrs Joyce, Hayward & Richards could travel with dogs & light sledge to Bluff Depot more easily returning to us with food of which there is a plentiful supply at the Bluff.

We now expect from that succour to reach us anytime from today in which case we will be saved from starvation & these lines unnecessary.

Yet I take precaution to leave this should I later become too weak & the cold make it harder to write.

Smith & myself are struck with scurvy – the former being helpless & weak. I am able to stand about yet becoming more feeble daily. Wild has signs of scurvy but is able to move his hands & feet & with a meal could travel, & this I am afraid cannot be the same for Smith & self.

We have not given up hope yet by any means, we trust in our comrades. We argue, say – talk cheery today and anyone coming along would imagine to be some picnic party.

(This was similar to Scott, who in one of his final letters wrote: 'It would do your heart good to be in our tent, to hear our songs and the cheery conversation as to what we will do when we get to Hut Point.'[32])

Now it may be wondered what has brought us to our present position. Briefly & I feel glad to say it has not been through any lack of organisation.

(Again, this was like Scott, who wrote: 'The causes of the disaster are not due to faulty organisation.'[33])

We have done the work we came down to do, this laying of a depot at Mt Hope, 82°, 81°, 80° for Sir Ernest Shackleton.

(Scott: 'It will be known that we have accomplished our object in reaching the Pole.'[34])

We made splendid progress homeward travelling as much as 10 miles a day & this with Smith on sledge. We filled up with a fortnight's provisions at 80° as our own experience had worried us against this region. Instead of doing the trip in a week we have had 17 days getting to within 9 miles of our own Bluff depot on 18 Feb since which date we have been camped.

With the exception of Smith we were all able to travel until the blizzard came upon us when we laid up 6 days after that period when we made a fresh start. I had to admit defeat owing to my inability to stand the strain. It is laying up that is making me weaker, legs black & blue, gums swollen & black.

The above roughly explains how we left here Wild who could have gone on preferred to remain & help us, the good unselfish fellow that he is.

It must be explained that with the exception of the first trip from Bluff we have had no fresh food since 9 October hence the disease has taken a stronger hold on us than the other party who had the opportunity of reaching Hut Point.

But I leave it on record all have done their duty nobly & well. This is all I can say & if it is God's will that we should here give up we do so in the true British fashion my own tradition holds us in power to do.

(Scott: 'We have no cause for complaint, but bow to the will of Providence, determined still to do our best to the last ... which would have stirred the heart of every Englishman.'[35])

Scott finished his 'Message to the Public' note with: 'Surely, a great rich country like ours will see that those who are dependent on us are properly provided for.'[36] Mackintosh finished with: 'Goodbye friends. I feel sure our people, my own dear wife & children will not be neglected.'[37]

(Scott's final journal entry was: 'For God's sake look after our people.'[38])

In addition to this note, Mackintosh also wrote a letter, to his brother George. Once again, the words and sentiments expressed in this most personal letter are strikingly similar to Scott's final letters to his friends.

28 Feb: 1916. The Ice Barrier – My dear old George

Well, old man, it's come to this – at least it looks like it. That I have to say farewell to my kith & kin, to peg out on this god-forsaken hole, with youth and hope cast aside.

However I pray for my own ideas. I had visions that all would go well with us when I returned having accomplished something, to have kept my beloved darlings in comfort & worthy to the state of life they ought to be brought up in instead of the drudgery & hand to mouth existence we lived, but now it seems I did not know when I was well off! Ah! Well, dear George, I have not time or is it a place here to write much, so must be brief. You have ever been too good to me. I know you will have a watchful eye on my ones. I feel sure too that they will not be neglected by those who know us. Good luck to you. May you meet as loving & dear a soul as I now lose – God keep you – is the last wish & farewell from your brother

Aeneas [39]

These were Mackintosh's final written words that have survived. His main expedition journal, which he started in October 1915, has never been found.

29 February 1916

On the morning of 29 February the weather cleared, enough for Richards to spot the other party's tent. He recalled that in the morning they rolled up their sleeping bags and sat inside the tent. From time to time they would go outside the door to have a look and then one time he 'saw this little dark spot to the south'. In Richards's mind they had 'accomplished something that at times had seemed to us to be quite impossible'.[40]

It took them a few hours to reach the others' camp, where Wild and then Mackintosh came out of the tent. In an interview in 1976 Richards tells us about Wild. When Wild heard them coming he came out of the tent, put on his canvas harness and walked out to meet Joyce, Richards and Hayward. He then tied his harness onto their sledge and helped them pull it the last short distance. Richards tells us that Wild did this without any emotion or fanfare. He simply wanted to give them a hand in.[41] Richards knew that Wild, Spencer-Smith and Mackintosh might have had a day's food when they were stopped by the blizzard, because he, Joyce and Hayward had one day's food left. So these three men had now been without food for a number of days. Richards believed that nine out of ten men would have simply stood at the door of the tent and said 'Thank God', but not Wild.[42] Richards said later: 'We had had three days of food by then while he had just about been out of food for six days. Several of us broke down and cried at his action.'

Richards says he never forgot how he felt at this time, and he even became overcome with emotion in an interview when relating Wild's actions, and this was sixty years after the event. Richards thought that Wild's action was incredible, something he could not put a name to. He simply described it as 'courage or just spirit'.[43]

Spencer-Smith's condition had not improved. Richards thought he might not have even survived because he was so weak when they had left him six days before.[44] Mackintosh tried to walk ahead while the others lifted Spencer-Smith up onto a sledge.

Joyce: 'It cleared up a little to the south about 8 o'clock, when Richards sighted something black to the north of us, but could not see properly what it was. After looking round sighted camp to the south, so we got under way as soon as possible.'[45]

Hayward:

Weather slightly better @ 6 o/c AM we started preparations for getting under way. We were overjoyed on the weather clearing considerably to see the camp, apparently not very far ahead, the going was very heavy & it took us considerably longer than we had anticipated to reach it.[46]

Joyce sets the scene:

Got up to the camp about 12.45, when Wild came out to meet us. We gave him a cheer, as we fully expected to find all down. He said he had taken a little exercise every day; they had not any food left.

The Skipper then came out of the tent, very weak + as much as he could do to walk. He said, 'I want to thank you for saving our lives'.

I told Wild to go + give them a feed + not to eat too much at first in case of reaction, as I am going to get under way as soon as they have had a feed. So we had lunch.[47]

Hayward noted that Spencer-Smith was in poor shape:

We were pleasantly surprised to see Wild appear at the rear of the tent & he came out a little way to meet us as we approached the Skipper managed to stagger out

& of course was very thankful at his deliverance & thanked us accordingly. Smith seems very bad. However no time was lost in preparing them a feed, all of us feeling very grateful at our altered condition.[48]

Richards: 'Picked up party after striking camp ... and thank the fates all are alive – Wild in good condition considering.'[49]

Hayward:

Smith was in a hole 2 feet deep where he had been lying & I can assure you that it was as much as we could do by our united efforts, owing to our weakened condition to lift him onto the sledge.

We impressed upon the party the vital necessity of getting under way without undue delay, & they were all anxious to assist in this immediately on finishing lunch, the Skipper was encouraged to go ahead as far as possible with the aid of a stick whilst we were stowing sledges (we had brought back with us the sledge we depoted at the Bluff).[50]

Joyce: 'The Skipper went ahead to get some exercise, and after an hour's digging out got everything ready for leaving. When we lifted Smith we found he was in a great hole which he had melted through. This party had been in one camp for twelve days.'[51]

Hayward continues the story:

Overtaking the Skipper who altho' struggling gamely could hardly stand. We put him in his bag on the back sledge & what is more we were able to haul the whole load much to our surprise, we feeling certain that it would mean relaying, the dogs are pulling splendidly now they are on the home trail.[52]

There were now four men and four dogs hauling the two sledges, with Spencer-Smith on the first and Mackintosh on the rear sledge.

The evening of 29 February 1916

Camping was now more difficult, as the fitter men had to first erect Mackintosh's tent and carry Spencer-Smith inside before attending to their own tent and feeding the dogs. In reality there were now three men down with scurvy, three other very weak men also with scurvy but not so serious. They were within 76 miles of Hut Point. Their next goal was to reach the Minna Bluff depot (again), 6 or 7 miles away. Not surprisingly Wild and Spencer-Smith's diary entries that day were full of joy.

Wild:

> Full belly once more. Saw the others at 12.30 and they got up to us about 2.10. We had a feed & started on our way again. I am not so weak as I thought I should be thank goodness. We had to put the Skipper on the sledge. Luckily they brought a spare sledge from the Bluff as there is Smith and he on now.
>
> I think seeing them was the most welcome sight I have ever seen.[53]

Spencer-Smith concluded his notes with a Latin quote: 'God giveth the increase':

> Blew and drifted all night and most of morning. Hard pressed – but at 12.30 Wild looked out of a peep-hole and saw black speck which was the other party – and now we are bursting with thankfulness and food.
>
> Joyce & Co. have had a terrible time: travelling at every possible moment they were on their last legs when they got to the depot (about ten miles). The dogs were splendid – they actually barked on route when they saw bamboo ahead: and in the evenings they did not bark for sugar, as if they knew that there was none for them.
>
> We have had the closest of close calls – 'Deus datincrementum'.[54]

Joyce summarised the day's events:

> We got under way and picked the Skipper up; he had fallen down, too weak to walk. We put him on the sledge we had brought out + we camped about 8 o'clock.

I think we did about three miles – rather good with two men on the sledges + Hayward in a very bad way.

I don't think there has been a party either N. or South in such a strait 3 men down + 3 of us very weak. But the dogs seemed to have new life since we turned north. I think they realise they are homeward Bound. I am glad we kept them even when we were starving. I knew they would have to come in at the finish.[55]

Hayward was also pleased: 'After 2½ hrs travelling we camped. All feeling very satisfied at the day's proceedings.'[56]

Joyce:

Hayward in a very bad way. His gums are protruding + black + his legs + feet are giving him great trouble. He just hangs onto the sledge.[57]

I am more than pleased that Wild is well. Richy is more than splendid & always cheerful. I could not have better pals in this misfortune. Poor Smithy has been helpless for 38 days + he is always cheerful.[58]

Spencer-Smith: 'We travelled about 2½ miles this evening at fair speed, so as to get a new pitch. I was sunk at least a foot into the ground at Starvation Camp – and very wet. We have three weeks of food now, so all seems well.'[59]

Joyce was now looking ahead:

We have now to look forward to southerly winds for help, which I think we shall get at this time of year. Let us hope the temperature will keep up, as our sleeping-bags are wet through and worn out, and all our clothes full of holes + Finneskoe in a dilapidated condition; in fact, one would not be out on a cold day in civilization with the rotten clothes we have on.

Wild will have his work cut out. If the Skipper can assist a little, if only to help himself, it will be something.

Turned in 11 o'clock, wet through, but in a better frame of mind. Hope to try and reach the depot to-morrow, even if we have to march overtime.[60]

The remarkable achievement of rescuing Mackintosh, Spencer-Smith and

Wild is best explained by Richards. In an interview in 1976 he said that he has never ceased to marvel that in such a blizzard they found the small speck that was the depot and then on the return journey found the even smaller speck that was the tent. They travelled about 18 miles in six days. He self-consciously claimed 'no credit for under the prevailing conditions it could only be written down as a fluke'.[61]

The six men were back together. Joyce, Richards and Hayward were in one tent, Mackintosh, Spencer-Smith and Wild in the other. Joyce, Richards and Wild were now the only fit men but they now had ample food. Hut Point was approximately 76 miles away.

Chapter 15

'WE ARE ALL
RAPIDLY GOING DOWN
WITH SCURVY'

1 March 1916

O<small>N THE PREVIOUS</small> day (29 February) they had travelled 2 or 3 miles after picking up Mackintosh, Spencer-Smith and Wild, which meant on the morning of 1 March, the six men were only a few miles from the Bluff depot.

They were away reasonably quickly, with Spencer-Smith and Mackintosh on the sledges. In the afternoon the tail-wind was stronger, enabling them to reach the Bluff depot that evening, 70 miles from Hut Point. The men started to see familiar sights and for Richards, to see Mount Erebus was just like seeing home; to him it was a lovely mountain.[1]

It was a tiring day for Richards and it remained fixed in his mind. He remembered hauling hard all day and Spencer-Smith, who was watching him from the sledge said: 'For God's sake, Richy, stop or you'll bust your heart.'[2] He recalled being completely exhausted when they arrived at the depot; however, his day was not over. When they stopped they found some tent poles were missing. Because of their worsening condition over the past few weeks, they had not been as particular with the packing and lashing of items on the sledges, and that was how the tent poles had come to fall off. They could not put up the tent without them and Richards says he did not know what they would have done if they had lost them. He remembers standing on the sledge with his glasses to look back over their track and he could see them some distance away. He recalled that he went back to pick them up and that this walk was 'the hardest damn journey I ever made', even though it was only about a mile. Richards was the youngest in the party and he liked to ease any load for Joyce, who he called 'old Joycey'. He said: 'You know what you are when you're in your twenties, you see a bloke forty; you reckon he's an old man.'[3] Richards wrote later that he was more spent that evening than at any other time on the whole journey.[4]

Hayward: 'Under way 8 o/c proceeding in same manner. Smith on first sledge, Skipper on rear sledge. Splendid breeze helping us considerably & by lunch we estimated that we were not more than 5 M from depot.'[5]

Joyce:

> Set sail; put the Skipper on rear sledge. The temperature has gone down and it is very cold. Bluff in sight. We are making good progress, doing a good mileage before lunch.
>
> After lunch a little stronger wind.
>
> H--- still hanging on to sledge. Skipper fell off twice.[6]

Spencer-Smith: 'It is homely to see the old place again. Erebus and Terror have been visible all day – for the first time for many weeks. Sunshine, southerly, and drift: surface indifferent, but dogs splendid being now bound northward and we reached the Bluff Depot tonight (about 8 miles).'[7]

Hayward:

> After lunch going good & made depot in about 3½ hrs.
>
> When we came to pitch our tent we found that somehow our tent poles had fallen off the back sledge where they had been stowed this seemed the last straw however Richards looked back the track through the glasses & made out something approx half a mile away, which proved to be the poles.[8]

Joyce did not acknowledge Richards's efforts:

> When camping found we had dropped our tent-poles, so Richards went back a
> little way + spotted them through the binoculars about half a mile off + brought
> them back. Hayward and I were very cold by that time, the drift very bad. Moral:
> See everything properly secured. We soon had our tent up, cooked our dinner in
> the dark + turned in about 10 o'clock.[9]

Richards: '…Had a very hard day's work and straining to pull the men …
is difficult. My legs are in fair condition so far. Haywood finds difficulty in
walking. Dogs in good condition.'[10]

Hayward knew they all now had scurvy:

> I should mention that we are all, more or less, suffering from scurvy, our gums being
> much swollen. I feel it very badly in the limbs particularly in the groin, knees &
> ankles; the only cure of course is a diet of fresh meat & this we cannot procure till
> we get in, so one sees the vital necessity of quick progress.[11]

2 March 1916

On the morning of 2 March the six men, with their four dogs, Oscar, Towser,
Con and Gunner, left the Bluff depot with 70 miles to travel to reach Hut
Point. A strong wind helped push them along. They guessed the number
of miles they had travelled each day, and their estimates varied considerably (they now had no sledge-meter). By the evening they were less than
60 miles from Hut Point.

Without the assisting wind, which allowed them to use a sail, Richards
had doubts they would have survived. They always had a tent floor cloth
on one of the sledges ready to be used – and with a southerly breeze behind
they had no trouble hauling two sledges. Richards remembered that on
that day the wind was so strong that the sledges would overrun the men
and dogs, rather than having to pull them. The men could jump on board,
although they were very hard to steer.[12]

Spencer-Smith never made a fuss and this attitude impressed Richards. In a letter he wrote fifty years afterwards Richards described how he was tied directly to the sledge so he believed that he probably saw more of Spencer-Smith than the others, and had opportunity for the occasional word with him. Richards would see him sink into a coma and at times heard him wandering with his thoughts, but he was amazingly cheerful. Richards never heard him complain and was sure that Spencer-Smith never at any time lost hope.[13]

Here's Joyce on the start to the day:

> Up as usual. Strong south-west wind with heavy drift.
>
> Took 2 weeks' provisions from the depot. I think that will last us through, as there is another depot* about 50 miles north from here; I am taking the outside course on account of the crevasses, and one cannot take too many chances with two men on sledges + one crippled.[14]

Hayward:

> There seems to be no end to this awful weather & we left the Bluff Depot in a howling gale accompanied by drift, of course.
>
> The wind helps us along considerably but the process of striking tents & stowing sledges under these conditions is harder than a day's heavy hauling & from the time we started till lunch was a chapter of accidents.
>
> First Smith then the Skipper edging so far over to the side of the sledge on which they are lying as to capsize it, which meant considerable delay before things were righted.[15]

Richards: 'Good heavy southwest wind accompanied by heavy drift. Sledges went well in the afternoon. Sometimes carrying 4 men so strong was the wind. One sail only set.'[16]

Joyce: 'Wind and drift very heavy; set half-sail on the first sledge and under way about 3.30. The going is perfect; sometimes sledges overtaking

---

*   'Another depot' was the Cope Number 3 depot. It was about 30 miles away, not 50.

us. Carried on until 8 o'clock, doing an excellent journey for the day; distance about 11 or 12 miles.'[17]

Spencer-Smith:

We did about 3 miles before lunch. Amazing drift – we were in it just after lunch, but 5 yards to the east there was none! A 45 knot breeze and high drift all thro' afternoon.

With the merest rag of a sail on the forward sledge both H. and R. had to sit on the sledge so as to make the pace reasonable. We must have done anything between 8 and 10 miles.[18]

At the end of the day Joyce was still apprehensive:

Gives one a bit of heart to carry on like this only hope we can do this all the way. Hard to cook our meals in the dark but still we did not mind turned in about 11 o'clock. Pleased with ourselves although we were wet through with snow as it got through all the holes in our clothes + the sleeping bags are worse than awful.[19]

3 March 1916

The weather now started to take another turn for the worse, and they were unable to travel. Their sleeping bags were now filled with ice and their footgear and clothing were worn out – it was second-hand when they commenced sledging.

Wild: 'Blizzard and nothing doing.'[20]

Richards: 'Heavy wind and drift. Laying up.'[21]

Spencer-Smith: 'Regular hurricane blowing this morning, and obscured everywhere. Nothing doing all day.'[22]

Hayward: 'We are unable to get under way this morning wind being so violent as to make the striking of tents dangerous. We are hoping for a lull. Weather continued too thick to enable us to start & we had to remain in camp.'[23]

Joyce:

> Up the usual time. It has been blowing a raging blizzard all night. Found to our dis-
> gust utterly impossible to carry on. Another few hours of agony in these rotten bags.
>
> Later. Blizzard much heavier. Amused myself mending Finneskoe + Burberrys,
> mitts + socks. Had the Primus while this operation was in force. Hoping for a fine
> day to-morrow.[24]

4 March 1916

Even though the blizzard was still howling they had to keep moving. Hayward
was now unable to help and even Spencer-Smith noted his poor condition.
He was now riding on the sledges at times, with Spencer-Smith and Mackintosh. Mackintosh had reached the stage where he could only stumble along in
a squatting position under his own steam for a few yards. He tried to stay on
his feet by hanging on to the back of the sledge but unfortunately his legs had
got to such a state he could only hobble – even Joyce was now sympathetic
towards him. Richards after the event gave both Mackintosh and Hayward
'full marks' because after they stopped for lunch or for any reason, both men
would set off with a couple of ski-sticks while the others were packing up.[25]

Richards's mind was more at rest and he may have considered at this stage
that their troubles were over as he reverted to what he called his 'unfortunate practice in not keeping a detailed personal diary'.[26]

Richards: 'Fine wind – fair progress.'[27]

Joyce:

> Up 5.20. Still blizzarding, but have decided to get under way as we will have to try
> and travel through everything.
>
> Hayward is getting worse, and one doesn't know who is the next. No mistake it
> is scurvy, and the only possible cure is fresh food.
>
> Got under way 9.35. It took some two hours to dig out dogs and sledges, as they
> were completely buried. It is the same every morning now. Set sail, going along
> pretty fair. Hayward gets on sledge now and again.[28]

Wild: '10 miles in a blizzard. Hayward is done now so we have got three men to pull three more. I have just been making a new primus that is why I am so late.'[29]

Hayward:

The scurvy from which we are suffering is playing us up badly. Joyce, Richards, Wild luckily are not very stiff & I sincerely hope that they will get in without getting worse.

As for myself my knees & ankles have stiffened right up & it is as much as I can do to get over the ground at anything like a fast pace however so far by shutting my eyes & getting my head down I usually find myself somewhere around most of the time.[30]

Spencer-Smith:

Still blowing and drifting in the morning, but after a great deal of excavating we made a late start and did about 5 miles. The afternoon slightly better – though very hard work for the pullers, Hayward almost being hors de combat now – and the day's total should be about 11m.

Very uncomfortable morning and good afternoon. Our primus is playing Old Harry now and it sometimes takes 1½ hours before we really get into a meal.[31]

Joyce:

Lunched as usual; sledges got buried again at lunch-time. It takes some time to camp now, and in this drift it is awful.

In the afternoon wind eased a bit and drift went down. Found it very hard pulling with the third man on sledge, as Hayward has been on all the afternoon. Wind veered two points to south, so we had a fair wind.

An hour before we camped Erebus and Terror showing up, a welcome sight. Only hope wind will continue. Drift is worst thing to contend with as it gets into our clothes, which are wet through now.

Hayward's symptoms are gums very swollen + turning black. Joints of legs swollen + black feet. Cannot hardly press on them. Elbows stiff + sore. Pupils of eye enlarged so no mistake it is scurvy + the only possible cure is fresh food + I sincerely hope the ship is in – if not we shall get over the hills by Castle Rock which is rather difficult + will delay another couple of days.

Smith is still cheerful he has not hardly moved for weeks he has to have every-thing done for him.

Skipper is not so cheerful. He seems to be worsening. day before yesterday when we were travelling he fell off the sledge 2 or 3 times + in this heavy wind + drift it is impossible to hear anyone shout. I told him if he did not shout as soon as he fell he would be left behind he said it would be a good job.[32]

They were now within 50 miles of Hut Point.

5 March 1916

Like the previous day they struggled on. With a mild blizzard blowing they could see nothing, so they would just plod along in the thick blank whiteness. It was very depressing work. And conditions at night were becoming abhor-rent, with the ice in their sleeping bags melting as they lay in them. Richards recalled that this particular time, early March 1916, was one of the saddest periods of the whole sledging journey. It was very cold and the nights were closing in earlier and earlier every day. From about four o'clock in the after-noon it would be dark and they had no lights inside the tents. Richards's strongest memory was that at night time they 'did nothing but shiver'. They were in iced-up sleeping bags and wearing worn clothing so they had very little sleep. They would put on a woollen helmet and Richards remembered vividly the little bit of ice around his face would melt but he would 'sort of get used to it dripping' on his face. He recalled shivering violently all night long some nights. When he shivered, it was not just a shiver; to Richards 'it was a jumping of the body'. His whole body shook as it tried to keep a blood circulation going.[33]

Twelve months earlier, Mackintosh, on the way back to Hut Point with Joyce and Wild, often wrote on the trials and tribulations of a frozen sleeping bag:

As a matter of fact the bags are bags in name only for as we straighten them out it crackles and crunches like as if we were breaking a piece of wood and it is more in the form of a board when laid out. When all else is done we get in! The inside fur is a mass of ice, congealed from my breath.

One creeps into the bag, toggles up with half-frozen fingers, and hears the crackling of the ice. Presently drops of thawing ice are falling on one's head. Then comes a fit of shivers. You rub yourself and turn over to warm the side of the bag which has been uppermost. A puddle of water forms under the body.

After about two hours you may doze off, but I always wake with the feeling that I have not slept a wink.[34]

And here is another Mackintosh mid-March diary note from the year before:

Had a hoosh and a yarn and then unfolded our frozen boards (bags once!) and placed our bodies inside, the prior greeting – the cold ice against your fingers as you separated the flap of the bag, open it then in go your legs followed by the rest of your body so apart from the ice crackling as you get in nothing happens, but after this down goes your head which meets a shower of snow and ice, you ease the flap over and toggle up – the toggling generally takes a little time as the fingers 'go' but this is eventually accomplished you are prepared for sleep.

The warmth from the body now sets up a thaw, you turn and shift position, but all is damp while at this stage, the ice resting against the helmet close to cheek, made that part so cold that it started my tooth going. I turned helmet round and made things better; all our clothes, the top ones, are damp.

Towards early morning the temperature falling, everything froze again, this caused feet to get cold, the cold gradually creeping up body, until shivering commenced and then you shivered until till getting up time brought relief.[35]

Hayward had written then:

It is really unfair to tax anybody's imagination, to the extent required to obtain anything like a fair average idea of the hideous night, the weather & the sleeping bag contrived to make last night for me, I will only say that I have never had to contend with anything like it & hope I may never have to again.[36]

Spencer-Smith was now taking opium. In an interview in 1976 Richards thought back and remembered they had a medicine chest with some poisons in it: some cocaine tablets, opium and strychnine. He had no idea what the strychnine was for.[37] They could not yet see the next food depot yet, one of three that Cope and his party had laid down in 1915, all within 40 miles of Hut Point.

Hayward summed up the day in a few words: 'Bright. Under way 9 o/c AM all started, drift very hard going in places. 10 M for day.'[38]

Wild: 'Saw a skua gull this morning.'[39] (This indicated they were now close to the sea.)

Joyce maintained his diary:

> Sledge going hard, especially in soft places. If Hayward had not broken down we should not feel the weight so much. Wind and drift very heavy. A good job it is blowing some, or else we should have to relay. All land obscured.
>
> Sun shining brightly + no wind, it seemed strange last night. no flapping of tent in ones ears, about 8.30 came on to drift again under way 9.20 both sails set. sledge going hard especially in soft places if Hayward had not give in we should not feel the weight so much. Lunch 12.45.
>
> Under weigh at 3 wind + drift very heavy a good job it is blowing some or else we should have to relay all land obscured Distance about 10 or 11 miles a very good performance Camped 7.10 in the dark.
>
> Patients not in the best of trim. I hope to get in bar accidents in 4 days.[40]

Spencer-Smith:

> Calm till breakfast and then a good southerly (with drift) and sunshine helped a lot. The afternoon was dull and overcast, but the days trek is about 10 m.: no sign of Cope's No. 3 Depot.
>
> I am on the rear sledge now – a skittish little thing. Bad gripes. 1 gr. opium afternoon and evening.[41]

6 March 1916

On 6 March the six men were less than 40 miles from Hut Point. In the morning they picked up supplies from Cope's No. 3 depot. It had taken them two hours to reach there, only a mile and a half from where they set off in the morning. Their progress after lunch was even worse. They had lunched at 12.30 and were under way at two o'clock but there was less of a wind, making it difficult for Joyce, Richards and Wild and their four dogs to haul three sick men on the sledges. Even with assistance from a gentle wind for part of the day they had managed only 8 miles, putting them around 30 miles from Hut Point by evening.

Joyce: 'Going with a fair wind in the forenoon which eased somewhat after lunch which caused very heavy work in pulling. It seems to me I shall have to Depot someone if the wind eases at all.'[42]

7 March 1916

7 March was a difficult day, made up of a number of stages: from 5 a.m. to 9 a.m. – four hours packing up camp; from 9 a.m. to 11 a.m. – they travelled only one and a half miles; from 11 a.m. to 2 p.m. – they camped for lunch where they then decided to dump one of the sledges and any unnecessary gear; from 2 p.m. to 8 p.m. – over these six hours they only managed only another one and a half miles. At 8 p.m. they camped, having travelled approximately 3 miles for the entire day.

Joyce:

> Although we turn out at 5 it seems a long time to get under way. There is double as much work to do now with our invalids.
>
> This is the calmest day we have had for weeks. The sun is shining + all land in sight. It is very hard going. Had a little breeze about 11 o'clock, set sail, but work still very, very heavy.
>
> Hayward and Skipper going on ahead with sticks, very slow pace, but it will buck them up and do them good. If one could only get some fresh food! [43]

Hayward at lunch: 'Anyhow we were forced to camp, having only trundled about 1½ M. At this camp we depoted everything possible including personal gear – 1 sledge, decreasing the load by perhaps 200 lb.' [44]

Then Hayward on their afternoon:

> We were again under way by 1.30, the Skipper having gone on ahead. This new arrangement was not the success expected & going still very difficult, being … 2 men & dogs, on overtaking the Skipper he was whacked & was put on the sledge, this added weight proved too much.
>
> It was plainly sure that unless our speed can be improved the result will be disastrous & the six of us will never get in. [45]

Joyce: 'Distance about three and a half miles.' [46]

The evening of 7 March 1916

That evening they made the decision to leave Mackintosh. After their meal Joyce and Richards called Wild to their tent to discuss the situation. They knew they could not keep going and after talking it over Richards tells us he said: 'Well, there's only one thing to do, Smith's almost at his last gasp, we've got to get in with him, we can't get in as it is, we may not get in at all.' [47] Spencer-Smith was weakening rapidly and Mackintosh was unable to walk, being on the sledge all the time, and Hayward most of the time. They had reached the stage where progress had become almost impossible if there was no following wind. If they did not quickly make Hut Point, Richards thought it 'might be fatal'. [48] They guessed that fate would now play its part.

Richards thought later, when speaking about this stage of their journey, that Mackintosh may have lost his capacity for clear thought at this time and was prepared to leave decisions to others. When Richards, Joyce and Wild decided that the correct thing to do was to leave him in the tent Mackintosh acquiesced without any complaining or comment at all. Richards was sure that he could see that if they did not do something they might all perish, even though they were close to Hut Point. The three fitter men thought that, at the time and in their judgement, the right thing to do was to try to get Spencer-Smith (and Hayward) to Hut Point as they felt that Spencer-Smith was near death. If they could get him to Hut Point they would save his life, because they believed that seal meat would quickly cure his scurvy.[49]

Hayward was now badly off his food and was eating only a little of his pemmican. His lips were discoloured and he was almost incapable of moving his legs.[50] In his diary note that day he admitted that he was now of no value to the others – and he expressed his concern – what would his fiancée think of him?

Joyce:

After a consultation decided to Depot the Skipper + proceed in with Smith + Hayward + leave him with 3 weeks provisions + I told him when we camped what we proposed to do + I could not see any other way out it he said:

'do anything you like with me Joyce'.

It may be blowing hard tomorrow as we can take him on further it seems hard only about 30 miles away + yet cannot get any assistance. Our gear is absolutely rotten, no sleep last night shivering all night in wet bags. I wonder what will be the outcome of it all after our struggle 'Trust in Prove'.[51]

Hayward:

We camped & things were talked over & everybody naturally being anxious of finishing on what would best help matters to a safe conclusion.

It was decided that the Skipper remain here in camp & the rest of us push on with full speed as we are all more or less unwell at any time & further men needing Back up. In any case it is absolutely necessary that we get fresh food quickly & of course we hope that we may obtain assistance at Hut Pt.

Anyhow it's a cinch that drastic measures are required for such a drastic position & this seems the best thing to be done.

Am now out of the team, my legs having become so swollen, stiff & painful as to make my pulling any weight in the trace impossible, in fact it is as much as I can do to keep up even with this slow pace.

I do not know what you will think of me, & I will not try to describe my feelings.[52]

Richards: 'We are all rapidly going down with scurvy. Hayward particularly bad. Decided to depot Skipper here and march onto Hut Point and out again as soon as possible.'[53]

Wild: 'We have decided to leave the Skipper here & struggle onto Hut Point with the other two & then come back for the Skipper. I think that's the only way we can possibly do it.'[54]

Spencer-Smith's diary – 7 March 1916

He started with a Many Happy Returns of the Day to 'F' – his sister Fredrica Ethel, who was born this day in 1875.[55]

He goes on to explain that the O.M. (Mackintosh) would be left here. H. (Hayward) and he would remain at H.P. (Hut Point) and the others would come back with seal-meat, and with C. (Cope) their doctor, who Spencer-Smith expected to be at Hut Point.

> To F. M. H. R. O. T. D.
>
> A bitterly cold night: bag frozen stiff in a bad position. Glorious weather but only for about 3 miles, as the wind dropped.
>
> Decided to depot O.M. tomorrow and push on to H.P. with the invalids – Hayward's legs are very bad now and even Wild has a touch in the teeth.
>
> H. and I will be left at H.P. and the others will come back at top speed with seal-meat and C. and fetch the O.M. with whom we leave 3 weeks' food.[56]

The six men were just 30 miles from Hut Point.

Chapter 16

'WEARY, WORN, AND SAD'

8 March 1916

IN THE MORNING of 8 March Mackintosh was left behind, 30 miles from Hut Point. Joyce, Richards and Wild, and the four dogs were then to haul the sledge with both Spencer-Smith and Hayward on board, although Hayward was hobbling along at times.

They pitched the conical tent over Mackintosh and set him up with provisions. In Richards's memory he was comfortable there, quite willing to comply with the others and made no complaint or any comment. He thought Mackintosh seemed 'a bit dull', as though he didn't seem to know what was happening.[1]

Spencer-Smith made no diary entry.

Richards clearly remembered the night of 8 March. They turned in at about 10.30 p.m., very cramped for space as there were five in a three-man tent. It was a terrible night; pitch dark and so cold that they all shivered violently the whole night through. Their sleeping bags were threadbare and filled with ice condensed in the fur.[2] Mackintosh had written previously about the cold nights of March, how he 'shivered most of the night' and the 'lower temperature caused the bags which were moist to freeze hard'. None of the men slept and spent the night 'twisting and turning'. To Mackintosh: 'sleep in these conditions is impossible'.[3]

Spencer-Smith said he had stomach pains, and he was bleeding from the bowels. They could see the blood seeping through his sleeping bag.[4]

Joyce: 'Wished the Skipper goodbye. Took Smith + Hayward on. Had a fair wind, going pretty good. Hope to arrive in Hut Pt in 4 days. Lunched at Copes No. 2 depot. Did about 4½ miles.'[5]

Hayward:

> 5.30 pm. Blowing hard with drift. Fixed up Skipper in camp & got under way 10 o/c going difficult.
>
> I manage to get along somehow but the pain in my legs is excruciating. We made No 2 depot at lunch & camped. After lunch going improved & we camped having travelled 9 M for day.[6]

Richards: 'Marched approximately 8 miles. Haywood just staggering.'[7]

Wild wrote: 'Very cold.'[8]

They camped 20 miles from Hut Point.

9 March 1916

Spencer-Smith died in the early morning. Even though he had taken some opium, Richards believed this was to relieve his stomach pains, not to take his own life. Richards remembered taking a vial of opium tablets out of Spencer-Smith's vest pocket and saw that it was full except for four. Richards was sure he had not poisoned himself. He did not believe Spencer-Smith took enough tablets – four would not have hurt him even if he had taken them all that night.[9]

Richards wrote more on Spencer-Smith in his book *The Ross Sea Shore Party*. He tells us that from 29 January, until 8 March when he died, Spencer-Smith was on the sledge. They tried to do what they could to make life more comfortable for him and they were upset that they had not done more. Richards felt that the jolting of the sledge must have been almost unbearable at times. Now, within two days' march of comparative safety, his loss seemed so tragic after what he had been through.[10]

Richards believed that Spencer-Smith had a high sense of duty and this led to him losing his life. He no doubt felt that the final depot just had to be made for Shackleton and he pushed himself to the limit to carry this out. Richards felt that a man with a lesser sense of obligation would have turned back earlier.[11]

They dug a grave and buried him. They had to roll his body (in his sleeping bag) to the grave dug in the snow as they were too weak to lift it. Hayward sat against the sledge with his back towards the operations refusing to look.[12]

Wild: 'Woke up this morning and found poor Smith dead at 6am.'[13]

Joyce:

> Had a very bad night, cold intense. Temperature down to -29 all night.
>
> Smith was groaning + singing out practically the whole time as he was in pain with gripes for which he was taking opium. 4 o'clock AM he asked Wild the time + started laughing at him + asked him if he lost his bearings.[14]

Richards remembered that Spencer-Smith spoke to Wild in a jocular manner, as Wild got up from his sleeping bag to relieve himself, saying: 'Have you lost your bearings Tubby?'[15]

Wild: 'He asked me the time at 4 o'clock and spoke to Richards afterwards. It was very cold last night, that and all the hardships he has gone through did it.'[16]

Richards:

> Smith died at about 5am. At about 4am he asked Wild the time (we were all unable to sleep owing to the extreme cold and iced conditions of the bags) and somewhere about 4.15 – 30 as I was up on my bag he said:
>
> 'If your heart's [behaving] funny what is the best thing to do, sit up or lie down?'
>
> I said that I did not know but thought it best to lie still...[17]

Sometime later Richards looked across at Spencer-Smith. Joyce said Richards called out: 'I think he has gone.'[18]

They thought he had been dead for some little time as ice had formed on his eyelashes and beard.[19] Here's Hayward: 'On getting up we found that Smith had died during the night & we're able to fix the time from various incidents at about 5 o/c AM.'[20]

Joyce:

> Poor chap after being ill for 57 days. We left him at 83° for a week + carried him on the sledge for 40 days. He had a strenuous time in his wet bag + the jolting of the sledge on a very weak heart was not too good for him. Sometimes when we lifted him on the sledge he would nearly faint, but during the whole time he never complained.
>
> Wild looked after him from the start.[21]

Wild:

> We had carried him for 40 days & he was laid up for a week before that, so he was very weak & his bag was wet through (as was all of ours) & that made him colder. He was complaining about the cold during the night but we couldn't do anything.[22]

Richards:

> … All night he had been restless but he expressly told us not to take notice of him the night previously. He had been suffering from pains in the stomach for some days and he took say 10 tablets of opium all told … The night before he died he had a severe attack and took 4 tablets.
>
> We have pulled him helpless for 40 days over a distance of 300 miles. He has been laid up for 47 days and complained some 10 days previously. He should never have been allowed to go beyond 81S.[23]

Joyce: 'We buried him in his bag at 9 o'clock at the following position: Ereb. 184 – Obs. Hill 149 Dis 93. We made a cross of bamboos + built a mound + cairn, with particulars.'[24]

Richards: 'Bearings Erebus 184°, Observation Hill 149°, Mt Discovery 93°.'[25]

Hayward: 'We buried him at 9 o/c erecting a cairn & cross. It was bitterly cold in the night, & this combined with his weak condition was no doubt the cause of death.'[26]

And Wild, a day later, wrote: 'We buried Smithy as reverently as possible at 9am, yesterday. We built a cairn over him, & put a rough cross made of two bamboos. It's a great pity, him dying within 20 miles of Hut Point.'[27]

(A January 1917 medical report by Cope stated: 'Spencer-Smith's death. Although he was in such good spirits and so near safety, his death was due to the effects of scurvy reaching his heart, an almost invariable effect in prolonged cases. But it is also possible that his previous heart trouble may have made this organ liable to an early attack. Another factor which aggravated his case was that he took opium to send him to sleep.'[28])

A sad party heads for Hut Point, only 20 miles away

Their mood of the four men was understandably sombre as they set off for Hut Point without Spencer-Smith, and with Mackintosh out on the Barrier on his own. If the dogs were in good spirits there would have been a joyous clamour of welcome as the men arose for the day but they too were tired. On the march the men saw the lack of effort from the dogs by their low-carried heads and trailing tails, showing an utter weariness of life.

Typically Joyce was out in front for the day's march, with the harness slung over his shoulder, bent forward with the whole weight of the trace. Now and again he would raise and half turn his head to cheer on the others. That night there was little joy in their diaries.

Richards: 'We marched perhaps 10 miles today and made very hard work of it.

'We are weak and the dogs too have scurvy, I think. They have no heart.'[29]

Hayward: 'All realizing the necessity of getting into Hut Pt if we are to save our lives & of course that of the Skipper. Dogs do not seem to do anything much & progress is slow. Put up 9 M for day.'[30]

Joyce:

After that got under way with Hayward on sledge. Found going very hard, as we had a northerly wind in our faces, with a temperature below 20. What with frost-bites, etc., we are all suffering.

Even the dogs seem like giving in; they do not seem to take any interest in their work.

We have been out much too long, and nothing ahead to cheer us up but a cold, cheerless hut. We did about 2½ miles in the forenoon; Hayward toddling ahead every time we had a spell. During lunch the wind veered to the south with drift, just right to set sail. We carried on with Hayward on sledge and camped in the dark about 8 o'clock.

Turned in at 10, weary, worn, and sad.

Hoping to reach Depot tomorrow.[31]

10 March 1916

On the morning of 10 March Joyce, Richards, Hayward and Wild were only 10 miles from Hut Point. They had 5 miles to travel across the last of the Great Ice Barrier and from there it would be a few more miles around the edge of the sea-ice to be within 2 miles of Hut Point. These 2 miles would be a last small step, if the sea was frozen over, otherwise it would be a two-day trek around the hills to get to Hut Point.

The first part of their day went well, as did the trek to the edge of the sea-ice, but the sea-ice was not frozen, which meant they could not walk directly to Hut Point. They then had no alternative but to climb the steep slopes and camp for the night. They were so exhausted they could take no more than a couple of steps up the hills before having to rest. They even thought of sleeping in the snow.

A serious problem now confronted them – how would they get the incapacitated Hayward around the slopes to Hut Point the next day?

Joyce:

Turned out as usual. Beam wind, going pretty fair, very cold. Came into very soft snow about 3; arrived at Safety Camp 5 o'clock.

Got to edge of Ice Barrier; found passage over in a bay full of seals. Dogs got very excited; had a job to keep them away. By the glass it looked clear right to Cape Armitage, which is 4½ miles away.

Arrived there 8 o'clock, very dark and bad light. Found open water.[32]

Hayward: 'We were disheartened to find that a big lane of open water & fissures barred further progress forcing us to turn.'[33]

Joyce:

Turned to climb slopes against a strong north-easterly breeze with drift. Found a place about a mile away, but we were so done up that it took until 11.30 to get gear up. This slope was about 150 yds up, + every 3 paces we had to stop and get breath.[34]

Wild:

Well we got there after the most strenuous day ever I've done in my life. We got up there. I've never been more done up.

I took my sleeping bag up last and after every two steps I fell on top of it and had a spell. I rolled it up, was too weary to carry it. I was in a good mind to open it out & turn in & chance it. We finished at 11.30pm all done in.[35]

Hayward, stricken with scurvy, was aware that he was of little help: 'After getting tent up they returned for bags &c. whilst I fixed the camp & we all turned in exhausted & utterly played out.'[36]

Joyce: 'I think this is the worst day I ever spent. What with the disappointment of not getting round the Point, and the long day and the thought of getting Hayward over the slopes, it is not very entertaining for sleep.'[37]

Mackintosh spent the night alone in his tent, out on the Barrier, 30 miles from Hut Point.

11 March 1916

The next day started well when Joyce, and then Richards with Wild, checked the state of the sea-ice from the hills and saw that it looked secure.

This meant they might be able to descend the hills and cross to Hut Point over the ice. They found a way down to the sea-ice and even though the sea-ice was not firm they took the risk and kept going. Finally, they arrived at *Discovery* hut.

The hut was only an empty wooden shed with no heating or bunks. However, they were now safe, and to these four men the hut represented security. As Richards wrote in his book: 'There was no one there, and of course we had expected no one'. They found that snow had seeped into the hut and they had to pass Hayward through a window to enter.[38]

Many years later he recalled having an overwhelming desire for fresh meat when they were getting close to seals. He tells us it was rather extraordinary how his system reacted when they crossed a crack in the ice to go into the hut and there were several seals there. He says he had a strong urge to kill one of them 'and to drink the blood'. To him it was an amazing feeling, an almost overpowering one and he believed that if the hut had been further away than just a hundred yards he would have killed one of the seals there and then. He remembers that his system was crying out for the blood – and that feeling he had never forgotten – it remained very vividly in the forefront of his mind, sixty years later.[39] But their first step on arrival was to have a meal of cooked dried vegetables, and then to kill seals for fresh meat.

Richards also remembered feeling sombre for the first half-hour after he reached Hut Point. He says that this was unusual for him. It was the only time he could recollect being somewhat sorry for himself. Mackintosh was still out on the Barrier, they were weak and low in spirits having just buried Spencer-Smith and they could hardly eat anything because their gums just about covered their teeth. He remembers thinking then of other returning parties in former expeditions who would have come back to warm greetings and some reasonable amenities of civilisation; food, comfort and medical care. But he says this mood passed very quickly.[40] Joyce had similar feelings.

Joyce:

Up at 7 o'clock; took binoculars and went over the slope to look around the Cape.

To my surprise found the open water and pack at the Cape only extended for about a mile.

Came down and gave the boys the good news. I think it would take another two hard days to get over the hills, and we are too weak to do much of that, as I am afraid of another collapsing.[41]

Hayward:

Richards & Wild reconnoitred & found that the fissures which prevented us getting round Cape Armitage last night did not extend for more than 400 yds & we decided to try again.

Under way 11.30 hell of a job getting gear down on the sea-ice (afternoon) rounded the Cape & were pleased to find R & W report correct.[42]

Joyce: 'We went round the Cape and found ice; very slushy, but continued on. No turning now; got into hard ice shortly after, eventually arriving at Hut Point about 3 o'clock.'[43]

Wild: 'Hut Point at last.'[44]

Joyce:

It seems strange after our adventures to arrive back at the old hut.

This place has been standing since we built it in 1901, and has been the starting-point of a few expeditions since. When we were coming down the bay I could fancy the '*Discovery*' there when Scott arrived from his Farthest South in 1902, the ship decorated rainbow fashion, and Lieu Armitage giving out the news that Capt Scott had got to 82 17. S. We went wild that day getting slightly intoxicated. But now our homecoming is quite different.

Hut half-full of snow through a window being left open + drift getting in; but we soon got it shipshape and Hayward in. I had the fire going + plenty of McDoddies dried veg there.

After we had had a feed, Richards and Wild went down the bay and killed a couple of seals.

I gave a good menu of seal meat at night + we turned in about 11 oclock, full in the tummy – too full in fact.[45]

Hayward: 'Richards was not long in killing a seal & we had our first meal of fresh food for months at 5 o/c & we are all grateful for our safety.'[46]

Richards: 'Arrived Hut Point – killed seals and had first decent feed.'[47]

Wild: 'I haven't mentioned before but we all have a touch of scurvy & are on fresh food now trying to get rid of it.'[48]

Joyce: 'As there is no news here of the ship, and we cannot see her, we surmise she has gone down with all hands. I cannot see there is any chance of her being afloat or she would be here. I don't know how the Skipper will take it.'[49]

Hayward: 'There is no news of the ship & there can be no doubt that she has perished with all hands.'[50]

Hayward's scurvy

Hayward had concerns for his health. He wrote at this time: 'I am hoping that my legs will soon get better.'[51]

Hayward had been working under the same conditions as Joyce and Richards since October 1915 but he had fallen ill before them. It seems that he had not eaten fresh meat as often as Joyce and Richards. In November 1915 the three men returned to Hut Point a number of times and Hayward would have had the opportunity to eat fresh meat then. However, at an interview in 1980 Richards said that Hayward, like Mackintosh and Spencer-Smith, was not as keen to eat seal meat as the others. His words were that these three men 'were the ones never too endured with seal meat' and he went on to say that he, Joyce and Wild all liked seal meat and ate it whenever they could.[52]

From photographs Hayward was a far bigger man than the others, Richards called him burly and physically strong,[53] and this may have been a cause of Hayward falling ill before Joyce and Richards. As a bigger man he may have needed a larger share of the food ration. In Cope's medical report on the party's health in January 1917, he wrote: 'In the case of Hayward his constitution was not strong, and from 6 Jan (1916) when Mackintosh's party joined them he was pulling very heavy loads. Thus

Hayward succumbed despite the favourable auspices under which he had previously been working.'[54]

Cope, however, could understand why Mackintosh's and Spencer-Smith's conditions weakened well before those of Joyce, Richards and Hayward:

> Up to 13 Dec, 1916 Joyce's party enjoyed the rests made at Hut Point whereas Mackintosh's party only enjoyed one such rest. With this it must be remembered that during each rest stop fresh food was eaten, and on the fourth journey southward made by Joyce's party to the Bluff Depot freshly cooked meat (and part boiled meat for the dogs also) was taken which was all finished by 6 Jan, 1917 at 80° S.[55]

Cope also gives a logical reason why Mackintosh and Spencer-Smith succumbed before Wild; their 'dislike' of seal meat.

> About 12 miles from the Bluff Depot on Joyce's fourth journey southwards the party met that of Capt Mackintosh and some freshly cooked meat which had been brought out for them was given over to the party.
>
> Wild was the only man in this party who took full advantage of this opportunity of renewing his acquaintance with fresh food, both Mackintosh and Spencer-Smith exhibiting their dislike of seal meat they had both shown during the previous winter at Cape Evans, a point which must not be lost sight of seeing it would at least explain an early tendency to scurvy.

Cope also adds: 'The mildness of W's attack was probably due to his strong constitution and to his mode of life, he having before been used to doing hard work on a diet consisting considerably of artificial foods.'[56]

He concluded his report with: 'The Southern party had lime juice with them both in liquid (fortified) and pastille form but the taking of it had no apparent effect on the scurvy. This was because it was not taken early enough when the scurvy had attacked them.'[57]

Four men were now safe at *Discovery* hut at Hut Point. Mackintosh still had to be rescued but he was located only 30 miles south, on the Barrier, a few miles from where they had buried Spencer-Smith.

Chapter 17

'AS HAPPY AS A PICCADILLY MASHER'

12 March 1916

AT HUT POINT, Joyce, Richards and Wild recuperated and made ready for their trek back to rescue Mackintosh. Hayward was to stay at the hut because he could not walk. In his interviews Richards explained that they did not immediately head south again to bring in Mackintosh because they had to recover, and mend their clothes and fur boots. In addition the sea-ice had come into the shore at Hut Point and was liable to go out at any moment. Once this happened there would be less seals about and it was essential to get a good store of meat and blubber while they could. Some of the meat they would cook to take with them when they went out to pick up Mackintosh.[1]

Joyce was happy:

Heard groans proceeding from the sleeping all night. All hands suffering from overeating.

Turned out 8 oclock, good breakfast. Porridge Seal + Veg + Coffee more like a Banquet to us. After breakfast Richy + Wild killed a couple of seals.

Hayward not very well all limbs swollen + black Gums very prominent. Hayward cannot hardly move. All of us in a very bad state but we must keep up exercise. my ankles + knees badly swollen, gums prominent. Wild very black around Joints + Gums very black. Richards is about the best off.

After digging hut out which made the hut a bit comfy prepared food which will keep the scurvy down.

The dogs have lost their lassitude + are quite frisky, except Oscar who is suffering from overfeeding.

After a good strenuous days work turned in 10 o'clock.[2]

Hayward: 'We are all engaged drying out togs &c & Joyce Richards & Wild preparing for their trip to bring in the Skipper. I need hardly say how disappointed I am at being unable see this thing through to the end.'[3]

13 March 1916

Joyce, Richards and Wild spent a second full day recovering, and making ready to go out for Mackintosh.

Wild: 'Spent the day drying bag & killing seals & getting ready to go for the Skipper. Today it has been blowing & drifting. We've been cooking seal meat to take with us & mending bags & finneskos, etc. We hope to make a start for the Skipper in the morning.'[4]

Richards: 'Hayward could only hobble.'[5]

Hayward: 'Having plenty of fresh meat & find it improving us all pretty rapidly. The others have decided to start to-morrow, so far sea-ice remains in.'[6]

Joyce:

Turned out 7 o'clock. Carried on much the same as yesterday bringing in seal blubber + meat. Preparing for departure tomorrow. Hope everyone will be alright. Made new dog harness + prepared sledge in afternoon cooked sufficient seal meat for our journey out and back + same for dogs, turned in 10 o'clock feeling much better.[7]

14 March 1916

On 14 March, Joyce, Richards, Wild and the four dogs set off south. In his book Richards tells us they left Hayward with a supply of cooked seal meat and everything he needed close by. At this time Hayward could only just move about but the others felt he would be able to manage well enough until they returned.[8] The three men made excellent progress for the day to reach Safety Camp on the Barrier. They were a wild-looking party – note Joyce's 'racist' description.

Hayward: 'Joyce R & W pulled out about 2 o/c & I start my arbitrary bachelordom for a week. How I wish I was fit & able go out again. I absolutely cannot bend my knees & to walk is agonizing.'[9]

Richards: 'Left Hut Point for Skipper.' He added later: 'It was necessary to recuperate before turning South again and repair some of our gear.'[10]

Joyce:

> A beautiful day. Under way after lunch. One would think, looking at our party, that we were the most ragged lot one could meet in a day's march; all our clothes past mending, our faces as black as niggers – a sort of crowd one would run away from. Going pretty good.
>
> As soon as we rounded CA* a dead head wind with a temp of -18 so we are not in for a pleasant time. Arrived at Safety Camp 6 o'clock, turned in 8.30 – after getting everything ready.[11]

15 March 1916

Richards: 'Good march. Cold at night. Dogs better than thought.'[12]

Joyce: 'Under way as usual. Nice calm day. I had a very cold night temp going down to -30. Going along at a rattling good rate in spite of our swollen limbs we done about 20 miles. Very cold when we camped temp -20 turned in 9 o'clock.'[13]

They were now camped within 10 or 15 miles from Mackintosh.

---

*   Cape Armitage.

16 March 1916

They travelled well and in the early afternoon they could see Mackintosh's tent. Richards recalled at interviews that Mackintosh seemed a little dazed when they came up to him and gave him the news of Spencer-Smith's death. It did not seem to make a big impression on him. Mackintosh 'didn't say bad luck or what have you' and Richards put this down to his lonely vigil on the ice shelf. Mackintosh told them that at times his mind had been wandering and he found himself talking to imaginary people in the tent during their absence.[14] Richards explained that it was fairly unemotional when they came up to Mackintosh because they were quite sure they would find him and quite sure he would be alright. To Richards it was 'just all in a day's work'; nothing like he felt when they went back and found the tent with Mackintosh, Spencer-Smith and Wild during the long blizzard.[15]

They found Mackintosh could only shuffle along with the aid of two sticks so they put him on the sledge and headed back towards Hut Point.[16]

Joyce:

> Up before the sun 4.45 had a very cold night. Not much sky under way early. Good going passed Smith's grave 10.45 + had lunch at Depot. Saw Skippers camp just after + looking through the glasses found him outside the tent much to the joy of all hands as we expected him to be down.
>
> Picked him up 4.15. broke the news of Smiths death + no ship he took it very well + said it was the best time of his life to see us. I gave him the date of the 17th to look out for our returning. So he had a surprise.[17]

Wild: 'We got to the Skipper's camp about 4 o'clock yesterday & packed up & came a little way on the home track. He can still manage to get about hobbling.'[18]

That night Joyce wrote:

> We struck his camp + went N. for about a mile + camped. We gave the Skipper + banquet of seal veg + blackcurrent jam, the feed of his life.

He explained every morning in his sleep as semi conscious state he had most peculiar dreams + always found himself talking to supposed people in the tent. I looked at him pretty straight + though he was still a little ... [indecipherable] but I think he is all right. He seems in a very bad way all his legs badly swollen + black, eye distended gums very swollen + black. I hope to get home in 3 day's + I think fresh food will improve him. We turned in 8 oclock. Distance done during day 18 miles.[19]

17 March 1916

Joyce: 'Up at 5 oclock under way 8 – Skipper feeling much better after feeding him up. Lunched a few yards past Smiths grave. Had a good afternoon going fair. Dist about 20 miles.

'Very cold night temp -30, what with wet bags + clothes rotten -----------.'[20]

Back at Hut Point Hayward wrote nothing more than: 'Reading Thinking Eating.'[21]

18 March 1916

Joyce, Richards and Wild, with Mackintosh, reached Hut Point safely. Joyce:

Turned out 5 oclock. Had rather a cold night. Temp -39 Surface very good, got the Skipper to have a walk for a little way which done him good. Lunched as usual. Pace good after lunch, going good arrived at Safety Camp 4.10. To our delight found the sea ice in the same conditions + arrived at Hut Pt 7 oclock.[22]

Wild:

Hut Point again. Hooray.

We have exceeded our utmost expectation. Getting back here last night at 6.30

doing about 84 geo miles in two days with the Skipper on the sledge. Skipper and
Hayward can just manage to get about. We others are just about all right now.[23]

Richards: 'Hut Point. Hayward safe. He had been left behind when we
returned for the Skipper.'[24]

Hayward was very pleased: 'Joyce & party with Skipper who I am glad to
say is no worse, got back about 6 pm having made a jolly good trip of it.'[25]

Joyce wrote that evening:

> Found Hayward still about the same, yet he made a good dinner + all hands seem
> in the best of spirits. Now we have arrived + got the party in remains to them-
> selves to get better plenty of exercise + fresh food ought to do miracles. We have
> been out 202 days (* with September sledging) + done a distance of about 1900
> miles a good record. I think the irony of fate was poor Smith going under a day
> before we got in.
>
> Had a thorough exam of the Skipper + found from his right hip bone down to
> knee a heavy blue + hard (swollen) from the knee to ankle (blue stripe) ankle swollen
> out of proportion. gums swollen but not so black, white of eye distended. Appetite
> extraordinary good. Feels in himself a different man– a good improvement
>
> Hayward, gums very swollen + black eyes as usual. Knees cannot bend at all not
> swollen or just slightly black walks like a bent up old man.
>
> Richards right leg + gums slightly swollen.
>
> Wild right leg behind knee black, slightly swollen gums very swollen.
>
> Myself right leg behind knee still + gums slightly swollen I think we shall all soon
> be well turned in 10.30.
>
> Before turning in Skipper shook us by the hand with great emotion thanking us
> for saving his life + said his wife + children will bless us.[26]

Always the realist, Wild wrote: 'We shall settle down here now for a couple of months.'[27]

The five remaining men of the Mount Hope Party were now safe. Conditions at *Discovery* hut were primitive but they knew they would soon
recover from scurvy on their diet of seal meat. Once mid-winter came they
would be able to walk safely over the sea-ice to Cape Evans.

Mid-March to late April 1916

Their long journey was now over, and successful, except for the loss of Spencer-Smith. Joyce remembered being 'as happy as a Piccadilly masher'.*[28]

Many years later Richards was still very proud of the work they had accomplished. In his book he wrote that they had the satisfaction of knowing that they had completed their task and that Shackleton would have had sufficient food over the latter part of his journey. He also added that man-hauling sledges for 1,500 miles with poor equipment and no support from a well-established base was a very notable task. To Richards it was an Antarctic journey that 'could rank with most that had gone on before'.[29]

The hut was full of ice and snow which had come in through a broken window so they cleared out a small corner to live in. In their first two weeks at Hut Point, from 19 March to early April, they slowly recovered and their diary entries were sparse. They knew they would be there until mid-winter, at least.

It would be June or July before they could expect the open water between Hut Point and Cape Evans to freeze over. It was possible to go around the land to Cape Evans but they never thought of attempting to travel that way, and certainly not without the right equipment. Plus, the light was poor and by mid-April it was dark for twenty-four hours of the day. The only way they intended to cross the 13 miles to Cape Evans was directly over the sea-ice, and during a full moon; and then only when the sea-ice had frozen firmly. With two invalids they resigned themselves to a protracted stay at Hut Point.[30] [31]

Hayward: 'There will not be much to record, these days of residence at Hut Pt. Skipper & I did the goose step for an hour or so by way of exercise. His legs are very much worse than mine, being practically blue all over.'[32]

Richards: 'Fixing Hut for winter. Rubbed Mackintosh and Haywood with spirit to ease their legs. Skipper brighter. Haywood less cheerful.'[33]

Joyce:

---

* 'Piccadilly masher' – a dandy man about town.

Up at 7 oclock. Got a good scones breakfast of seal liver porridge scones etc. All hands to judge by appetites found are in better health than one thinks to see the way that they are stowing away. Spent all day in living quarters, fixing up things. Sent the invalids out for exercise. Lunch at 2 oclock same store of provisions. Carried on again fixed up the living room by 7 oclock had dinner. Turned in 1 oclock.

After enquiring found all hands in about the same condition except appetite much better, that is can eat twice as much as ordinary man. Skipper right ankle swelled a little more + legs are a bit stiffer. I think he had too much exercise to-day.[34]

20 March 1916

Joyce:

Up 8 oclock. Cooked break appetites marvelous [sic] after break un packed took stock of stores. Shall have to allow until the middle of June so have got to allowance until then. Found in some things full + plenty but dripping the most essential thing found only 9 tins so shall have to have more boiled stews.

Patients could not go out on as of the cold wind + drift from SE. Everyone in good spirits. Richards massaging which seems to ease the muscles greatly. Gums gradually going down except Hayward's which are black. Turned in 9 oclock.[35]

Hayward: 'Blowing pretty hard & not much doing.'[36]

22–29 March 1916

In his book Richards wrote that he, Joyce and Wild were able to go about their daily tasks with reasonable efficiency, but Mackintosh and Hayward required looking after. Mackintosh still had some internal haemorrhaging and neither he nor Hayward could straighten their legs more than a little past a right angle. At first everyone's teeth were barely visible owing to the gums coming down over them. Richards remembered that it was impossible to eat a biscuit without first soaking it in tea first.[37]

In an interview six decades later Richards could still paint a word picture of their life in the hut. He says they 'lived the life of troglodytes' (ancient people who lived in caves) and that it would take a lot of imagination for anyone to realise just how primitive the conditions were. *Discovery* hut was only a shell with one layer of wooden boards between them and the outside. Richards remembered that most of the hut was full of ice and snow so they lived in one small area on the northern side which had been partially partitioned off with some empty cases. This enclosed a small portion of the hut and that was their living space. The hut was not windproof so the men lived in their clothes and stayed inside their sleeping bags when they were in the hut. Their sleeping bags rested on planks raised above the floor by wooden provision cases. Richards tells us it was not warm enough to even sit up in the bag; they would get down inside their bags 'and get a bit of warmth that way'.[38] [39]

Their sole heating came from burning seal blubber chunks, each chunk about 6 inches square and 2 inches thick, which they would simply throw into the stove (a plate on top of a few bricks). The blubber would flare up, melt and then burn with a fierce heat. Richards remembered that some of the blubber oil would run out of the back of the bricks and onto the floor and every so often, when there was too much on the floor they would shovel it up into a tin, and use it again for fuel. He explained that as soon as they put any blubber into the stove the hut filled up with smoke.

Their clothes soon became saturated with blubber and seal blood. When they were out sealing they would cut the throat of the seal and the seal's arteries would spurt out blood all over them. In Richards's words the blood came out 'like a hose'. He says they never noticed the smell but they were all in a filthy condition, never taking their off their clothes or washing their hands – they had no facilities for heating water or any soap.[40]

There was virtually nothing at Hut Point in the way of food apart from a few dried vegetables which only lasted a few days. They had only a little flour, but no bread or cake or biscuits. They found some old biscuits that had been left there by Scott in 1901 but they found them so anaemic and musty they could not eat them. Virtually their sole food from the middle of March until the middle of June was seal meat. In Richards's memory that was all they had, 'morning, noon and night'.[41]

They had no lighting; all they could do was make an improvised blubber lamp – a bit of string in some blubber oil, in an old tin. When the wind forced the smoke down the flue of the stove it was difficult to even see the other side of the tiny partitioned off area in the dim light.[42] Richards reminisced, when looking at an old photograph of the inside of the hut, that in his mind he could still see the dim figures of Mackintosh and Joyce crouching with hands outstretched over the blubber stove to get a bit of warmth.[43]

Joyce: 'Wed 22nd – 29th. Patients recovering rapidly doing good exercise appetites not ceased one iota. Bay freezing + going out again. Richards + Wild still providing fuel + food killed 10 seals. Everything carrying on harmoniously.'[44]

Hayward: '22 Mar: Less windy & brighter, hope again to take some exercise later.'

In March and April of 1915 Mackintosh had painted a picture of living at Hut Point:

Here we are all huddled up alongside of the stove, applying lumps of blubber as the last piece gets burnt away, the stove being below us we are sitting over it in a bent up position like Indians over a fire, the blubber gurgles and splutters, the delightful sound of heat which one gets to know besides the feel.[45]

But the dirt, it's too terrible, everything we touch is blubber which, added with the smoke is as a dirty a mixture for blackening one as could be manufactured, the worst of this is that it soaks into one's clothes.

Already we are absorbed with it. What will it be like in another month, if we should be here? I can't say. Meals somehow seem to be the principal event of the day.[46]

We can see the wind has blown all the surrounding ice out of the Sound. Chances of reaching Cape Evans are consequently postponed again. Hope not for long.[47]

Do so hope the sea will freeze over and release us. What a crowd of utter tramps we look; long matted hair, un-cropped straggling beards, grease all over ourselves, clothes – dirtiness personified. The weather continues fine, light Northerly air, sea frozen in patches.

Oh! For the weather to continue fine for a few days and the sea to freeze.[48]

Prisoners once more we remain.[49]

Oh! This filth – when will be released?[50]

We have now got into a state of savagery. I find myself having no scruples at picking up my food with blubbery fingers.[51]

A significant diary entry then was his observation that a gale could take
away the sea-ice between Hut Point and Cape Evans: 'The wind today is
blowing fresh and later increasing to gale force; with this our slender hopes
have vanished for the ice in the Sound has gone out en mass. Cape Evans
is as distant as ever.'[52]

April 1916

Mackintosh recovered from his condition quickly but Richards tells us in an
interview that he did not really assume command again.[53] They had expected
Mackintosh to lead the sledge parties and in the early stages of sledging his
position as leader was never queried. However, as he became progressively
weaker on the way back to Hut Point, Richards recalled that he seemed incapable of making any decisions, deferring to him, Joyce and Wild.[54]

The seal meat proved remarkably effective in curing their scurvy and
Richards remembered the size of their meals as being truly prodigious.
They did not plan it that way; their bodies seemed to demand an inordi-
nate amount of meat. They could see each other gaining strength rapidly
from day to day.[55]

Richards recalled that as the winter closed in they experienced blizzards
with increasing frequency which prevented them from sealing and forced
them to stay in the hut. During these periods there was little they could
do, other than lie in their sleeping bags and 'try to doze the time away'.[56]

Their diary entries were sparse in April.

Joyce:

Wed 5th to 12th. Everyone now seems to be better. Skipper still black back of legs.

No pain. Had hair cut. 1st time for 19 mths seem to be walking on air + also whiskers trimmed seem like a smooth faced boy. Appetites still the same. Richy + Wild can just cope with the seal supply. Everyone quite cheerful. Seals killed 19. Temp -20 to 20.[57]

Wed 19th – 26th. Been blowing for a whole week. Ice gone out I forgot to mention I walked out for 4 miles over the new ice on Thursday + found it about 2 inches thick and in about 2 days would have been able to traverse to C Evans but fate forbade. Wind eased about noon all hands out. Patients able to take long walks. The Ice has gone out within ½ mile of hut. In fact it seems that the whole lot is going out. Let us hope not Seals killed up to date 26 rather a good supply.[58]

26 to 3 May Ice all gone out up to point. Been blizzarding for days not been able to go out much for xercize [sic]. Invalids practically better. Skipper still black back of leg. Gums better all our nails seem to be indented.

Party of 30 Penguins paid us a visit 24 Returned. 6 kept us company in our … [indecipherable] Found heart + livers one of the best things we have tasted since civilization Everything same as usual time passing quickly Everyone sociable – Seals 39.[59]

Hayward: '10 April: Lovely day – out (-20° getting cold).'[60]

Towards the end of April Hayward's diary notes were even less detailed: '22 April: Could not go out. 27 April: Out 30 April: Good Out.'[61]

At the end of April 1916 the five men were safe and recovering their health. There was now only one final scene to be played out.

Chapter 18

'SO THE FATE OF THESE FOOLISH PEOPLE WE DO NOT KNOW'

6–10 May 1916

DIARY ENTRIES FOR early May tell us that the weather was fine. Hayward and Mackintosh were taking walks, to check the state of the sea-ice. Joyce was clearly unhappy that Mackintosh and Hayward were contemplating walking across the sea-ice so early in the winter season.

6 May 1916

Hayward: 'Sat 6: Weather fine do Sea-ice Good.'[1]

7 May 1916

Joyce: 'Blizzard still carrying on for a couple of days then cold snap. Temp below -30. Bay again frozen. Wild + Richy still butchering seals. Skipper + Hayward went over sea ice on the 7th + found it bearable.'[2]

8 May 1916

Mackintosh announced at breakfast that he and Hayward were going to make the trip across to Cape Evans that day. The weather was fine and calm but the others were still surprised by Mackintosh's decision. He and Hayward were now walking freely but they had not walked more than a mile or two at one time. Richards tells us they were confident in their strength to be able to walk the 13 miles to Cape Evans, and they planned to travel light. Joyce (with Mackintosh) then checked the weather and for Joyce, the weather over the Bluff indicated that a blizzard would arrive soon.[3]

Joyce: 'I don't know why these people are so anxious to risk their lives again but it seems to me they are that way inclined for at breakfast the 8th he asked me what I thought about him going to C. Evans with Hayward.'[4]

Richards clearly remembered the discussion with Mackintosh, even sixty years later:

> It was just twilight in the middle of the day and I distinctly remember Mackintosh saying when we were having our morning food: 'Hayward and I are going to Cape Evans today.'
>
> And old Joycey got up and he went out through the passage-way and had a look down south to Minna Bluff, which you could see from there, and we always knew if it was obscured, there was bad weather coming.
>
> He came back and he said: 'Now look, Sir (he called him Sir), you may call me old cautious (which he sometimes did because Mackintosh was the reverse of that, he was terribly impetuous) but I wouldn't go to Cape Evans today for all the tea in China.'
>
> And Mack says: 'Oh nonsense, Joyce, we'll be alright'.
>
> And Joyce said: 'Well, I'll make you up some seal meat'.

And he made up some fried seal meat in a calico bag and gave it to him.

They knew we didn't want them to go, but Mack was the leader and he said:

'I'm going.'[5]

Joyce: 'I told him he could please himself, but I thought it was not a day for it, but still they shoved off + half an hour after leaving it came on a howling Blizzard.'[6]

Mackintosh and Hayward leave for Cape Evans

Richards related in his interviews that Mackintosh and Hayward went without any gear at all; they were just walking across, and in his opinion it was madness. He tells us that he, and Joyce and Wild, did not even consider joining them. In fact if Mackintosh had ordered them to join him Richards says they would have told him 'you go to hell'. In any case they could not go. Young ice has what the men called 'ice flowers' on it, which were ice crystals that look like small flowers. The crystals grow on freshly formed sea-ice and the sledges would not run on them.[7]

Although Richards, Joyce and Wild were not in favour there was not much they could do about his decision. Mackintosh was still in charge of the party and short of forcibly restraining him they could only urge him not to go.[8] Richards believed that Hayward may not have been as keen as Mackintosh. He thought Hayward looked dubious but possibly he did not wish to 'lose face'. Richards remembered the uncertain look on Hayward's face when Joyce said: 'I wouldn't go there for all the tea in China'.[9]

Richards's thoughts on the departure of Mackintosh and Hayward, revealed in an interview so many years afterwards, were that he, Joyce and Wild were extremely unhappy with Mackintosh's decision. He told his interviewer that the three of them had really worked their 'guts out' to get them to the safety of Hut Point and they did not want anyone to risk going to Cape Evans before the sea-ice was firm. Richards said he 'felt a little bit of bitterness' because by that time not only did he think it was a needless risk, but he was starting to feel the strain of the journey.[10] Richards thought that the two men took with them no more than a bag of cold seal meat and their personal diaries, which were carried in a wide pocket on the front of their sweaters.[11] (In fact, Hayward left his diary at Hut Point.)

Joyce, Richards and Wild walked up to the top of a small hill next to *Discovery* hut to watch the two men head north. (The hill has a cross on it, Vince's Cross, in memory of George Vince, who was a member of the *Discovery* Expedition. He died in 1902, the first man known to have lost his life in the McMurdo Sound region.)

There was just a dim twilight in the middle of the day and Richards remembered seeing Mackintosh and Hayward 'in the distance rather dimly', and looking almost 'pygmy-like' as they grew fainter walking across the expanse of sea-ice to the north.[12]

Joyce, Richards and Wild watched them for a while without saying a word to each other.[13]

Final words on 8 May 1916

Wild: 'If the other two get lost, I shall be sorry we humped them back here over the barrier. However, let's hope they get there alright.'[14]

Richards: 'So we turned back and went back to the hut.[15] Sure enough, in little more than an hour, the wind began to rise and before long the blizzard Joyce had predicted had arrived and we were confined by it to the hut until 10 May.'[16]

Joyce:

> Whether they got there or no they deserved to be badly frostbitten or lose their lives. After dragging them back from death they seem to think they can court it again ah well such is life + what fools we got to put up with.
>
> Carried on blowing + still the same outside open water to the N perhaps they have gone out on a flow [sic]. We are quite happy here + do not intend to leave until safe. There is no need to risk ones life without a cause.[17]

10 May 1916

Of course Richards, Joyce and Wild did not know then what had happened to Mackintosh and Hayward, but they did describe what happened after the two men left.

Joyce:

> On the 10th, the first day possible the three left behind walked over the ice to the North to try to discover some trace as to the fate of the others. Their footmarks were seen clearly enough raised up in the ice and these we followed for about 2 miles in a direction leading to CE [Cape Evans]. Here they ended abruptly and in the dim light a wide stretch of open water very lightly covered with ice was seen as far as the eye could see, no doubt one night's freezing. It was evident at once that part of the ice over which they had travelled had gone out to sea.[18]

Wild:

> There were 2 sets of them going to CE and one set turning which had been made on the 7th.
>
> Both sets of marks stopped suddenly about 2 miles from HP and we could see that the ice had all gone out from there, after they had passed. One set of marks was much nearer the land than the other.[19]

Richards:

> On 10th the three remaining members walked over the sea-ice to the North tracing the footsteps on the soft slushy ice. These ended abruptly in a sheet of water very lightly frozen as far as the eye could see.
>
> The footsteps often keeping into land for a little suddenly turned heading directly for CE as though a sudden decision had been made. Before leaving M had promised Joyce that if the weather changed for the worse he would return.[20]

Why did Mackintosh tempt fate?

Mackintosh took the risk to walk from Hut Point to Cape Evans in spite of a near-death experience on floating sea-ice seven years previously.

On the *Nimrod* Expedition in 1908 Mackintosh had been sent back to New Zealand after the accident where a boat hook hit his right eye, but in January 1909 he returned to McMurdo Sound. Due to pack ice the ship was stopped 25 miles away from the hut where the shore party was based so Mackintosh and three sailors left the ship to take the mail to the hut. They were pulling a sledge as they needed to carry a large postage bag, plus their tent, sleeping bags, cooking equipment and food. After four hours of hauling one of the sailors began to show signs of fatigue so he and another sailor returned to the ship, while Mackintosh and the remaining sailor, McGillan, pushed on.

That night they camped on the sea-ice but the next morning they came across open water, so they started back for the ship. However, they soon came across more open water. We have Mackintosh's own words from his diary at that time. He provides a graphic description of their predicament, and how close they came to losing their lives when caught on a floating sheet of ice:

> The first intimation that everything was not well was the sight of a whale sprouting. I thought it was just a Killer coming up as they often do to breathe in a seal hole, so no further notice was taken and on we trudged.
>
> Ten minutes later to my horror I saw water ahead and the ice moving rapidly. It seemed impossible and to make quite sure I had a good look from an elevated position. There was no room left for doubt for the immense ice sheet had formed into floes by the numerous cracks developing into lanes of open water.
>
> The cold knowledge that we were very much adrift was anything but cheering. We thought we were then about two and a half miles from shore but it must have been four in the least.

Mackintosh and his companion McGillan were now in a precarious situation, on sea-ice that was breaking up, and facing the possibility of being carried out to sea. Mackintosh continues:

There was water to the southward, water to the northward and we were between the two, and would before long be floating out to sea! So a bee line was made for the nearest shore. Across floes, hummocks, and deep snow we dragged our sledge, both realising the necessity of a speedy arrival at the nearest land.

The two men struggled to pull their sledge over the ice floes, towards the shore.

At places we had to lift the sledge bodily over the rough ice face. In spite of the cold weather we were sweating freely the extra work that now came upon us was back breaking. I cannot express the keen and ready way in which McGillan stood by me, and the way in which he showed his willingness to assist me in every way.

Now the situation had become dire, with the size of the ice floes diminishing. Through Mackintosh's words we can imagine what must have been going through his mind at this critical time:

Our arrival at the first point of land filled us with horror and disgust as we found an impassable lane of water stopping our progress! With all out strength we dragged on to the next point which appeared to be safe.

How we pulled: the floes were getting square in shape and smaller. At about every 200 yards we had to drag our sledge to the edge of a floe and then jump on to the next one ourselves, and with a big effort pull it to safety.

For an hour this kind of work lasted, our hands were cut and bleeding, our clothes wet through to the waist which of course froze as stiff as boards on us, for we had, when crossing from floe to floe, frequently fallen and slipped on the edge.

Finally they came close to a glacier that allowed them to jump onto solid ground:

Luck however was with us at last, and it cheered me when my companion told me that he had always had good luck. At 2.30pm we were near to the land and came to a piece of detached glacier that formed a bridge apparently to the shore. The floe that we were on was moving rapidly, so we had to make a great effort and drag our sledge over the six feet breach.

Our luck was in and we pulled the sledge a little way up the face of the ice and unpacked it. We were on terra firma! But none too soon for fifteen minutes later there was open water where we had gained the land! [21]

Why did he risk his life in May 1916? Eleven months earlier, in early June 1915, Mackintosh (with others including Hayward) had crossed from Hut Point to Cape Evans on the sea-ice so he knew the journey was possible at that time of the year. Richards believed that Mackintosh must have imagined that in May 1916 he could 'nip across' again – while the ice was in.[22]

Mackintosh had talked about a way to make the journey, by simply walking back on his own, or with one companion and taking nothing with them. Wild had diarised these thoughts of Mackintosh (in May 1915); how his plans were to simply lie down and cover himself with a jacket if a blizzard came on quickly. At that time Wild wrote that he had no idea what Mackintosh meant. Wild called it an impractical scheme.[23]

Mackintosh knew of the fragility of the weather. He even noted in his diary on 30 July 1915 that it could change from 'Paradise to Hades in a few hours'.[24] Richards tells us that all of the men including Mackintosh had seen blizzards take out the middle 7 miles of the sea-ice of the route between Cape Evans and Hut Point.[25]

In Richards's opinion Mackintosh's desire to risk a crossing to Cape Evans was based on his dislike of the primitive conditions at Hut Point, when compared to those at Cape Evans. He knew Mackintosh was quite fond of comfort and there was none whatsoever at Hut Point; it was just horrific. Cape Evans seemed a palace, with acetylene lighting, bunks to sleep in and blankets. Richards thought that Mackintosh must have said to himself: 'I could get across to Cape Evans; the Sound seems to be frozen over all the way.'[26] As leader he may have also been anxious to find out whether the four men at Cape Evans were safe but he (Richards) was more inclined to believe that Mackintosh could not put up with the conditions at Hut Point. Richards thought that outweighed everything else on his mind.[27]

It is hard to disagree with Richards's opinion considering the large number of diary entries Mackintosh wrote on the filthy conditions at *Discovery* hut. He dreaded staying at Hut Point any longer than was absolutely necessary.[28] He wrote continually on the putrid conditions, how their faces were black with soot and how everything they touched was blubber. He hated the smoke-filled hut and living a life of what he called 'primitive people'.[29]

Chapter 19

'ARE MACKINTOSH AND HAYWARD HERE?'

July 1916

I T WAS 15 July before Joyce, Richards and Wild (with their four dogs) crossed the sea-ice to Cape Evans. Richards tells us that the first thing they asked Cope, Stevens, Jack and Gaze was: 'Are Mackintosh and Hayward here?' They were told no and Richards says that they were not surprised but he adds that Cope, Stevens, Jack and Gaze were shocked to hear that Mackintosh and Hayward had attempted to cross earlier.[1]

All the men were absolutely convinced that Mackintosh and Hayward were lost and dead. They could not have lived for more than a few hours in the blizzard because they had no equipment of any sort. There was the barest chance that after the return of the sun they might find their bodies so during the spring and summer (August 1916 to January 1917), searches were carried out.

Mackintosh and Hayward were never seen again. No trace of their bodies was found. It was a tragic death for these two men, and heartbreaking for Joyce, Richards and Wild, who had heroically brought them back to the safety of Hut Point. Richards later named it as the final fatal tragedy of the expedition.[2]

Joyce, Richards and Wild, with Cope, Stevens, Jack and Gaze, then lived on at Cape Evans in reasonable comfort. As well as seal meat, penguin meat and penguin eggs they had stores that Scott had left (tinned vegetables, jams, sugar, flour and biscuits), beds to sleep on, an insulated hut with lighting and a few books and papers to read. They never washed or shaved and slept in their clothes inside their sleeping bags and under Jaeger blankets.[3]

There the dog Con was killed by the other three dogs – as a result of a long-standing feud between the huskies and him. Richards wrote later that Con was a general favourite of all the men who returned from Mount Hope and his death saddened them.[4]

Richards fell ill soon after they reached Cape Evans. In his book, *The South Polar Trail*, Joyce tells us that one day Richards suddenly collapsed. He simply threw up his arms, gave a cry, and fainted. Cope, who had become something of a recluse at Cape Evans, rallied and nursed Richards back to health. Joyce believed that the long journey had strained Richards's heart.

In August 1916 Richards scribbled a message on the wall next to his bunk, with an incorrect spelling of Spencer-Smith's name. The message is still faintly visible after almost 100 years: '*R. W. Richards, 14 August 1916, Losses to date, Hayward, Mack, Smyth, ship?*'

In his book Richards tells us that all they could do was wait at Cape Evans for the following January and February and see what came in the way of relief. They were not optimistic as they thought the *Aurora* had been lost but they all looked forward to seeing what the new year would bring. They scrounged some 'luxury items' like matches and soap, from a visit to a third hut at Cape Royds which was a few miles to the north of Cape Evans. Their stores at Cape Evans would last them for another 12 months, plus what they could obtain from seals and penguins. Killing seals for meat and fuel took up most of their time.[5]

10 January 1917

They were rescued on 10 January 1917 when the *Aurora* arrived at McMurdo Sound, with Shackleton on board. Richards tells us he was looking out for seals that morning and he saw what he termed 'some sort of shape' about 7 miles out to sea, which he thought might have been an iceberg. Then he saw a plume of smoke from the ship's stack so he called to the others that 'the ship's here'. He tells us that the others did not believe him, calling him a 'bloody fool'. But someone did get up and look and Richards remembered that man said: 'By Jove, there is something there'. He explains that there was then a 'terrific scurrying around' for a couple of hours to load up the sledges with the things that had to be taken back. They then set off to travel across the 7 miles of sea-ice to the ship. After a couple of hours walking they saw three tiny dots, which turned out to be three men, coming across the ice from the ship and Richards tells us that Joyce recognised one as Shackleton.[6]

In his book *The Ross Sea Shore Party* Richards wrote that Shackleton immediately asked how many men had been lost and on being told three, the three men lay down on the ice, which was a signal back to the ship indicating the number of lives lost.[7]

For Richards it was the first time he had met Shackleton. After being told of the loss of the *Endurance*, before even landing Shackleton on the Weddell Sea side of the continent, Richards remembered that it did not even register with them that all their labours and suffering had been for nothing. He said later: 'I don't look on our struggle as being futile. It was something that the human spirit accomplished.'[8]

The *Aurora* was under command of Captain John King Davis and he wrote later that he was astonished at what a profound effect such a long period of isolation had on the Mount Hope Party men. He says they were 'about the wildest looking gang' that he had ever seen. He described them as men with smoke-bleared eyes looking out from grey haggard faces with beards and uncut matted hair impregnated with soot and grease. He saw that their eyes had a strained and harassed look and he was not surprised given what they had endured. They had lost their ship eighteen months before; there was the toll of two seasons sledging, the loss of three companions, a lack of suitable clothing and proper food and the almost incessant storms and blizzards. To Davis what would have been worst of all were the weary months waiting for a rescue that might be delayed for another year.

All these factors combined to change the men into individuals unlike any he had ever met. He went on to state that the mark of their physical and mental hardships went far deeper than their appearance. He said: 'Their speech was jerky, semi-hysterical and at times almost unintelligible.'[9]

Joyce gave a report to Shackleton on the steps he and the others had taken to try and discover the bodies of Mackintosh and Hayward. Then Shackleton, Joyce and Wild searched again, unsuccessfully. Davis conducted an inquiry with Joyce, Richards and Wild and their statements are included in his 'Report of the Proceedings of the 'Aurora' Relief Expedition 1916–17' notes. Davis's conclusion was that because Mackintosh and Hayward had only been on their journey to Cape Evans for two hours before the blizzard overtook them, it appeared unlikely that they would have had the time to reach land. The thinness of the ice suggested that it would have broken up quickly into detached floes. In Davis's opinion this would have lessened their chances of being carried more than a very short distance before they would have lost all support.[10]

A memorial cross was erected on the hill behind Cape Evans. There was no inscription put on the cross but a sheet of paper was left at the Cape Evans hut with these words, in Shackleton's handwriting.

I. T. A. E.

1914–1917

Sacred to the Memory

Of Lieut. Aeneas Lionel A. Mackintosh, RNR,

V. G. Hayward

And

The Rev. A. P. Spencer-Smith, BA,

Who perished in the service of the Expedition.

'Things done for gain are nought

But great things done endure.'

'I was ever a fighter so one fight more

The best and the last

I should hate that death bandaged

my eyes and bid me creep past.

Let me pay in a minute Life's glad
arrears of pain darkness & cold'.[*]

The three Mount Hope survivors leave Antarctica

On 17 January Joyce, Wild and Richards left McMurdo Sound on the *Aurora*.

Shackleton presented Richards (and Joyce) with a prismatic compass, and on the back of Richards's he engraved an inscription, using his diamond ring:

'To R. W. Richards

From E. H. Shackleton.'

Richards said later that the compass was 'the greatest keepsake I have from those days in the Ross Sea'. It had emotional associations for him, particularly in the difficult six days of the blizzard in February 1916 when they searched for the Bluff depot and then turned south again to try and locate Mackintosh, Spencer-Smith and Wild. Richards said: 'Our lives definitely depended on it.'[11]

Ernest Wild died in March 1918. The *Sydney Morning Herald* newspaper of 16 March 1918 reported that he had been killed on a minesweeper in the Mediterranean. However, Wild's naval records show that he died on 10 March 1918 of 'Enteric Fever' – typhoid.[12]

In 1923 Joyce, Richards, Wild and Hayward were each awarded the Albert Medal in bronze, for saving life on land. Richards wrote to a colleague in 1956 stating that he could never quite figure out why they were awarded the medal as they were only saving their own lives, and they could scarcely do that and leave the others behind.[13] In 1971 the Albert Medal ceased and living recipients were invited to exchange their Albert Medal for the George Cross.

Joyce's book, *The South Polar Trail*, was published in 1929.

---

[*]   The poem is 'Prospice' by Robert Browning, a favourite poet of Shackleton and many men of that era.

In 1940 Ernest Joyce died aged sixty-five.

Richards's book *The Ross Sea Shore Party* was published in 1962. He said it was 'an attempt to set down my personal story of the fortunes and misfortunes of the Ross Sea Party of the Imperial Trans-Antarctic Expedition after the lapse of 40 years'.[14]

Richards was interviewed a number of times late in his life and at one interview he was asked what was the biggest moment; what registered most in his mind some sixty years later? Richards replied that it was finding the tent with Mackintosh, Spencer-Smith and Wild. For Richards it was 'probably the most emotional moment and reached deeper into me than anything else'.[15]

In 1985 Dick Richards died aged ninety-one.

Chapter 20

'THE GREATEST QUALITIES OF ENDURANCE, SELF-SACRIFICE, AND PATIENCE'

The Mount Hope Party

THE EARLY 1900s is known as the Heroic Age of Antarctic Exploration, and if we look at the British expeditions at this time we see many facets of heroism. The first was Scott's *Discovery* Expedition of 1901–04. In late 1902, Scott, Wilson and Shackleton set out, bravely and without fear, across the unknown of the Great Ice Barrier. On some days they managed to cover 15 miles, but on others only 5. Occasionally blizzards held them stationary for one or two days. They reached 82° 15´S and then turned back, but their return journey was grim as they were showing signs of scurvy and they struggled to reach each food depot that they had put down on their trip south. Scott and Wilson were left to haul the sledge as Shackleton weakened. An ill Shackleton returned home a year before Scott and was hailed as a hero, as were Scott and his men when they returned. Scott, Wilson and Shackleton had walked where no man had walked before, out across the unwelcoming Great Ice Barrier, and their exploits entranced the British public.

The second British expedition in the Heroic Age was Shackleton's *Nimrod* Expedition of 1907–09. Up on the polar plateau Shackleton and his men had reached a point 88° 23´S before they turned back. Their return trek to Hut Point had been left dangerously late and they encountered blizzards and near escapes searching for food depots before two of the four men reached their hut. Two men had been left out on the Barrier, but were rescued a few days later. On his return to England in 1909 the newspapers hailed Shackleton with headlines such as: 'The Hero of the Farthest South Expedition Reaches England' and 'The Return of the Heroic Explorer Who Went Furthest South'.[1] Shackleton was knighted, the Royal Geographical Society awarded him a Gold Medal and all men of his shore party received silver Polar Medals.

Scott's *Terra Nova* Expedition of 1910–12 was the third expedition of the time and Scott is remembered not so much for his achievements but for his heroic death. To the British nation Scott was the symbol of heroism and courage. 'Captain Scott's Four Heroic Comrades Who Died on Their Way Back from the Pole', and 'Heroes at the South Pole, The Terra Nova Returns to New Zealand with the Tragic News', ran the 1913 newspaper headlines.[2]

The final expedition of the Heroic Age was Shackleton's 1914–17 expedition. It is incontestable that the actions of Shackleton and his small party of men were heroic. They risked their own lives by sailing across 800 miles of the Southern Ocean, and then walking across South Georgia, so their colleagues on Elephant Island could be saved.

A number of aspects of heroism are evident in these earlier expeditions. First of all, the men were not only courageous and strong willed, but they worked under extreme physical conditions, in a hostile environment. It was precisely the same for the men of the Mount Hope Party, who travelled not simply the 360 miles out to Mount Hope and back but another seven or eight hundred miles as they placed provisions at various depot points and then returned to base for more.

A second feature of the men of earlier expeditions, which also gave rise to their heroic status, is that they apparently knew no fear, as did the men of the Mount Hope Party. Mackintosh and his men had no one to turn to if a catastrophe struck or if insurmountable difficulties arose. There were four men at Cape Evans but they were in no position to help. The six men of the Mount Hope Party, with four dogs, were completely alone on the Great Ice Barrier. In their diaries there is nothing written about trepidation or panic as they encounter crevasses, whiteout conditions, severe food shortages and a seemingly never-ending blizzard. Even when circumstances demanded that men be left behind, firstly Spencer-Smith alone, then Mackintosh, Spencer-Smith and Wild, and then Mackintosh alone, there is only angst and concern for their well-being.

The return journey of the Mount Hope Party had remarkable similarities to that of Scott's fateful final days. However, when they were stopped by a prolonged blizzard they refused to give in and wait in their tents for death to take hold. Close to starvation, three of the men, with the dogs, gallantly went out in the blizzard to search for a food depot.

Another feature that is evident in both Scott's and Shackleton's earlier expeditions was the camaraderie of the men. Similarly, the six men of the Mount Hope Party could not have achieved what they did, and performed so heroically, if they had not worked well together. And it is easy to imagine there could be disharmony in the group given that they were men of such different characters and backgrounds. However, through their diaries, we see that for the majority of the time, they thought positively of each other. Mackintosh often praised the men, adding special notes on Wild and Spencer-Smith, the two men usually in his three-man sledging team. Richards echoed Mackintosh's praise of Wild, particularly in relation to Wild's untiring efforts when looking after an incapacitated Spencer-Smith.[3] All the Mount Hope men had kind words to say about Spencer-Smith, particularly his fortitude and cheerfulness. He was known affectionately as 'Smith' or 'Smithy' and to Richards those names were as useful an appreciation of his character as he could give. They saw him as a 'good' man in the best sense of the word. His Christianity was not obtrusive but it was there all the time and he was always ready to help anyone in difficulty.[4] There is little comment on Hayward through their diaries but Richards tells us he got on well with people although seldom advanced any opinions of his own. He was even-tempered but not an unduly intellectual type, in Richards's opinion.[5] In his book Joyce mentioned his friendship with Richards, when Richards collapsed at Cape Evans in late 1916. Joyce wrote: 'He had been my constant companion for ten months, and a better pal amidst toil and trouble never existed.'[6] Richards in later years also gave his opinion on Joyce. He tells us he was bombastic, a bit of a swashbuckler and a rather flamboyant character.[7] [8] However, there was a strong bond between them. They shared a tent for six months and Richards stressed that 'you learn a man inside out in that period'.[9] He admitted to having a very soft spot in his heart for the man he called 'old Joycey'.[10]

Heroically, they channelled their energies into ensuring they carried out their goal. Differences in experience, age, upbringing and education all seem to have been put aside for the common good. In all their time of sledging and being confined to a hut over the dark months of winter, there are few diary entries of the Mount Hope Party that mention any serious disagreements or conflict. Even at Hut Point at the end of their trek back from Mount Hope Joyce noted that everything was going along harmoniously.[11] In later years Richards remembered that the spirits of the whole party were quite normal and personal relationships were usually very good. He believed that the long polar nights had not affected their spirits or created any particular psychological problems among the men.[12] All the men had empathy with each other's injuries and ailments and particularly with Spencer-Smith, Mackintosh and Hayward as they succumbed to scurvy. Even Joyce's hard-nosed attitude towards Mackintosh appeared to soften when Mackintosh's health was failing. Joyce and Richards were critical of Mackintosh's logistical decisions but the only significant negative diary comments on anyone's personal behaviour are in Wild's diary where he made notes on Mackintosh being selfish.[13] [14] Only in later correspondence and interviews was Richards critical of Mackintosh as the leader. At one interview he stated that in his opinion Mackintosh was a weak character, with no personality and no judgement. He was brave, 'as game as Ned Kelly', but not the man to lead.[15] These criticisms were not published in Richards's book *The Ross Sea Shore Party*.

Finally, if a definition of heroism is to risk one's own life to save the life of another, then it is self-evident that the efforts of the Mount Hope Party were heroic. Their mission was not for glory. All their efforts were geared towards placing provisions they believed were crucial for Shackleton's survival. In their minds the men coming across from the Weddell Sea side would be dependent on the depots, so they simply had to be laid, at all costs. Undeterred by the loss of the *Aurora* and most of their dogs they set about that task. Wearing boots made from old sleeping bags, trousers made from a canvas tent and using old equipment, they succeeded. If Shackleton's party had crossed Antarctica, the depots would have most likely saved their lives.

It appears undeniable that the Mount Hope Party was as heroic as other British expeditions of the era, possibly even more so. The six men were not only strong willed and gallant but they were never daunted by the work to be done. They were not simply men who performed with an indomitable spirit in the most challenging of times. They were men who risked their own lives so other men would survive.

Individual heroes

In his book *South*, Shackleton singled out only three men, Joyce, Wild, and Richards. They were Shackleton's heroes: 'Mackintosh and Hayward owed their lives on that journey to the unremitting care and strenuous endeavours of Joyce, Wild, and Richards, who, also scurvy-stricken but fitter than their comrades, dragged them through the deep snow and blizzards on the sledges.'[16]

It is arguable that Mackintosh, Spencer-Smith and Hayward should be added to Shackleton's list.

Mackintosh was the leader of the party, the man who planned the depot-laying programme. Without his leadership in the early stages, the depots may have never been laid. He managed his men to work cohesively over the winter of 1915 to prepare for the final sledging season. He helped with the sledge-hauling all the way to Mount Hope and ensured the last depot position was located correctly as instructed to him by Shackleton. Even though he was starting to falter on the way out to Mount Hope, he refused to give in. After his health failed he made every effort to help the others by hobbling along next to the sledge rather than sitting on it. He accepted being left behind with Spencer-Smith and Wild, and then later on his own. He made no diary reference of any pain or discomfort for having only one eye. Losing his life, in recklessly making a dash to Cape Evans in May 1916, unfortunately cast a long shadow over his achievements.

Spencer-Smith too was a man of stature and through all the diaries he comes across as a dedicated, hard-working member of the party. In November 1915 he knew he was unwell but he continued to assist in man-hauling supplies onto the Great Ice Barrier until late January 1916. After breaking down he was carried on the sledge for over 300 miles, lying in a wet and frozen sleeping bag, being jolted continuously day after day as the sledge bounced over the rough surface. The others had nothing but admiration for the way he accepted his condition, and how he remained cheerful and pleasant throughout.

There is also no reason for Hayward not to be recognised in the same light as Joyce, Wild and Richards. He was certainly seen by others as a hero, being awarded the British civilian medal for bravery, the Albert Medal, for his efforts to save the lives of Mackintosh and Spencer-Smith. From diary entries he was obviously an active member of the team that man-hauled provisions out to Mount Hope. He helped lay all the depots, battled with Joyce and Richards to reach the Bluff depot in the long blizzard and then returned to pick up Mackintosh, Spencer-Smith and Wild. It was only after this time that he became so stricken with scurvy that he was unable to help the others.

Joyce was undeniably a true hero. His willingness and dedication to lay the depots out to Mount Hope at all costs is apparent. He accepted every situation as it was and worked tirelessly. He was the front man on a rope leading the party the majority of the time, suffering snow-blindness and frostbite. He was the only man at Mount Hope to help locate the correct depot position and to place the provisions for Shackleton. He made the decision (with Richards and Hayward) to try to make the Bluff depot rather than die in their tent. He helped drag the sick men to safety and worked tirelessly to help others when they did reach Hut Point.

Wild certainly comes across as a quiet hero. He seemed to accept the situation in which he was placed, whatever that may be. He looked after the ailing and bed-ridden Spencer-Smith for weeks on end. He shared a tent with Mackintosh, whose actions at times he clearly found hard to fathom, but he did not upset the harmony of the team. He was the one to wait with two sick men while Joyce, Richards and Hayward searched for the Bluff depot, and then he helped these three to bring in the sledge when they did return. He was one of three men able to help Hayward and Mackintosh to reach Hut Point. He seemed to be always longing for a smoke and a drink, and made diary entries with humour even at the most critical of times.

To Shackleton, and from the diaries, Richards was certainly a hero. As a 22-year-old he shouldered a share of the leadership when Mackintosh started to falter, and when critical decisions had to be made. It was he and Joyce who pushed Mackintosh to use the dogs. He and Joyce were the two men to pull the party through at the most life-threatening times. They steered the party in blizzard conditions. Richards made the decision to take bearings on the back cairns to give them a direction to steer by on their return journey. It was he (with Joyce and Hayward) who had the strength of mind to make a move after being tent bound for six days, to find the Bluff depot and return to rescue Mackintosh, Spencer-Smith and Wild. He was one of the three men with the will-power to drag Mackintosh and Hayward to the safety of Hut Point.

All their endeavours were in vain; but without doubt the six men of the Mount Hope Party were heroic.

In *South* Shackleton wrote that the *Aurora* would land six men at McMurdo Sound and 'lay down depots on the route of the Transcontinental party'. He knew that the men of the Mount Hope Party would be crossing over 'well-travelled ground' and he expected them to encounter some 'difficulties and dangers' but he could not have anticipated what eventuated.[17]

In Shackleton's words: 'The result was that in making this journey the greatest qualities of endurance, self-sacrifice, and patience were called for.'[18]

Antarctica after 1917

The trek of the Mount Hope Party was the last great adventure in the Heroic Age of Antarctic Exploration.

No one attempted to emulate Shackleton's planned crossing of the Antarctic continent until forty-two years after the deaths of Spencer-Smith, Mackintosh and Hayward. In 1957, a private expedition, supported by various Commonwealth governments, set off to cross the Antarctic continent overland. This expedition was planned along similar lines to Shackleton's 1914–17 expedition. The main party, led by British explorer Dr Vivian Fuchs, left Shackleton Base, on the Weddell Sea side, and they had a support party led by New Zealander Sir Edmund Hillary based in McMurdo Sound. Like Mackintosh's 1916 men, Hillary's team were responsible for laying a line of supply depots towards the South Pole, for Fuchs to use on the final leg of his journey.

Fuchs's party arrived at McMurdo Sound on 2 March 1958, travelling with and on a number of motorised vehicles. They took ninety-nine days to cross from the Weddell Sea to McMurdo Sound – a distance of 2,160 miles.

The men of the Mount Hope Party remembered

A wooden cross on the hill behind the Cape Evans hut was erected to commemorate the loss of Mackintosh, Spencer-Smith and Hayward, but there are Antarctic landmarks dedicated to five of the six men of the Mount Hope Party:

Mount Mackintosh is an Antarctic mountain, at 74° 20´S 162° 15´E, and is the northern-most peak in the Prince Albert Mountains range, within the Trans-Antarctic Mountains.

Mount Joyce is a prominent, dome-shaped mountain, 6,000 feet high, standing on the south side of David Glacier, 8 geographical miles north-west of Mount Howard in the Prince Albert Mountains of Victoria Land.

Joyce Lake lies along the northern side of Taylor Glacier in Pearse Valley, Victoria Land.

Cape Spencer-Smith is a cape on White Island at 78° 00´S 167° 27´E.

Mount Hayward is a mountain, also on White Island, at 78° 06´S 167° 21´E.

Richards Inlet (83° 20´S 168° 30´E) is a large ice-filled inlet at the mouth of Lennox-King Glacier, opening to the Ross Ice Shelf just south-east of Lewis Ridge.

Apart from the Albert Medals, later replaced with George Crosses, awarded to Joyce, Richards, Wild and Hayward, these are the landmarks that recognise the efforts of the Mount Hope Party which laid the depots required by Shackleton.

Depots that were never needed.

POSTSCRIPT BY
DR D. L. HARROWFIELD

To ENTER AND then experience the solitude and subdued light of Captain R. F. Scott's 1910–13 expedition hut at Cape Evans is a unique personal experience that few have enjoyed. To have also been a friend of one of the later occupants, Dick Richards GC Polar Medal, last survivor of the subsequent occupants, the Ross Sea Shore Party 1914–17 led by Lieutenant A. L. A. Mackintosh, was a further privilege. Perhaps the culmination of a life-long interest concerned with Antarctica's brief human history.

In recent years several books and chapters in books, along with a few papers in journals, have been published on the Ross Sea Party Expedition during World War One. This expedition had the allotted task given by Sir Ernest Shackleton, of placing essential depots of food and fuel for his Imperial Trans-Antarctic Expedition 1914–17.

The writings by various authors, including myself, conveyed overviews and reassessments of the expedition, including that of the drift of the *Aurora* in the Ross Sea and Southern Ocean during 1915–16. The Ross Sea Party expedition, however, continues to be largely unknown. Only a few authors have located and used original manuscripts in private ownership or public institutions to assist in conveying this history. More will perhaps surface in years to come.

The men cast ashore on Ross Island in 1915 made do with either cast-off or improvised clothing, second-hand equipment along with food around six years old, all salvaged from that abandoned by the earlier expeditions to Ross Island, of Scott and Shackleton. They also put up with a diet mostly deficient in essential components for life, including the necessary calorific value required for good health. It was not until the end of the depot-laying and return to the hut erected at Hut Point for Scott's first expedition 1901–04 that fresh seal meat provided the necessary sustenance to relieve swollen and blackened gums and joints which slowly faded.

In the end the task by only six men was achieved, although during the eventual struggle to the safety of a fifteen-year-old wooden hut in a hostile environment, sadly cost the lives of three men. The Reverend Arnold Spencer-Smith died a few miles from safety and Mackintosh, leader of the expedition, along with dog handler Victor Hayward, although reaching Hut Point and regaining strength, were then lost in their desperate struggle for the better environment of the hut at Cape Evans.

The six men had sledged into history over the great expanse of the Ross Ice Shelf, the area of France, for 170 days and had covered 1,330 miles (2,465 km). One must not however forget supporting party members Irvine Gaze, Alexander Stevens, Keith Jack and John Cope, in the early stages.

During my work, including that for Canterbury Museum, Antarctic Heritage Trust and more recently Heritage Expeditions, I have often stood outside *Discovery* hut and gazed over the sea ice in the direction of Cape Evans. I have tried to imagine in the late austral summer, the bleak setting as Mackintosh and Hayward slowly faded in the limited light on 7 May 1916.

One can only imagine the sadness, pain and perhaps anger, felt by Richards, Ernest Joyce and Ernest Wild who, having done their best to save the men, then saw them lost forever. This new account by Wilson McOrist is compiled solely from original manuscript material. It has focused on the epic struggle of a small group of six men, which included Dick Richards, who in the face of adversity and incredible odds, set out to achieve their goal. They were not to know that Shackleton was in serious trouble on the other side of the continent, that he would lose his ship, and fail to achieve his goal of the first crossing of Antarctica, a dream not realised until four decades later.

Wilson's book is also of significance as for the first time the sledging accomplishment of the men who ensured the final depot was laid for Shackleton beside Mount Hope is told through their written accounts. One can feel very close to each of them. The words of these young men convey hardship and suffering, along with times of sadness and perhaps contentment, in a way that now brings this aspect of the expedition to life.

This book is a lasting tribute to the men of the Ross Sea Shore Party, their great courage and also the four dogs; Oscar, Gunner, Con and Towser who completed the almost impossible task, along with those who helped make this possible. Wilson McOrist has done them a service. In 1916 the *Aurora*, refitted at Port Chalmers, New Zealand, returned to McMurdo Sound and in January 1917 rescued the seven survivors. Many went on to serve in World War One.

David L. Harrowfield
Oamaru
New Zealand

TIMELINE

1914

In England, Shackleton recruits Mackintosh, Joyce, Spencer-Smith, Wild and Hayward

11 November	The *Aurora* arrives in Sydney
1 December	Mackintosh recruits Richards
14 December	The *Aurora* leaves Sydney
24 December	The *Aurora* leaves Hobart

1915

1 January	The *Aurora* enters the Ross Sea, Antarctica
10 January	The *Aurora* arrives at McMurdo Sound
24 January	The first season of sledging commences
9 February	Joyce's team lay supplies at Minna Bluff depot, near 79°S
11 February	Mackintosh's team also reach the Bluff depot
19 February	Mackintosh, Joyce and Wild put down the 80°S depot

21 February–6 March	Hayward and Richards, and others, place depots close to Hut Point
12 March	Spencer-Smith and Richards, and others, are back at Cape Evans
14 March	Hayward and others arrive at *Discovery* hut, Hut Point
24 March	Mackintosh, Joyce and Wild also reach *Discovery* hut
6 May	The *Aurora* is swept away from Cape Evans
2 June	The men at *Discovery* hut make the crossing to Cape Evans
22 August	The sun appears over the horizon
September	All the depot stores are taken from Cape Evans to *Discovery* hut
October	The depots laid earlier close to Hut Point are replenished
November	The depots continue to be replenished, using two teams, led by Mackintosh and Joyce
24 December	Mackintosh's team leaves Bluff depot and heads south. Joyce's team is approaching the Bluff depot
31 December	Both teams are together

1916

6 January	At 80°S, Gaze, Cope and Jack are sent back, leaving the six men of the Mount Hope Party
12 January	The 81°S depot is laid
18 January	The 82°S depot is laid
22 January	Near 83°S, Spencer-Smith is left behind
26 January	The final depot at Mount Hope is put in place
29 January	Mackintosh, Joyce, Wild, Hayward and Richards return to Spencer-Smith
2 February	The six men reach the 82°S depot and pick up provisions
7 February	They reach 81°S (209 miles to Hut Point)

11 February	They reach 80°S (155 miles to Hut Point)
17 February	A blizzard stops their progress, 10 miles from the Bluff depot (80 miles to Hut Point)
17–22 February	The blizzard continues
23 February	Mackintosh, Spencer-Smith and Wild are left behind
23–26 February	Joyce, Richards and Hayward, with the four dogs, trek to the Bluff depot
29 February	Joyce, Richards and Hayward return to Mackintosh, Spencer-Smith and Wild
1 March	The six men are at Bluff depot (70 miles to Hut Point)
6 March	The six men are 40 miles from Hut Point
8 March	Mackintosh is left behind (30 miles to Hut Point)
9 March	Spencer-Smith dies, early that morning (20 miles from Hut Point)
11 March	Joyce, Wild, Richards and Hayward reach *Discovery* hut at Hut Point
14 March	Joyce, Wild and Richards set off to bring in Mackintosh
16 March	Mackintosh is rescued
18 March	The five remaining men of the Mount Hope Party are at Hut Point
March–April	The men recover, and wait for the sea-ice to freeze so they can walk to Cape Evans
8 May	Mackintosh and Hayward leave, to walk to Cape Evans
15 July	Joyce, Wild and Richards, and the four dogs, walk to Cape Evans
July 1916–January 1917	Joyce, Wild and Richards (with Cope, Gaze, Jack and Stevens) are at Cape Evans

1917

10 January	The relief ship arrives

SOURCES

ABBREVIATIONS

ATL: Alexander Turnbull Library, Wellington, New Zealand
RGS-IBG: Royal Geographical Society (with the Institute of British
  Geographers), London, United Kingdom
CM: Canterbury Museum, Christchurch, New Zealand
NMM: National Maritime Museum, Greenwich, London, United Kingdom.
SPRI: Scott Polar Research Institute, Cambridge, United Kingdom

PRIMARY SOURCES

Diaries

1. Hayward, Victor George, original field diary. JOD/231/1. NMM.
2. Joyce, Ernest Edward Mills, original field diary, private collection
    of Betsy Krementz. Log transcript of Ernest E. Joyce (MS-
    Papers-0217-01, microfilmed at MS-Copy-Micro-0629), ATL.

3. Mackintosh, Aeneas Lionel Acton, diary notes 31 Dec 1914–24 Jan 1915, and 5 Jun 1915–30 Sep 1915, SPRI. MS 1537/4/1/1; D Mackintosh Aeneas, Diary 5 Jun 1915 to 30 Sep 1915 and diary notes, 25 Jan–15 Apr 1915. SSC/112 (Mackintosh, A. L. A. Journal of 1915). RGS-IBG.

4. Richards, Richard Walter, original field diary. Imperial Trans-Antarctic Expedition [Ross Sea Party] 1914–1917, Richard W. Richards's papers, MS 285. Item 3, 1 February 1915–19 February 1915, and MS 154, 23 February 1916–19 March 1916, CM.

5. Spencer-Smith, Arnold Patrick, original field diary. Diary 25 Jan 1915–11 Mar 1915, and 1 Oct 1915–7 Mar 1916. MS 1390; BJ. SPRI.

6. Wild, Harry Ernest, original field diary. 31 Oct 1914 to 19 Mar 1916. MS 928/3; BJ. SPRI.

SECONDARY SOURCES

Other diaries and 1914–1917 related documents

Cope, J. L. 'Medical Report of the Ross Sea Base ITAE, January 1917'. MS 1537/4/4/3; D. SPRI.

Gaze, I. O., diary note, January 1916, MS 105, CM.

Hayward, postcard to his parents, 16 November 1914. JOD/231/2. NMM.

Hayward, radio telegram to Ethel Bridson, 31 December 1914, MS 1590/2/133. SPRI.

Joyce, letter to James Paton, 2 October 1915. ATL.

Joyce, letter to Mackintosh, 15 November 1915. MS 1537/4/4/6/7;D. SPRI.

Joyce, letter to Mackintosh, 6 January 1916. MS 1537/4/4/6/7;D. SPRI.

Joyce, transcripts of his field diary, ATL.

Mackintosh, letter to G. Marston, 27 February 1913. SPRI.

Mackintosh, letter, written 28 February 1916, transcribed by Richards, MS 285. Item 1 & Item 2, CM.

Mackintosh, letters to Ernest Joyce of 28 October 1915, 25 November

1915, 5 December 1915 and 1 January 1916. MS 1537/4/4/6/1-8;D. SPRI.

Richards Agreement with Shackleton, written 18 January 1916 in Antarctica. MS 99, CM.

Richards Agreement with Shackleton, written December 1914, at Sydney, Australia. MS 1537/4/5/1;D. SPRI.

Richards, letter-gram to Mackintosh, 2 December 1914. MS1590/2/120; D. SPRI.

Richards, letters to Mackintosh, 21 November 1914. MS 1590/2/26;D. and 26 November 1914. MS 1590/2/27;D. SPRI.

Richards, telegrams to Mackintosh, 30 November 1914. MS 1590/2/118;D and 2 December 1914. MS1590/2/120; D. SPRI.

Shackleton, letter to A. L. A. Mackintosh. 18 September 1914. MS 1537/4/4/22;D. SPRI.

Shackleton, letter to his wife Emily, 17 August 1914. MS 1537/2/30/42;D. SPRI.

Spencer-Smith, A. P., letter to parents November 1914, MS 277, ITEM No 22. CM.

Stevens, A. Report 1914–1917 ATAE. MS 100 / 136; BJ. SPRI.

Letters, audio and other manuscript sources

Hayward, Peter John, grand-nephew of Victor Hayward, private papers.

Horsman, Debby, grand-niece of Arnold Patrick Spencer-Smith, private papers.

Phillips, Anne, granddaughter of Aeneas Mackintosh, private papers, and interview, 5 July 2011. Twickenham, UK.

Naval Service Record of Ernest Edward Mills Joyce, No: 160823. Naval Historical Branch, Ministry of Defence, Portsmouth, UK.

Naval Service Record of Harry Ernest Wild, No: 181904. Naval Historical Branch, Ministry of Defence, Portsmouth, UK.

P&O Officers Register, NMM.

Report of Proceedings of the Aurora Relief Expedition 1916–1917. MS 1598/1–2;D. SPRI.

Richards, interview with L. Bickel, 1976. TRC 495, National Library of Australia.

Richards, interview with P. Lathlean, 1976.

Richards, interview with P. Law, December 1980.

Richards, interview, Australian Broadcasting Commission, *Verbatim* programme, 1977. Broadcast in 2002.

Richards, papers at the Art & Historical Collection, Federation University (formerly University of Ballarat), Victoria, Australia.

Richards, various letters to historians A. J. T. Fraser and L. B. Quartermain, from 1956 to 1969. MS 1, 285 and 303. CM.

Newspapers, journals and periodicals

Australasian Post, Wellington, New Zealand.

Daily Mirror, London, UK, 1909, 1913.

Old Woodbridgian, school magazine, Woodbridge School, Suffolk, UK.

Scottish Geographical Magazine, Vol. 30, No. 2, 1914.

The Argus, Melbourne, Australia.

The Dial, college magazine, Queens' College, Cambridge, UK, 1907.

The Eagle, school magazine, Bedford Modern School (BMS Archives). Journal of 1917.

The Mercury, Hobart, Tasmania, 12 December 1911.

Sydney Morning Herald.

The Times, London, UK.

The West Australian, Perth, WA, 13 July 1914.

Willesden Chronicle, Willesden Green, UK.

Published works

Antarctic Historic Huts, New Zealand Antarctic Heritage Trust booklet.

Ballantyne, R. *The World of Ice*. London, Thomas Nelson, 1860.

Caesar, A. *The White: Last Days in the Antarctic Journeys of Scott and Mawson, 1911-1913.* Picador, Sydney, 1999.

Davis, J. K., *With the* Aurora *in the Antarctic 1911-1914.* Andrew Melrose, London, 1919.

Debenham, F., *In the Antarctic: Stories of Scott's Last Expedition.* John Murray, London, 1952.

Joyce, E. *The South Polar Trail: The Log of the Imperial Trans-Antarctic Expedition.* Duckworth, London, 1929.

Mackintosh, A. L. A., *Shackleton's Lieutenant: The Nimrod diary of A. L. A. Mackintosh, British Antarctic Expedition, 1907–09,* ed. Stanley Newman. Polar Publications, Christchurch, 1990.

Marston, G. & Murray, J., *Antarctic Days: Sketches of the Homely Side of Polar Life by Two of Shackleton's Men.* Andrew Melrose, London, 1913.

Mawson, D. *Antarctic Diaries.* Unwin Hyman, London, 1988.

Mills, L., *Frank Wild.* Caedmon of Whitby, 1999.

Priestley, R. E. *Antarctic Adventure.* T. Fisher Unwin, London, 1914.

Richards, R. W. *The Ross Sea Shore Party 1914–17.* Scott Polar Research Institute, Cambridge, 1962.

Scott, Capt. R. F., *Scott's Last Expedition: The Journals,* Location and Catalogue: 51024-42, 46272. British Library.

Scott, R. F., *The Voyage of the Discovery.* Smith Elder, London, 1905.

Shackleton, E. H., *South.* Heinemann, London, 1919.

Shackleton, E. H., *The Heart of the Antarctic, Vol. 1.* Heinemann, London, 1909.

Wilson, E., *Antarctic Notebooks,* Reardon, Cheltenham, 2011

Unpublished works

Jones, A. G. E., 'Tubby', Polar Record, Vol. 18, pp. 43–45. SPRI.

Fraser, A. J. T., 'Antarctic Padre', Canterbury Museum, New Zealand.

Richards R. W., 'Four Dogs', provided by D. Harrowfield.

ENDNOTES

Introducton

1. E. H. Shackleton, *South* (London: Heine-mann, 1919)

2. Ibid.

Chapter 1

1. R. W. Richards, *The Ross Sea Shore Party 1914–17* (Cambridge: Scott Polar Research Institute, 1962)
2. R. F. Scott, *The Voyage of the Discovery* (London: Smith Elder, 1905)
3. New Zealand Antarctic Heritage Trust booklet, *Antarctic Historic Huts*
4. Richards, interview with P. Lathlean, 1976
5. Richards, *The Ross Sea Shore Party*
6. E. H. Shackleton, *The Heart of the Antarctic, Vol. 1* (London: Heinemann, 1909)
7. Ibid.
8. Shackleton, *South*
9. Spencer-Smith letter to his parents, 8 November 1914
10. A. Phillips, granddaughter of Aeneas Mackintosh. Private papers
11. Ibid., interview, 5 July 2011, Twickenham, UK
12. *The Eagle*, Bedford Modern School (BMS) journal of 1917
13. National Maritime Museum. P&O Officers Register, Ref 75/8, p. 119
14. *Sydney Morning Herald*, 3 December 1907
15. P&O Officers Register
16. Anne Phillips, granddaughter of Aeneas Mackintosh. Private papers
17. National Archives. Naval Service Record of Ernest Edward Mills Joyce, No: 160823
18. Scott, *Voyage*
19. Naval Service Record of Ernest Edward Mills Joyce, No: 160823
20. Shackleton, *Heart*
21. G. Marston & J. Murray, *Antarctic Days: Sketches of the Homely Side of Polar Life by*

Two of Shackleton's Men (London: Andrew Melrose, 1913).

22. L. Mills, *Frank Wild* (Whitby: Caedmon of Whitby, 1999)
23. Shackleton, *Heart*
24. The *West Australian* newspaper, Perth, WA, 13 July 1914
25. The *Mercury* newspaper, Hobart, Tasmania, 12 December 1911
26. Naval Service Record of Harry Ernest Wild, No: 181904
27. Mills, *Frank Wild*.
28. A. G. E. Jones, 'Tubby', SPRI, Polar Record, Vol. 18, No. 112, 1976, pp. 43–5
29. Naval Service Record of Harry Ernest Wild, No: 181904
30. Ibid. Comment by Iain MacKenzie, Curatorial Officer, Admiralty Library, Naval Historical Branch (Naval Staff), Ministry of Defence, HM Naval Base, Portsmouth
31. 'Tubby', Polar Record, Vol. 18, pp. 43–5
32. Debby Horsman, great-niece of A. P. Spencer-Smith. Private papers
33. *Old Woodbridgian* school magazine, Woodbridge School, Suffolk, UK
34. A. J. T. Fraser, 'Antarctic Padre', unpublished
35. *The Dial*, Queens College Magazine, Queens College, Cambridge, UK, 1907
36. J. J. Hayward, grand-nephew of Victor Hayward. Private papers
37. *Willesden Chronicle*, Willesden Green, UK, 16 February 1917
38. R. Ballantyne, *The World of Ice* (London: Thomas Nelson, 1860)
39. P. J. Hayward, grand-nephew of Victor Hayward. Private papers
40. *Willesden Chronicle*, 16 February 1917, and from the private papers of P. J. Hayward, grand-nephew of Victor Hayward
41. P. J. Hayward, grand-nephew of Victor Hayward. Private papers
42. Richards papers at the Art & Historical Collection, Federation University (formerly University of Ballarat)
43. Richards, interview with P. Lathlean, 1976
44. Richards telegram to Mackintosh, 2 December 1914
45. Richards, interview with L. Bickel, 1976

Chapter 2

1. Shackleton, *South*
2. Mackintosh letter to G. Marston, 27 February 1913
3. A. L. A. Mackintosh, *Shackleton's Lieutenant: The Nimrod Diary of A. L. A. Mackintosh, British Antarctic Expedition, 1907–09* (Christchurch: Stanley Newman, Polar Publications, 1990)
4. Richards letter to L. B. Quartermain, 9 November 1960
5. Shackleton letter to Mackintosh, 18 September 1914
6. E. Joyce, *The South Polar Trail: The Log of the Imperial Trans-Antarctic Expedition* (London: Duckworth, 1929)
7. *Sydney Morning Herald*, 29 June 1914
8. Richards, *The Ross Sea Shore Party*
9. Spencer-Smith diary, July 1915
10. Hayward diary, July 1915
11. *Sydney Morning Herald*, 29 June 1914
12. George Smith, headmaster at Merchiston Castle, Edinburgh, written reference for A. P. Spencer-Smith, 4 June 1912, supplied by Debby Horsman, great-niece of A. P. Spencer-Smith
13. Naval Service Record of Harry Ernest Wild, No: 181904
14. P. J. Hayward, grand-nephew of Victor Hayward. Private papers
15. *Willesden Chronicle*, 11 September 1914
16. Ibid., 16 February 1917
17. Shackleton letter to his wife Emily, 18 August 1914
18. A. Stevens, report of the 1914–17 ATAE expedition, SPRI
19. J. K. Davis, *With the Aurora in the Antarctic*

1911–1914 (London: Andrew Melrose, 1919)

20. Richards, interview with P. Lathlean, 1976

21. The *Argus* newspaper, Melbourne, 11 November 1914

22. P. J. Hayward, grand-nephew of Victor Hayward. Private papers

23. Hayward postcard, 16 November 1914. NMM

24. Spencer-Smith postcard to his parents, November 1914. Debby Horsman, great-niece of A. P. Spencer-Smith. Private papers

25. Spencer-Smith, letter to his parents, 8 November 1914. Debby Horsman, great-niece of A. P. Spencer-Smith. Private papers

26. Richards, interview with L. Bickel, 1976

27. Richards telegram, 30 November 1914

28. Richards letter to Mackintosh, 21 November 1914

29. Richards letter to Mackintosh, 26 November 1914

30. Richards, *The Ross Sea Shore Party*

31. Richards, interview with P. Lathlean, 1976

32. Richards Agreement, 1 December 1914, SPRI

33. Richards, *The Ross Sea Shore Party*

34. Spencer-Smith cablegram, 1914. Debby Horsman, great-niece of A. P. Spencer-Smith. Private papers

35. Richards, *The Ross Sea Shore Party*

36. Joyce, *The South Polar Trail*

37. Richards, *The Ross Sea Shore Party*

38. Richards, interview with P. Lathlean, 1976

39. Richards, *The Ross Sea Shore Party*

40. Hayward radio telegram to Ethel Bridson, 31 December 1914

41. *The Times*, 1 April 1914

42. Joyce, *The South Polar Trail*

43. Mackintosh diary, 1 January 1915

44. Ibid., 2 January 1915

45. Ibid., 12 January 1915

46. Ibid., 8 January 1915

47. Richards interview with P. Lathlean, 1976

48. Mackintosh diary, 1 January 1915

49. Ibid., 3 January 1915

50. Ibid., 1 January 1915

51. Joyce, *The South Polar Trail*

52. Richards, *The Ross Sea Shore Party*

53. Mackintosh diary, 1 January 1915

54. Ibid., 7 January 1915

55. Shackleton letter to Mackintosh, 18 September 1914. In part this letter stated:

'I would here inform you that the T-C party will carry sufficient provisions & equipment to cross right across to McM Sound but it is all important as we cannot tell what delays may ensure and what accidents may occur that the Southern depot from the Ross Sea should be laid.

'I make the above remark as regards the TC party equipment in case some very serious accident incapacitates your party from making a depot so that you may not have the anxiety of feeling that the T-C is absolutely dependent on the depot that you are to lay, but it is of supreme importance, as ensuring the absolute safe return of the TC party to have this depot laid.'

(TC and T-C means Shackleton's Trans-Continental Party.)

56. Shackleton letter to Mackintosh, 18 September 1914

57. Mackintosh diary, 13 February 1915

58. Mackintosh diary, 16 June 1915

59. Shackleton letter to Mackintosh, 18 September 1914. This letter also stated:

'Para 18: This paragraph is for your information only and you are to discuss it with nobody but follow implicitly these directions. If the TC party has not come out, and you go north, you must leave at Cape Evans or Cape Royds in a position easy for six men to handle, the best lifeboat belonging to Aurora. You must deck her over the foreport with canvas, or even deck her halfway along with a canvas cover and framework , she must have a good mast and sail, 12 oars, anchor and oil bag, a water breaker empty, sufficient sledging stores, oil and Primus cooker, to last two months, also sleeping bag and Burberrys; in fact the full equipment of a sledging party for six men for two months. You will also leave a sextant. The TC party will be equipped chronometers, nautical almanacs, etc. You should also leave a general chart of the ocean south of NZ. The reason for the equipment is as follows – should by any chance the TC party have arrived at winter quarters at the Ross Sea, after the ship has gone, I may decide to go north in the lifeboat. Under these circumstances I will make for Cape Adare then Macquarie Island, &

thence to Auckland Island and so on to Stew-
art Island. I do not wish you to wait at either
M Island or A Island on the way up. If we can
cross the ocean south of these islands there
is nothing to prevent us reaching civilization
generally.'

60. Shackleton, *South*

61. Mackintosh diary, 1 January 1915

62. Joyce, *The South Polar Trail*

63. Richards, *The Ross Sea Shore Party*

64. Mackintosh diary, 9 January 1915

65. Richards, *The Ross Sea Shore Party*

66. Richards, interview with P. Lathlean, 1976

67. Mackintosh diary, 9 January 1915

68. Richards notes, Art & Historical Collection, Federation University (formerly University of Ballarat)

69. Mackintosh diary, 10 January 1915

Chapter 3

1. Richards, *The Ross Sea Shore Party*

2. Joyce, *The South Polar Trail*

3. Mackintosh diary, 12 January 1915

4. Joyce diary transcripts, 16 January 1915

5. Mackintosh diary, 16 January 1915

6. Shackleton letter to Mackintosh, 18 September 1914

7. Richards letter to L. B. Quartermain, unknown date

8. Joyce field diary, 24 January 1915

9. F. Debenham, *In the Antarctic: Stories of Scott's Last Expedition* (London: John Murray, 1952)

10. Mackintosh diary, 24 January 1915

11. Wild diary, 25 January 1915

12. Mackintosh, *Shackleton's Lieutenant*

13. Mackintosh diary, 25 January 1915

14. Spencer-Smith diary, 25 January 1915

15. Wild diary, 27 January 1915

16. Ibid., 9 October 1915

17. Joyce, *The South Polar Trail*

18. Richards, *The Ross Sea Shore Party*

19. Spencer-Smith diary, 27 January 1915

20. Richards, *The Ross Sea Shore Party*

21. Joyce diary transcripts, 30 January 1915

22. Joyce, *The South Polar Trail*

23. Caesar, A., *The White* (Sydney: Picador, 1999)

24. Joyce field diary, 27 January 1915

25. Ibid., 30 January 1915

26. Wild diary, 28 January 1915

27. Ibid., 30 January 1915

28. Spencer-Smith diary, 28 January 1915

29. Ibid., 29 January 1915

30. Mackintosh diary, 28 January 1915

31. Joyce field diary, 9 February 1915

32. R. E. Priestley, *Antarctic Adventure* (London: T. Fisher Unwin, 1914)

33. Spencer-Smith diary, 30 January 1915

34. Wild diary, 30 January 1915

35. Mackintosh diary, 30 January 1915

36. Wild diary, 31 January 1915

37. Mackintosh diary, 1 February 1915

38. Ibid., 2 February 1915

39. Spencer-Smith diary, 31 January 1915

40. Ibid., 7 February 1915

41. Richards diary, 23 January 1915

42. Hayward diary, 31 January 1915

Chapter 4

1. Debenham, *In the Antarctic*

2. Richards, *The Ross Sea Shore Party*

3. Debenham, *In the Antarctic*

4. Mackintosh diary, 1 February 1915

5. Spencer-Smith diary, 2 February 1915

6. Wild diary, 2 February 1915

7. Debenham, *In the Antarctic*

8. Spencer-Smith diary, 3 February 1915

9. Mackintosh diary, 3 February 1915
10. Ibid., 4 February 1915
11. Spencer-Smith diary, 5 February 1915
12. Ibid., 6 February 1915
13. Mackintosh diary, 7 February 1915
14. Ibid., 8 February 1915
15. Ibid., 9 February 1915
16. Ibid., 10 February 1915
17. Spencer-Smith diary, 10 February 1915
18. Ibid., 11 February 1915
19. Ibid., 14 February 1915
20. Ibid., 15 February 1915
21. Ibid., 16 February 1915
22. Ibid., 17 February 1915
23. Hayward diary, 18 February 1915

24. Spencer-Smith diary, 22 February 1915
25. Richards, *The Ross Sea Shore Party*
26. Mackintosh diary, 20 February 1915
27. Priestley, *Antarctic Adventure*
28. Joyce field diary, 11 February 1915
29. Wild diary, 14 February 1915
30. Mackintosh diary, 15 February 1915
31. Ibid., 17 February 1915
32. Ibid.,18 February 1915
33. Ibid., 19 February 1915
34. Ibid., 20 February 1915
35. Wild diary, 19 February 1915
36. Joyce field diary, 21–23 February 1915
37. Mackintosh diary, 21 February 1915
38. Ibid., 22 February 1915

Chapter 5

1. Mackintosh diary, 24 February 1915
2. Ibid., 25 February 1915
3. Ibid.
4. Joyce field diary, 25–26 February 1915
5. Ibid.
6. Ibid., 25 February 1915
7. E. Wilson, *Antarctic Notebooks* (Cheltenham: Reardon, 2011)
8. Mackintosh diary, 27 February 1915
9. Joyce field diary, 1 March 1915
10. Mackintosh diary, 1 March 1915
11. Joyce field diary, 2 March 1915
12. Wild diary, 28 February 1915
13. Ibid., 2 March 1915
14. Mackintosh diary, 2 March 1915 Wild diary, 3 March 1915
15. Mackintosh diary, 2 March 1915
16. Ibid., 6 March 1915
17. Joyce field diary, 6 March 1915
18. Wilson, *Antarctic Notebooks*
19. Debenham, *In the Antarctic*
20. Mackintosh diary, 10 March 1915
21. Ibid., 12 March 1915
22. Ibid., 13 March 1915
23. Ibid., 14 March 1915
24. Joyce field diary, 12 March 1915
25. Ibid., 14 March 1915
26. Ibid., 8–12 March 1915
27. Mackintosh diary, 15 March 1915

28. Joyce field diary, 8–12 March 1915
29. Ibid., 15 March 1915
30. Mackintosh diary, 15 March 1915
31. Ibid., 18 March 1915
32. Ibid.
33. Ibid., 22 March 1915
34. Priestley, *Antarctic Adventure*
35. Mackintosh diary, 23 March 1915
36. Joyce field diary, 22, 23 March 1915
37. Mackintosh diary, 24 March 1915
38. Joyce field diary, 24 March 1915
39. Mackintosh diary, 24 March 1915
40. Joyce field diary, 24 March 1915
41. Richards letter to L. B. Quartermain, 25 November 1961
42. Hayward diary, 9 February 1915
43. Ibid., 10 February 1915
44. Richards diary, 11 February 1915
45. Hayward diary, 10 February 1915
46. Ibid., 12 February 1915
47. Richards diary, 12 February 1915
48. Ibid.
49. Hayward diary, 12 February 1915
50. Ibid., 14 February 1915
51. Ibid., 15 February 1915
52. Richards diary, 15 February 1915
53. Hayward diary, 17 February 1915
54. Ibid., 18 February 1915
55. Ibid., 19 February 1915

56.   Richards diary, 19 February 1915
57.   Hayward diary, 21 February 1915
58.   Priestley, *Antarctic Adventure*
59.   Hayward diary, 23 February, 1915
60.   Ibid.
61.   Ibid., 24 February 1915

62.   Ibid., 25 February 1915
63.   Ibid., 26 February 1915
64.   Ibid., 28 February 1915
65.   Ibid., 3 March 1915
66.   Ibid., 6 March 1915
67.   Ibid., 7 March 1915

Chapter 6

1.   Hayward diary, 11 March 1915
2.   Ibid., 12 March 1915
3.   Ibid., 13 March 1915
4.   Ibid., 14 March 1915
5.   Ibid., 15 March 1915
6.   Ibid., 21 March 1915
7.   Ibid., 22 March 1915
8.   Joyce field diary, 25 March 1915
9.   Hayward diary, 25 March 1915
10.   Mackintosh diary, 25 March 1915
11.   Joyce field diary, late March 1915
12.   Ibid., April 1915
13.   Mackintosh diary, 26 March 1915
14.   Ibid., 27 March 1915
15.   Ibid., 28 March 1915
16.   Ibid., 30 March 1915
17.   Hayward diary, 30 March 1915
18.   Joyce field diary, April 1915
19.   Ibid.
20.   Mackintosh diary, 27 January 1915
21.   Richards, interview with P. Lathlean, 1976
22.   Hayward diary, 1 April 1915
23.   Ibid., 5 April 1915
24.   Ibid., 15 April 1915
25.   Ibid., 23 April 1915
26.   Ibid., 25 April 1915
27.   Ibid., 29 April 1915

28.   Mackintosh diary, 1 April 1915
29.   Ibid., 4 April 1915
30.   Ibid., 7 April 1915
31.   Ibid., 8 April 1915
32.   Ibid., 11 April 1915
33.   Ibid., 12 April 1915
34.   Ibid., 13 April 1915
35.   Ibid., 15 April 1915
36.   Richards, interview with L. Bickel, 1976
37.   Richards letter to L. B. Quartermain, 16 April 1963
38.   Mackintosh diary, 6 April 1915
39.   Ibid., 15 April 1915
40.   Wild diary, 28 December 1915
41.   Joyce diary transcripts, 1915
42.   Wild diary, 28 December 1915
43.   Richards, interview with P. Lathlean, 1976
44.   Richards, *The Ross Sea Shore Party*
45.   Spencer-Smith diary, 4 March 1915
46.   Ibid., 6 March 1915
47.   Ibid., 23 March 1915
48.   Ibid., 12 March 1915
49.   Ibid., 2 May 1915
50.   Richards, interview with P. Lathlean, 1976
51.   Richards, interview with L. Bickel, 1976
52.   Richards, *The Ross Sea Shore Party*
53.   Ibid.

Chapter 7

1.   Hayward diary, May 1915
2.   Joyce field diary, 9 May 1915
3.   Hayward diary, May 1915
4.   Joyce field diary, May 1915

5.   Wild diary, 24 May 1915
6.   Ibid.
7.   Hayward diary, 1 June 1915
8.   Joyce field diary, June 1915

9. Richards, *The Ross Sea Shore Party*
10. Hayward diary, 1 June 1915
11. Wild diary, 2 June 1915
12. Joyce field diary, June 1915
13. Joyce letter to James Paton, a member of *Aurora*'s crew, 22 October 1915
14. Joyce field diary, June 1915
15. Richards, *The Ross Sea Shore Party*
16. Stevens, report of the 1914–17 expedition
17. Mackintosh diary, 5 June 1915
18. Ibid., 13 June 1915
19. Ibid., 8 June 1915
20. Hayward diary, 2 June 1915
21. Ibid., 5 June 1915
22. Ibid., 21 June 1915
23. Ibid., 22 June 1915
24. Spencer-Smith diary, 22 June 1915
25. Richards, *The Ross Sea Shore Party*
26. Mackintosh diary, 26 June 1915
27. Hayward diary, 26 June 1915
28. Joyce diary transcripts, July 1915
29. Spencer-Smith diary, July 1915
30. Richards, *The Ross Sea Shore Party*
31. Wild diary, 28 December 1915
32. Joyce diary transcripts, 1915
33. Mackintosh diary, 5 June 1915
34. Richards, interview ABC radio, *Verbatim* programme
35. Mackintosh diary, 1 July 1915
36. Ibid., 16 July 1915
37. Ibid., 30 July 1915
38. Hayward diary, July 1915
39. Spencer Smith diary, July 1915
40. Mackintosh diary, 23 August 1915
41. Ibid., 26 August 1915
42. Richards, *The Ross Sea Shore Party*
43. Cope Medical Report of the Ross Sea Base ITAE, January 1917

Chapter 8

1. Richards, *The Ross Sea Shore Party*
2. Hayward diary, 1 October 1915
3. Joyce field diary, 1 October 1915
4. Mackintosh diary, 8 September 1915
5. Ibid., 21 September 1915
6. Ibid., 30 September 1915
7. Spencer-Smith letter to his parents, 30 September 1915
8. Richards, *The Ross Sea Shore Party*
9. Joyce field diary, 10 October 1915
10. Ibid., 11 October 1915
11. Hayward diary, 11 October 1915
12. Wild diary, 11 October 1915
13. Richards letter to A. J. T. Fraser, 9 July 1961
14. Joyce field diary, 12 October 1915
15. Wild diary, 11 October 1915
16. Debenham, *In the Antarctic*
17. Joyce field diary, 12 October 1915
18. Ibid., 15–18 October 1915
19. Spencer-Smith diary, 17 October 1915
20. Wild diary, 20 October 1915
21. Joyce field diary, 23 October 1915
22. Spencer-Smith diary, 23 October, 1915
23. Joyce field diary, 26 October 1915
24. Richards, interview with L. Bickel, 1976
25. Richards, unpublished document, 'Four Dogs'
26. *Scottish Geographical Magazine*, Vol. 30, No. 2, 1914
27. Richards, unpublished document, 'Four Dogs'
28. Richards, interview with L. Bickel, 1976
29. Joyce field diary, 28 October 1915
30. Hayward diary, October 1915
31. Mackintosh letter to Joyce, 28 October 1915
32. Joyce field diary, 5 November 1915
33. Ibid., 6 November 1915
34. Wild diary, 16 October 1915
35. Ibid., 21 October 1915
36. Ibid., 1 November 1915
37. Ibid., 2 November 1915
38. Ibid., 9 November 1915
39. Ibid., 17 November 1915
40. Ibid., 19 November 1915
41. Ibid., 9 December 1915
42. Spencer-Smith diary, 5 November 1915
43. Ibid., 7 November 1915
44. Hayward diary, 15 November 1915
45. Spencer-Smith diary, 9 November 1915
46. Ibid., 17 December 1915

47. Ibid., 2 January 1916
48. *The Eagle*, Bedfordshire Modern School magazine, March 1917
49. Naval Service Record of Harry Ernest Wild
50. P&O Officers Register
51. Mackintosh diary, 2 February 1915
52. Spencer-Smith diary, 12 November 1915
53. Wild diary, 12 November 1915
54. Ibid., 14 November 1915
55. Joyce field diary, 17 November 1915
56. Joyce letter to Mackintosh, 15 November 1915
57. Mackintosh letter to Joyce, 25 November 1915
58. Joyce field diary, 25 November 1915
59. Richards letter to L. B. Quartermain, 19 November 1963
60. Joyce field diary, 28 November 1915
61. Mackintosh letter to Joyce, 4 December 1915
62. Spencer-Smith diary, November and December, 1915
63. Richards, *The Ross Sea Shore Party*
64. Joyce field diary, 13 December 1915
65. Hayward diary, 13 December 1915
66. Joyce field diary, 14 December 1915
67. Spencer-Smith diary, 15 December 1915
68. Wild diary, 15 December 1915
69. D. Mawson, *Antarctic Diaries* (London: Unwin Hyman, 1988)
70. Spencer-Smith diary, 22 December 1915
71. Wild diary, 24 December 1915
72. Spencer-Smith diary, 25 December 1915
73. Wild diary, 25 December 1915
74. Spencer-Smith diary, 27 December 1915
75. Wild diary, 27 December 1915
76. Spencer-Smith diary, 27 December 1915
77. Wild diary, 29 December 1915
78. Spencer-Smith diary, 29 December 1915
79. Wild diary, 30 December 1915
80. Spencer-Smith diary, 29 December 1915
81. Joyce field diary, 25 December 1915
82. Gaze field diary, 29 December 1915
83. Joyce field diary, 29 December 1915
84. Wild diary, 31 December 1915
85. Spencer-Smith diary, 31 December 1915
86. Joyce field diary, 31 December 1915

Chapter 9

1. Wilson, *Antarctic Notebooks*
2. Jack diary, 5 January 1916
3. Mackintosh, letter to Joyce, 1 January 1916
4. Hayward diary, 1916
5. Wild diary, 1 January 1916
6. Joyce field diary, 1 January 1916
7. Spencer-Smith diary, 2 January 1916
8. Joyce field diary, 3 January 1916
9. Hayward diary, 1916
10. Wild diary, 3 January 1916
11. Spencer-Smith diary, 3 January 1916
12. Joyce field diary, 4 January 1916
13. Ibid., 5 January 1916
14. Gaze diary, January 1916. 'gave A. P. a pretty good a/c of what Joyce's intentions were – that he was out to play DIRT on the Skipper. Feel no compunction about speaking out to AP about Joyce (so that he can put the Skipper on his guard) because Joyce is not playing the game by any manner of means – nothing is done openly – all on the quiet – all the more dirty for it too. (Joyce … intends to push on and try and meet Shackleton first – intending the Skipper to do the Hack work. sincerely hope … the Skipper goes on (as originally intended) to the fartherest South and meets Shackleton himself – sending Joyce back (as intended) from 82'
15. Joyce field diary, 6 January 1916
16. Hayward diary, summary notes written January 1916
17. Spencer-Smith diary, 6 January 1916
18. Wild diary, 6 January 1916
19. Richards, interview with P. Lathlean, 1976
20. Joyce field diary, 7 January 1916
21. Hayward diary, 1916
22. Joyce field diary, 8 January 1916
23. Wild diary, 7 January 1916
24. Spencer-Smith diary, 7 January 1916
25. Joyce field diary, 8 January 1916
26. Hayward diary, 1916
27. Joyce field diary, 8 January 1916

28.   Richards, *The Ross Sea Shore Party*
29.   Ibid.
30.   Hayward diary, 1916
31.   Wild diary, 8 January 1916
32.   Spencer-Smith diary, 8 January 1916
33.   Richards, interview with L. Bickel, 1976
34.   Ibid.
35.   Mackintosh diary, 14 September 1915
36.   Joyce field diary, 20 October 1915
37.   Spencer-Smith diary, 9 January 1916
38.   Joyce field diary, 9 January 1916
39.   Ibid.
40.   Richards, interview with L. Bickel, 1976
41.   Spencer-Smith diary, 10 January 1916
42.   Joyce field diary, 13 January 1916
43.   Ibid., 10 January 1916
44.   Wild diary, 11 January 1916
45.   Spencer-Smith diary, 11 January 1916
46.   Joyce field diary, 11 January 1916
47.   Wild diary, 12 January 1916
48.   Joyce field diary, 12 January 1916
49.   Ibid., 13 January 1916
50.   Richards, *The Ross Sea Shore Party*
51.   Joyce field diary, 14 January 1916
52.   Hayward diary, 18 January 1916

53.   Joyce field diary, 14 January 1916
54.   Ibid., 15 January 1916
55.   Spencer-Smith diary, 14 January 1916
56.   Ibid., 15 January 1916
57.   Ibid., 18 January 1916
58.   Wild diary, 15 January 1916
59.   Ibid., 16 January 1916
60.   Ibid., 17 January 1916
61.   Richards, interview with L. Bickel, 1976
62.   Mackintosh agreement with Richards.
63.   R. F. Scott, *Scott's Last Expedition: The Journals*
64.   Richards, *The Ross Sea Shore Party*
65.   Richards letter to L. B. Quartermain, 8 August 1969
66.   Richards, *The Ross Sea Shore Party*
67.   Richards letter to L. B. Quartermain, 11 December 1960
68.   Spencer-Smith diary, January 1916
69.   Ibid.
70.   Joyce field diary, 19 January 1916
71.   Ibid., 20 January 1916
72.   Ibid., 21 January 1916
73.   Wild diary, January 1916

Chapter 10

1.   Richards, interview with L. Bickel, 1976
2.   Richards letter to A. J. T. Fraser, 9 July 1961
3.   Richards, interview with L. Bickel, 1976
4.   Ibid.
5.   Spencer-Smith diary, 22 January 1916
6.   Joyce field diary, 22 January 1916
7.   Hayward diary, 22 January 1916
8.   Wild diary, 22 January 1916
9.   Spencer-Smith diary, 22 January 1916
10.   Joyce field diary, 23 January 1916
11.   Hayward diary, 23 January 1916
12.   Wild diary, 23 January 1916
13.   Spencer-Smith diary, 23 January 1916
14.   Ibid., 24 January 1916
15.   Richards, *The Ross Sea Shore Party*
16.   Ibid.
17.   Joyce field diary, 25 January 1916
18.   Hayward diary, 25 January 1916

19.   Wild diary, 25 January 1916
20.   Spencer-Smith diary, 25 January 1916
21.   Wilson, *Antarctic Notebooks*
22.   Richards, interview with L. Bickel, 1976
23.   Richards, *The Ross Sea Shore Party*
24.   Ibid.
25.   Richards, interview with L. Bickel, 1976
26.   Hayward diary, 26 January 1916
27.   Joyce field diary, 26 January 1916
28.   Richards, interview with L. Bickel, 1976
29.   Richards, *The Ross Sea Shore Party*
30.   Wild diary, 26 January 1916
31.   Hayward diary, 26 January 1916
32.   Joyce field diary, 26 January 1916
33.   Hayward diary, 26 January 1916
34.   Spencer-Smith diary, 26 January 1916
35.   Richards, *The Ross Sea Shore Party*
36.   Richards, interview with L. Bickel, 1976

37.   Ibid.
38.   Ibid.
39.   Joyce field diary, 27 January 1916
40.   Wild diary, 28 January 1916
41.   Mawson, *Antarctic Diaries*

42.   Spencer-Smith diary, 27 January 1916
43.   Joyce field diary, 28 January 1916
44.   Hayward diary, 28 January 1916
45.   Spencer-Smith diary, 28 January 1916

Chapter 11

1.   Richards, *The Ross Sea Shore Party*
2.   Richards, interview with L. Bickel, 1976
3.   Richards, *The Ross Sea Shore Party*
4.   Ibid.
5.   Richards, interview with L. Bickel, 1976
6.   Richards, *The Ross Sea Shore Party*
7.   Richards diagram, provided by D. Harrowfield
8.   Richards, interview with L. Bickel, 1976
9.   Spencer-Smith diary, 29 January 1916
10.   Joyce field diary, 29 January 1916
11.   Wild diary, 29 January 1916
12.   Hayward diary, 29 January 1916
13.   Joyce field diary, 29 January 1916
14.   Spencer-Smith diary, 29 January 1916
15.   Ibid.
16.   Wild diary, 30 January 1916
17.   Hayward diary, 30 January 1916
18.   Mackintosh diary, 7 March 1915
19.   Joyce field diary, 30 January 1916
20.   Spencer-Smith diary, 30 January 1916
21.   Joyce field diary, 31 January 1916
22.   Spencer-Smith diary, 31 January 1916
23.   Hayward diary, 31 January 1916
24.   Mackintosh diary, 12 March 1915
25.   Ibid., 13 March 1915
26.   Wild diary, 31 January 1916
27.   Joyce field diary, 1 February 1916
28.   Joyce diary transcript, 1 February 1916
29.   Spencer-Smith diary, 1 February 1916
30.   Wild diary, 1 February 1916
31.   Joyce field diary, 2 February 1916
32.   Ibid.
33.   Spencer-Smith diary, 2 February 1916
34.   Hayward diary, 2 February 1916
35.   Richards, *The Ross Sea Shore Party*
36.   Richards, interview with L. Bickel, 1976
37.   Debenham, *In the Antarctic*

38.   Richards, interview with L. Bickel, 1976
39.   Joyce field diary, 3 February 1916
40.   Spencer-Smith diary, 4 February 1916
41.   Hayward diary, 4 February 1916
42.   Joyce field diary, 4 February 1916
43.   Spencer-Smith diary, 5 February 1916
44.   Joyce field diary, 5 February 1916
45.   Richards, interview with L. Bickel, 1976
46.   Spencer-Smith diary, 6 February 1916
47.   Hayward diary, 6 February 1916
48.   Wild diary, 6 February 1916
49.   Joyce field diary, 6 February 1916
50.   Richards, interview with L. Bickel, 1976
51.   Richards, *The Ross Sea Shore Party*
52.   Hayward diary, February 1916
53.   Ibid.
54.   Spencer-Smith diary, 7 February 1916
55.   Ibid., 8 February 1916
56.   Ibid., 9 February 1916
57.   Ibid., 10 February 1916
58.   Ibid., 11 February 1916
59.   Wild diary, 7–10 February 1916
60.   Joyce field diary, 8 February 1916
61.   Richards, *The Ross Sea Shore Party*
62.   Ibid.
63.   Joyce field diary, 12 February 1916
64.   Ibid., 14 February 1916
65.   Ibid., 17 February 1916
66.   Hayward diary, February 1916
67.   Ibid.
68.   Spencer-Smith diary, 14 February 1916
69.   Wild diary, February 1916
70.   Richards, *The Ross Sea Shore Party*
71.   Richards, interview with L. Bickel, 1976
72.   Ibid.
73.   Ibid.
74.   Wild diary, 17 February 1916

75. Joyce field diary, 17 February 1916
76. Spencer-Smith diary, 17 February 1916

Chapter 12

1. Hayward diary, February 1916
2. Wild diary, 18 February 1916
3. Ibid.
4. Joyce field diary, 18 February 1916
5. Spencer-Smith diary, 18 February 1916
6. Richards, *The Ross Sea Shore Party*
7. Joyce field diary, 19 February 1916
8. Hayward diary, 19 February 1916
9. Spencer-Smith diary, 19 February 1916
10. Richards, interview with L. Bickel, 1976
11. Hayward diary, 3 March 1915
12. Joyce field diary, 20 February 1916
13. Wild diary, 20 February 1916
14. Spencer-Smith diary, 20 February 1916
15. Richards, *The Ross Sea Shore Party*
16. Joyce field diary, 21 February 1916
17. Wild diary, 21 February 1916
18. Spencer-Smith diary, 21 February 1916
19. Hayward diary, 21 February 1916
20. Richards, *The Ross Sea Shore Party*
21. Richards letter to L. B. Quartermain, 7 March 1963
22. Richards, interview with P. Law, December 1980
23. Richards letter to L. B. Quartermain, 7 March 1963
24. Hayward diary, 22 February 1916
25. Joyce field diary, 22 February 1916
26. Joyce diary transcripts, 22 February 1916
27. Ibid.
28. Wild diary, 22 February 1916
29. Spencer-Smith diary, 22 February 1916
30. Richards, interview with L. Bickel, 1976
31. Richards, *The Ross Sea Shore Party*
32. Richards letter to L. B. Quartermain, date unknown.
33. Mackintosh, *Shackleton's Lieutenant*
34. Richards, interview with L. Bickel, 1976
35. Hayward diary, 23 February 1916
36. Joyce field diary, 23 February 1916
37. Spencer-Smith diary, 23 February 1916
38. Joyce field diary, 23 February 1916
39. Hayward diary, 23 February 1916
40. Ibid.
41. Richards diary, 24 February 1916
42. Richards, interview with L. Bickel, 1976
43. Richards, *The Ross Sea Shore Party*
44. Joyce field diary, 23 February 1916
45. Hayward diary, 23 February 1916
46. Richards diary, 24 February 1916
47. Richards, interview with L. Bickel, 1976
48. Ibid.
49. Richards, *The Ross Sea Shore Party*
50. Joyce field diary, 23 February 1916
51. Ibid.
52. Hayward diary, 23 February 1916
53. Richards diary, 24 February 1916
54. Joyce field diary, 23 February 1916
55. Scott, *Voyage*
56. Richards, interview with L. Bickel, 1976
57. Joyce field diary, 23 February 1916
58. Richards diary, 23 February 1916
59. Hayward diary, 23 February 1916
60. Wild diary, 23 February 1916
61. Spencer-Smith diary, 23 February 1916

Chapter 13

1. Joyce, *The South Polar Trail*
2. Richards, interview with L. Bickel, 1976
3. Richards, *The Ross Sea Shore Party*
4. Ibid.

5.　Ibid.
6.　Richards, interview with L. Bickel, 1976
7.　Richards, *The Ross Sea Shore Party*
8.　Ibid. Ibid.
9.　Joyce field diary, 24 February 1916
10.　Richards diary, 23 February 1916
11.　Joyce field diary, 24 February 1916
12.　Richards diary, 24 February 1916
13.　Joyce diary transcripts, 24 February 1916
14.　Richards, interview with L. Bickel, 1976
15.　Joyce field diary, 24 February 1916
16.　Richards diary, 24 February 1916
17.　Hayward diary, 24 February 1916
18.　Joyce field diary, 24 February 1916
19.　Richards diary, 24 February 1916
20.　Joyce field diary, 24 February 1916
21.　Richards diary, 24 February 1916
22.　Hayward diary, 24 February 1916
23.　Richards, *The Ross Sea Shore Party*
24.　Richards diary, 24 February 1916
25.　Ibid.
26.　Ibid.
27.　Ibid.
28.　Spencer-Smith diary, 24 February 1916
29.　Wild diary, 24 February 1916
30.　Richards, 'Four Dogs', unpublished document
31.　Hayward diary, 25 February 1916
32.　Joyce field diary, 25 February 1916
33.　Hayward diary, 25 February 1916
34.　Richards diary, 25 February 1916
35.　Richards, interview with L. Bickel, 1976
36.　Ibid.
37.　Hayward diary, 25 February 1916
38.　Richards diary, 25 February 1916
39.　Richards, *The Ross Sea Shore Party*
40.　Joyce field diary, 25 February 1916
41.　Spencer-Smith diary, 25 February 1916
42.　Wild diary, 25 February 1916
43.　Richards, *The Ross Sea Shore Party*
44.　Richards, interview with L. Bickel, 1976
45.　Ibid.
46.　Ibid.
47.　Richards, *The Ross Sea Shore Party*
48.　Richards, interview with L. Bickel, 1976
49.　Joyce field diary, 26 February 1916
50.　Hayward diary, 26 February 1916
51.　Richards diary, 26 February 1916
52.　Richards, interview with L. Bickel, 1976
53.　Joyce field diary, 26 February 1916
54.　Richards diary, 26 February 1916
55.　Joyce field diary, 26 February 1916
56.　Hayward diary, 26 February 1916
57.　Joyce field diary, 26 February 1916
58.　Richards diary, 26 February 1916
59.　Ibid.
60.　Hayward diary, 26 February 1916
61.　Richards diary, 26 February 1916
62.　Joyce diary transcripts for February 1916
63.　Hayward diary, 26 February 1916
64.　Richards diary, 26 February 1916.
65.　Joyce field diary, 26 February 1916
66.　Wild diary, 26 February 1916
67.　Spencer-Smith diary, 26 February 1916

Chapter 14

1.　Richards diary, 27 February 1916
2.　Hayward diary, 27 February 1916
3.　Joyce field diary, 27 February 1916
4.　Joyce diary transcripts for 27 February 1916
5.　Richards, interview with L. Bickel, 1976
6.　Joyce field diary, 27 February 1916
7.　Richards diary, 27 February 1916.
8.　Hayward diary, 27 February 1916
9.　Joyce field diary, 27 February 1916
10.　Hayward diary, 27 February 1916
11.　Richards, *The Ross Sea Shore Party*
12.　Richards diary, 27 February 1916
13.　Joyce field diary, 27 February 1916
14.　Richards, interview with L. Bickel, 1976
15.　Wild diary, 27 February, 1916
16.　Spencer-Smith diary, 27 February 1916
17.　Richards, *The Ross Sea Shore Party*
18.　Richards diary, 28 February 1916
19.　Hayward diary, 28 February 1916
20.　Joyce field diary, 28 February 1916
21.　Richards diary, 28 February 1916
22.　Hayward diary, 28 February 1916

23. Joyce field diary, 28 February 1916
24. Richards diary, 28 February 1916
25. Hayward diary, 28 February 1916
26. Richards diary, 28 February 1916
27. Ibid.
28. Ibid.
29. Spencer-Smith diary, 28 February 1916
30. Wild diary, 28 February 1916
31. Scott, *Scott's Last Expedition: The Journals*, Message to the Public, March 1912
32. Ibid., letter to Sir J. M. Barrie, March 1912
33. Ibid., Message to the Public, March 1912
34. Ibid., letter to Sir J. M. Barrie, March 1912
35. Ibid., Message to the Public, March 1912
36. Ibid.
37. Mackintosh letter, written 28 February 1916, later transcribed by Richards
38. Scott, *Scott's Last Expedition: The Journals*, Message to the Public, March 1912
39. Mackintosh, letter, 28 February 1916, later transcribed by his wife Gladys – from the private papers of Anne Philips

40. Richards, *The Ross Sea Shore Party*
41. Richards, interview with P. Lathlean, 1976
42. Richards, interview with L. Bickel, 1976
43. Richards, interview with P. Lathlean, 1976
44. Richards, interview with L. Bickel, 1976
45. Joyce field diary, 29 February 1916
46. Hayward diary, 29 February 1916
47. Joyce field diary, 29 February 1916
48. Hayward diary, 29 February 1916
49. Richards diary, 29 February 1916
50. Hayward diary, 29 February 1916
51. Joyce field diary, 29 February 1916
52. Hayward diary, 29 February 1916
53. Wild diary, 29 February 1916
54. Spencer-Smith diary, 29 February 1916
55. Joyce field diary, 29 February 1916
56. Hayward diary, 29 February 1916
57. Joyce field diary, 29 February 1916
58. Joyce diary transcripts for 29 February 1916
59. Spencer-Smith diary, 29 February 1916
60. Joyce field diary, 29 February 1916
61. Richards, interview with L. Bickel, 1976

Chapter 15

1.   Richards, interview with L. Bickel, 1976
2.   Ibid.
3.   Ibid.
4.   Richards, *The Ross Sea Shore Party*
5.   Hayward diary, 1 March 1916
6.   Joyce field diary, 1 March 1916
7.   Spencer-Smith diary, 1 March 1916
8.   Hayward diary, 1 March 1916
9.   Joyce field diary, 1 March 1916
10. Richards diary, 1 March 1916
11. Hayward diary, 1 March 1916
12. Richards, interview with L. Bickel, 1976
13. Richards letter to A. J. T. Fraser, 9 July 1961
14. Joyce field diary, 2 March 1916
15. Hayward diary, 2 March 1916
16. Richards diary, 2 March 1916
17. Joyce field diary, 2 March 1916
18. Spencer-Smith diary, 2 March 1916
19. Joyce field diary, 2 March 1916
20. Wild diary, 3 March 1916
21. Richards diary, 3 March 1916

22. Spencer-Smith diary, 3 March 1916
23. Hayward diary, 3 March 1916
24. Joyce field diary, 3 March 1916
25. Richards, interview with L. Bickel, 1976
26. Richards, interview with P. Lathlean, 1976
27. Richards diary, 4 March 1916
28. Joyce field diary, 4 March 1916
29. Wild diary, 4 March 1916
30. Hayward diary, 4 March 1916
31. Spencer-Smith diary, 4 March 1916
32. Joyce field diary, 4 March 1916
33. Richards, interview with L. Bickel, 1976
34. Mackintosh diary, 2 March 1915
35. Ibid., 20 March 1915
36. Hayward diary, 8 March 1915
37. Richards, interview with L. Bickel, 1976
38. Hayward diary, 5 March 1916
39. Wild diary, 5 March 1916
40. Joyce field diary, 5 March 1916
41. Spencer-Smith diary, 5 March 1916
42. Joyce field diary, 6 March 1916

43. Ibid., 7 March 1916
44. Hayward diary, 7 March 1916
45. Ibid.
46. Joyce field diary, 7 March 1916
47. Richards, interview with L. Bickel, 1976
48. Richards, *The Ross Sea Shore Party*
49. Richards, interview with L. Bickel, 1976
50. Cope Medical Report of the Ross Sea Base

ITAE. January 1917
51. Joyce field diary, 7 March 1916
52. Hayward diary, 7 March 1916
53. Richards diary, 7 March 1916
54. Wild diary, 7 March 1916
55. Debby Horsman, great-niece of A. P. Spencer-Smith. Private papers
56. Spencer-Smith diary, 7 March 1916

Chapter 16

1.   Richards, interview with L. Bickel, 1976
2.   Richards letter to A. J. T. Fraser, 9 July 1961.
3.   Mackintosh diary, 15 March 1915
4.   Richards, interview with L. Bickel, 1976
5.   Joyce field diary, 8 March 1916
6.   Hayward diary, 8 March 1916
7.   Richards diary, 8 March 1916
8.   Wild diary, 8 March 1916
9.   Richards, interview with L. Bickel, 1976
10. Richards, *The Ross Sea Shore Party*
11. Richards letter to A. J. T. Fraser, 9 July 1961
12. Cope Medical Report of the Ross Sea Base ITAE. January 1917
13. Wild diary, 9 March 1916
14. Joyce field diary, 9 March 1916
15. Richards letter to A. J. T. Fraser, 9 July 1961
16. Wild diary, 9 March 1916
17. Richards diary, 9 March 1916
18. Joyce field diary, 9 March 1916
19. Richards, *The Ross Sea Shore Party*
20. Hayward diary, 9 March 1916
21. Joyce field diary, 9 March 1916
22. Wild diary, 9 March 1916
23. Richards diary, 9 March 1916
24. Joyce field diary, 9 March 1916
25. Richards diary, 9 March 1916
26. Hayward diary, 9 March 1916
27. Wild diary, 10 March 1916
28. Cope Medical Report of the Ross Sea Base ITAE. January 1917.
29. Richards diary, 9 March 1916
30. Hayward diary, 9 March 1916
31. Joyce field diary, 9 March 1916
32. Ibid., 10 March 1916

33. Hayward diary, 10 March 1916
34. Joyce field diary, 10 March 1916
35. Wild diary, 10 March 1916
36. Hayward diary, 10 March 1916
37. Joyce field diary, 10 March 1916
38. Richards, *The Ross Sea Shore Party*
39. Richards, interview with L. Bickel, 1976
40. Richards letter to L. B. Quartermain, 19 November 1963
41. Joyce field diary, 11 March 1916
42. Hayward diary, 11 March 1916
43. Joyce field diary, 11 March 1916
44. Wild diary, 11 March 1916
45. Joyce field diary, 11 March 1916
46. Hayward diary, 11 March 1916
47. Richards diary, 11 March 1916
48. Wild diary, 11 March 1916
49. Joyce field diary, 11 March 1916
50. Hayward diary, 11 March 1916
51. Ibid.
52. Richards, interview with P. Law, December 1980
53. Richards letter to L. B. Quartermain, 27 January 1962
54. Cope Medical Report of the Ross Sea Base ITAE. January 1917
55. Ibid.
56. Ibid.
57. Ibid.

Chapter 17

1. Richards, *The Ross Sea Shore Party*
2. Joyce field diary, 12 March 1916
3. Hayward diary, 12 March 1916
4. Wild diary, 13 March 1916
5. Richards diary, 13 March 1916 Hayward diary, 13 March 1916
6. Joyce field diary, 13 March, 1916
7. Richards, *The Ross Sea Shore Party*
8. Hayward diary, 14 March 1916
9. Richards diary, 14 March 1916
10. Joyce field diary, 14 March 1916
11. Richards diary, 15 March 1916
12. Joyce field diary, 15 March 1916
13. Richards, interview with L. Bickel, 1976
14. Ibid.
15. Ibid.
16. Joyce field diary, 16 March 1916
17. Wild diary, 17 March 1916
18. Joyce field diary, 16 March 1916
19. Ibid., 17 March 1916
20. Hayward diary, 17 March 1916
21. Joyce field diary, 18 March 1916
22. Wild diary, 18 March 1916
23. Richards diary, 18 March 1916
24. Hayward diary, 18 March 1916
25. Joyce field diary, 18 March 1916
26. Wild diary, 18 March 1916
27. Joyce diary transcripts for 18 March 1916
28. Richards, *The Ross Sea Shore Party*
29. Ibid.
30. Richards, interview with L. Bickel, 1976
31. Hayward diary, 19 March 1916
32. Richards diary, 19 March 1916
33. Joyce field diary, 19 March 1916
34. Ibid., 20 March 1916
35. Hayward diary, 20 March 1916
36. Richards, *The Ross Sea Shore Party*
37. Richards, interview with L. Bickel, 1976
38. Richards, *The Ross Sea Shore Party*
39. Richards, interview with L. Bickel, 1976
40. Ibid.
41. Ibid.
42. Richards letter to L. B. Quartermain, 7 March 1964
43. Joyce field diary, 22 March 1916
44. Mackintosh diary, 28 March 1915
45. Ibid., 30 March 1915
46. Ibid., 1 April 1915
47. Ibid., 7 April 1915
48. Ibid., 13 April 1915
49. Ibid., 2 April 1915
50. Ibid., 10 April 1915
51. Ibid., 13 April 1915
52. Richards, interview with L. Bickel, 1976
53. Richards letter to L. B. Quartermain, 2 February 1964.
54. Richards, *The Ross Sea Shore Party*
55. Ibid.
56. Joyce field diary, 12 April 1916
57. Ibid., 26 April 1916
58. Ibid., 3 May 1916
59. Hayward diary, 10 April 1916
60. Ibid., April 1916

Chapter 18

1. Hayward diary, May 1916
2. Joyce field diary, 10 May 1916
3. Richards, *The Ross Sea Shore Party*
4. Joyce field diary, 10 May 1916
5. Richards, interview with L. Bickel, 1976
6. Joyce field diary, 10 May 1916
7. Richards, interview with L. Bickel, 1976
8. Ibid.
9. Ibid.
10. Ibid.
11. Richards letter to L. B. Quartermain, 10 August 1965
12. Richards, *The Ross Sea Shore Party*
13. Richards, interview with L. Bickel, 1976
14. Wild diary, 8 May 1916
15. Richards, interview with L. Bickel, 1976

16.   Richards, *The Ross Sea Shore Party*

17.   Joyce field diary, 10 May 1916

18.   Joyce, 'Report of the Proceedings of the "Aurora" Relief Expedition 1916–1917'

19.   Wild, 'Report of the Proceedings of the "Aurora" Relief Expedition 1916–1917'

20.   Richards, 'Report of the Proceedings of the "Aurora" Relief Expedition 1916–1917'

21.   *The Eagle*, Bedford Modern School journal, 1917, Mackintosh, *Nimrod* diary,

    5 January 1909

22.   Richards, interview with L. Bickel, 1976

23.   Wild diary, 24 May 1915

24.   Mackintosh diary, 30 July 1915

25.   Richards, interview with L. Bickel, 1976

26.   Ibid.

27.   Ibid.

28.   Mackintosh diary, 31 March 1915

29.   Ibid., 27 March 1915

Chapter 19

1.   Richards, interview with L. Bickel, 1976

2.   Richards letter to A. J. T. Fraser, 9 July 1961

3.   Richards, interview with L. Bickel, 1976

4.   Richards letter to L. B. Quartermain, 27 January 1962

5.   Richards, *The Ross Sea Shore Party*

6.   Richards, interview with L. Bickel, 1976

7.   Richards, *The Ross Sea Shore Party*

8.   Richards, interview with L. Bickel, 1976

9.   Davis, as quoted by L. Bickel in Richards

    interview 1976

10.   'Report of the Proceedings of the "Aurora" Relief Expedition 1916–1917'

11.   Richards, *Australasian Post*, Wellington, New Zealand newspaper, 25 February 1982

12.   Naval Service Record of Harry Ernest Wild

13.   Richards letter to L. B. Quartermain, 6 January 1956

14.   Richards, *The Ross Sea Shore Party*

15.   Richards, interview with L. Bickel, 1976

Chapter 20

1.   *Daily Mirror* newspaper, UK, 1909

2.   Ibid., 1913

3.   Richards, interview with L. Bickel, 1976

4.   Richards letter to A. J. T. Fraser, 9 July 1961

5.   Richards letter to L. B. Quartermain, 27 January 1962

6.   Joyce, *The South Polar Trail*

7.   Richards letter to L. B. Quartermain, 20 December 1963

8.   Ibid., 12 November 1960

9.   Richards, interview with L. Bickel, 1976

10.   Richards letter to L. B. Quartermain, 10 August 1966

11.   Joyce diary transcripts for March and April, 1916

12.   Richards, interview with L. Bickel, 1976

13.   Wild diary, 24 May 1915

14.   Ibid., 6 February 1916

15.   Richards, interview with L. Bickel, 1976

16.   Shackleton, *South*

17.   Ibid.

18.   Ibid.